Using Microsoft Office 4

Quick Start to Microsoft Office

Standard equipment for Microsoft Office windows

If you've never used Windows or Microsoft Office before (or even if you have!), here's some basic stuff you need to know before you get started.

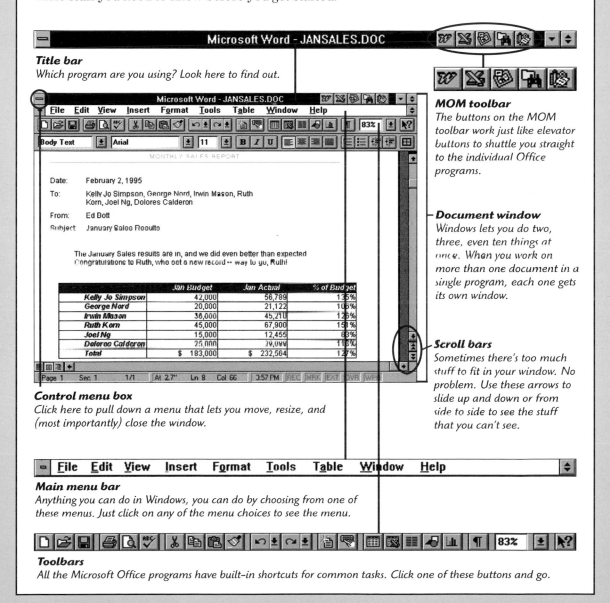

Title bar
Which program are you using? Look here to find out.

MOM toolbar
The buttons on the MOM toolbar work just like elevator buttons to shuttle you straight to the individual Office programs.

Document window
Windows lets you do two, three, even ten things at once. When you work on more than one document in a single program, each one gets its own window.

Scroll bars
Sometimes there's too much stuff to fit in your window. No problem. Use these arrows to slide up and down or from side to side to see the stuff that you can't see.

Control menu box
Click here to pull down a menu that lets you move, resize, and (most importantly) close the window.

Main menu bar
Anything you can do in Windows, you can do by choosing from one of these menus. Just click on any of the menu choices to see the menu.

Toolbars
All the Microsoft Office programs have built-in shortcuts for common tasks. Click one of these buttons and go.

que 201 W. 103rd Street • Indianapolis, IN 46290 • (317)581-3500
Copyright © 1994 Que Corporation

Excel

Excel shortcuts

Selecting worksheet areas	Shortcut
Select cells	⇧Shift+ movement key
Select current row	⇧Shift+ Space bar
Select current column	Ctrl+ Space bar

Editing data	Shortcut
Edit a cell	F2
Fill right	Ctrl+R
Fill down	Ctrl+D
Format numbers	Ctrl+1 (Number tab)
Align numbers	Ctrl+1 (Alignment tab)
Change fonts	Ctrl+1 (Font tab)
Add borders	Ctrl+1 (Border tab)
Add shading	Ctrl+1 (Patterns tab)
Fill selection of cell with current entry	Ctrl+↵Enter
Enter current date	Ctrl+;
Enter current time	Ctrl+⇧Shift+:
Insert a tab	Ctrl+Alt+Tab⇄

Formatting the worksheet	Shortcut
Hide current/selected row(s)	Ctrl+9
Show hidden rows	Ctrl+⇧Shift+(
Hide current/selected column(s)	Ctrl+0
Show hidden column(s)	Ctrl+⇧Shift+)

Other shortcuts	Shortcut
Display Function Wizard	⇧Shift+F3
Insert the autosum formula	Alt+=

PowerPoint shortcuts

Changing views	Shortcut
Change to slide view	Ctrl+Alt+N
Change to slide sorter view	Ctrl+Alt+P
Change to outline view	Ctrl+Alt+O
Change to master view	⇧Shift+click View button

Inserting	Shortcut
Insert new slide	Ctrl+M
Insert new slide with AutoLayout	Ctrl+⇧Shift+M
Insert date	Alt+⇧Shift+D
Insert page number	Alt+⇧Shift+P
Insert time	Alt+⇧Shift+T

Formatting text	Shortcut
Center paragraph	Ctrl+E
Justify paragraph	Ctrl+J
Left-align paragraph	Ctrl+L
Right-align paragraph	Ctrl+R

Drawing	Shortcut
Group objects	Ctrl+⇧Shift+G
Ungroup objects	Ctrl+⇧Shift+H

Slide show	Shortcut
Go to slide number	Number+↵Enter
Advance to next slide	Space bar
Return to previous page	←Backspace
Black screen on/off	B
White screen on/off	W
Show pointer on/off	A
Stop/restart automatic show	S
End show	Esc

Other shortcuts	Shortcut
Move from title to text	Ctrl+↵Enter

PowerPoint

Top keyboard shortcuts

Office

Shortcuts common in all Office programs

Moving and copying	Shortcut
Cut selection to Clipboard.	Ctrl+X
Copy selection to Clipboard.	Ctrl+C
Paste from Clipboard.	Ctrl+V

Editing	Shortcut
Oops! Undo what I just did.	Ctrl+Z
Repeat what I just did.	Ctrl+Y
Select all.	Ctrl+A
Clear the selection.	Del
Turn bold on/off.	Ctrl+B
Turn italic on/off.	Ctrl+I
Turn underline on/off.	Ctrl+U
Find some text or formatting.	Ctrl+F
Replace some text or formatting.	Ctrl+H
Check spelling.	F7

Managing files	Shortcut
Save this document.	Ctrl+S
Start a new file.	Ctrl+N
Open a file.	Ctrl+O
Print a document.	Ctrl+P

Other shortcuts	Shortcut
Choose OK.	↵Enter
Cancel a command.	Esc
Get help.	F1

Word shortcuts

Formatting	Shortcut
Change font	Ctrl+D
Change point size	Ctrl+⇧Shift+P
Center	Ctrl+E
Justify	Ctrl+J
Left align	Ctrl+L
Indent	Ctrl+N
Right align	Ctrl+R
Create hanging indent	Ctrl+T
Single space lines	Ctrl+1
Double space lines	Ctrl+2
One and one half space lines	Ctrl+5
Insert page break	Ctrl+↵Enter
Apply normal style	Ctrl+⇧Shift+N

Changing the view	Shortcut
Change to normal view	Ctrl+Alt+N
Change to outline view	Ctrl+Alt+O
Change to page layout view	Ctrl+Alt+P

Inserting special fields	Shortcut
Insert date field	Alt+⇧Shift+D
Insert page field	Alt+⇧Shift+P
Insert time field	Alt+⇧Shift+T

Other shortcuts	Shortcut
Print preview	Ctrl+F2
GoTo	F5
Repeat Find or GoTo	⇧Shift+F4
Start thesaurus	⇧Shift+F7

Mouse techniques

General Office techniques	How do I do it?
Display a pull-down menu.	Click on the menu choice in the menu bar.
Display a shortcut menu.	Right-click where you need the menu to appear.
Find out what a button does.	Move the mouse pointer over the toolbar button to display a ToolTip.
Display the Office Manager menu.	Click on the Office Manager button on the MOM toolbar.

Selecting stuff	How do I do it?
Select an icon or picture.	Point at it and click.
Select two things that aren't right next to one another.	Hold down the Ctrl key as you select the first one, and keep holding it down as you move from place to place, marking the selections with the mouse.
Deselect something.	Point somewhere outside the highlighted area and click.

Selecting text in Word	How do I do it?
Select a word.	Point to the word and double-click.
Select an entire sentence.	Hold down the Ctrl key, point to the sentence, and double-click.
Select an entire paragraph.	Move the mouse pointer to the left margin until it turns into an arrow, position it alongside the paragraph, and double-click.
Select the whole document.	Move the mouse pointer to the left margin until it turns into an arrow, and then triple-click.

Working with a single cell in Excel	How do I do it?
Select a cell.	Point and click.
Position the insertion point in a cell.	Point and double-click.
Select characters in a cell.	Double-click in the cell, then drag through the characters you want to select.
Select a word in a cell.	Double-click the word. (This also works with cell addresses, formula arguments, and other things that aren't "words."

Selecting multiple cells in Excel	How do I do it?
Select a range.	Click in the cell at one corner of the range and drag the pointer to the opposite corner.
Select a group of unconnected cells.	Select the first cell or range, then hold down the Ctrl key and select the next cell or range. Continue holding the Ctrl key down until you've selected all the cells you want.
Select an entire row or column.	Click on the letter or number in its heading.
Select multiple rows or columns.	Select the first row or column and hold down the mouse button while dragging through the rest.

Using

Microsoft® Office 4

Ed Bott

Using Microsoft Office 4

Library of Congress Catalog No.: 94-069628

ISBN: 0-7897-0091-3

98 97 96 95   6 5 4 3 2

Interpretation of the printing code: the rightmost double-digit number is the year of the book's printing; the rightmost single-digit number, the number of the book's printing. For example, a printing code of 95-1 shows that the first printing of the book occurred in 1995.

Publisher: *David P. Ewing*

Associate Publisher: *Don Roche, Jr.*

Associate Publisher—Operations: *Corinne Walls*

Managing Editor: *Michael Cunningham*

Credits

Publishing Manager
Charles O. Stewart III

Acquisitions Editor
Jenny L. Watson

Product Director
Kathie-Jo Arnoff

Production Editor
Nancy E. Sixsmith

Technical Editor
Gregory A. Dew

Novice Reviewer
Paul Marchesseault

Figure Specialist
Cari Ohm

Book Designers
Amy Peppler-Adams
Sandra Stevenson

Cover Designer
Jay Corpus

Acquisitions Assistant
Tracy Williams

Operations Coordinator
Patty Brooks

Editorial Assistant
Jill Pursell

Production Team
Stephen Adams
Stephen Carlin
Daryl Kessler
Elizabeth Lewis
Stephanie Mineart
Kaylene Riemen
Tina Trettin

Indexer
Rebecca Mayfield

Composed in *ITC Century*, *ITC Highlander*, and *MCPdigital* by Que Corporation.

Dedication

To my father, who patiently answered all my questions when I was a child, and then had a few hundred questions of his own—all about computers—when I became an adult.

—EB

Trademark Acknowledgements

About the Author

Ed Bott is Senior Contributing Editor of *PC/Computing* magazine. With two monthly columns and frequent cover stories on Microsoft Windows and other topics, his is one of the most recognized "voices" in the computing industry.

Acknowledgments

This book did not come into existence overnight. A hard-working and dedicated team compressed years of work into a few short months to turn hundreds of pages of raw manuscript and hundreds of megabytes of images into the polished package you hold in your hands.

Literally dozens of people—editors, artists, graphic designers, proofreaders, and others—worked on this book, and it's impossible to thank them all. So let me single out just a handful of individuals whose efforts were truly heroic.

Kathie-Jo Arnoff, Senior Product Development Specialist, provided constant feedback and sharp criticism to make sure that each chapter was the best it could be.

Nancy Sixsmith, Production Editor, turned a high-powered lens on the manuscript—and put in many hours of overtime to make sure that every sentence sparkled.

Jenny Watson, the world's most persistent Acquisitions Editor, pulled all the pieces together.

Greg Dew, Technical Editor, added valuable tips and made sure that no errors crept in.

A special thank you to Lisa Wagner, who reviewed several chapters and helped make mail-merge understandable—no small task; and to Nancy Stevenson, who helped put the finishing touches on several chapters.

I owe a special debt of gratitude to Yael Li-Ron, my colleague from *PC/Computing*, who helped bring the section on PowerPoint to life.

For help with the book's design, thanks go to Mirales/Ross, Inc., Mike Zender of Zender & Associates, Professor Elizabeth Keyes of Rensselaer Polytechnic Institute, and Amy Peppler-Adams of design Lab.

And I could not have finished this book without Chuck Stewart, Product Series Director, who provided vision, encouragement, a sympathetic ear, and—when necessary—truly great coffee beans to help me through many late nights. Thank you, Chuck.

Contents at a Glance

{ Table of Contents }

*How do I
start up
Office
(and shut
it down
safely)?*

see page 12

Chapter 3: Lost? Get Help Fast with a Single Click

Chapter 4: Saving Your Work (and Finding It Again)

Enough already! I just want to save this file!

see page 41

Chapter 5: MOM (the Microsoft Office Manager) Knows Best

Part II: Using Word

Chapter 6: Creating a New Document

What's in a Word window?
see page 60

Chapter 7: Opening, Organizing, and Editing Documents

Chapter 8: The Secrets of Great-Looking Documents

How can I make my words look more interesting?

see page 92

`70%`

Chapter 9: Let Word Do Your Work for You

*Word tables at a glance
see page 130*

Chapter 10: Lists and Tables

Chapter 11: Letters by the Dozen

*What's mail merge,
and how does it work?
see page 145*

Chapter 12: Fancy Word Stuff

Chapter 13: Putting It on Paper

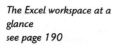

The Excel workspace at a glance
see page 190

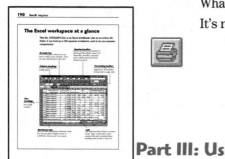

Part III: Using Excel

Chapter 14: Creating a New Worksheet

Chapter 15: Working with Worksheets and Workbooks

Chapter 16: Making Great-Looking Worksheets

I want to replace everything in a cell

see page 216

What can I do with the Formatting toolbar?
see page 234

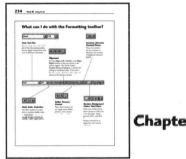

*Desper-
ately
searching
for data*

see page 249

Chapter 19: Printing Your Worksheets

My work-sheet's a little too big. Can I force it to fit?

see page 287

Chapter 20: Using Excel and Word Together

"oh-lay"

PowerPoint and its tools
see page 307

Part IV: Using PowerPoint

Chapter 21: Creating a New Presentation

Chapter 22: Making Great-Looking Presentations

*I want
smooth
transitions*

see page 330

Chapter 23: Using Word and Excel with PowerPoint

Chapter 24: It's Showtime! Giving a Great Presentation

*How do I
place an
Excel chart
in a slide?*

see page 348

Part V: Beyond the Basics

What is electronic mail, anyway?

see page 386

Introduction

I wrote this book for my father, the small business owner. And for my brother, the teacher, and my cousin, the biologist, and my insurance agent, and my accountant, and the UPS driver, and the guy who runs the Italian restaurant on Main Street, and a bunch of other people just like them.

What do these folks have in common? Well, all of them are bright, well-educated, and successful (especially my father). They've mastered the really hard stuff in life, like raising kids, running a business, killing crabgrass, and programming a VCR. They're all experienced computer users, but they're not computer experts. And at one time or another, each of them has asked me the exact same question: *What do I do now?*

If you're like a few million other people, you've been asking that question a lot lately, ever since a huge collection of Windows programs called Microsoft Office appeared on your PC. Maybe it was just there when you bought a new PC. Maybe it showed up on your department's network one day, along with a terse note telling you it's time to switch from WordPerfect or Lotus 1-2-3 or Harvard Graphics to these new programs.

What do I do now?

You could start pulling down menus, clicking mouse buttons, and pressing key combinations until you stumble on the right ones.

Or you could look in the manuals. *If* you could find them. And *if* they were written in plain English. And *if* you had the time to scour through several hundred pages of technotrivia in search of the answers you need.

Or you could look in this book, which was written specifically to answer one question: *What do I do now?*

What makes this book different?

You don't need an advanced degree in engineering or computer science to read this book. If you can tell the difference between the left and right mouse buttons, you've got all the technical background you need.

It's written in plain English, too. I promise not to bury you in detailed explanations and three-letter acronyms (TLAs). After all, you're not studying for a degree in computer science—you're trying to get some work done, with the help of some incredibly powerful and occasionally baffling computer programs.

With Office, as with all Windows programs, there are always *at least* four different ways to do everything. If you were planning to become a computer expert, you'd expect a computer book to give you step-by-step instructions for each of them. Not this book.

In this book, I focus on results. That means I'll tell you the best way to get each job done. There might be three other ways to do the same thing, but for most people, most of the time, the technique I describe is the one that will get results most quickly.

Oh, and there won't be a quiz.

How do I use this book?

This isn't a textbook. You don't have to start at page 1 and read all the way to the end. It's not a mystery novel, either, so if you want to skip to the last chapter first, be my guest.

You'll probably be surprised at some of the things that the three big Microsoft Office programs can do. That's why, if you have the time, it's worth flipping through the chapters, looking at the headings, and searching out references to the things you do at work. The people who published this book went to a lot of trouble to make sure that those interesting ideas would leap off the page and catch your attention as you browse. (It shouldn't take that long—after all, this isn't one of those 1200-page monster books that helps you build up your biceps every time you lift it.)

This book will come in especially handy when you have a big job to do and you're not sure where to begin. And if you get stuck, you'll probably find the way out in these pages.

How this book is put together

Some people will use all the programs in the Microsoft Office. Others will spend most of their time in one. It doesn't matter which type you are—you'll find exactly what you're looking for. You could look at this book as a sort of Dagwood sandwich, with three big chunks of information, one for each of the big three Office programs, stuffed between two slices of general information. These five parts are divided into chapters that get into the specifics of each program. And inside each chapter, you'll find tips, hints, and step-by-step instructions for getting your work done faster without having to ask what to do next.

Part I: Getting Started

What is this thing called Office? It's three big programs (plus a few little ones you get for free). Look here to discover all the things these programs have in common, like menus, toolbars, and helpful wizards.

Part II: Using Word

It's official—Microsoft Word is now the world's most popular software program. Word is filled with shortcuts and cool features—like a built-in spelling checker and thesaurus that make you look smarter; and ready-made templates that let you put together memos, letters, invoices, and brochures without breaking a sweat. So, for you and the 20 million or so other people who use Word, here's all you need to know to create a simple letter or your own professional-looking newsletter.

Part III: Using Excel

There are all sorts of accounting genes in my family, but I didn't get any of them, which is why I use Excel all the time. With Excel worksheets, I can type in row after row, and column after column of numbers—with full confidence that Excel will add, subtract, multiply, divide, and generally crunch them correctly. Check out these chapters for details on how to build budgets, turn numbers into great-looking graphs, and print out dazzling reports guaranteed to impress even non-accountants. Turn straight to Chapter 20 if you want pointers on using Excel and Word together.

Part IV: Using PowerPoint

How many times have you sat in a darkened room while someone else stands at an overhead projector, droning on and on and flipping boring black-and-white foils? Drone, flip, drone, flip, snore.... The next time *you* stand up in front of a crowd, use PowerPoint to help keep your audience awake and on the edge of their seats. If you ever have to sell anything—products, services, or ideas—you'll find PowerPoint's dazzling electronic slide shows irresistible.

Part V: Beyond the Basics

And then there's the complicated stuff. Look here for helpful advice on using Office with your company's electronic mail. You can also get a brief introduction to all the little Office programs here, including one that lets you manage the collection of clip art you didn't even know you had, and another that lets you create official-looking charts showing who's who in your company. If you want to rework any part of Office to match the way you work, check out Chapter 25.

Special book elements

This book contains a number of special elements and conventions to help you find information quickly—or skip stuff you don't want to read right now.

Tips either point out information often overlooked in the documentation, or help you use your software more efficiently, like a shortcut. Some tips help you solve or avoid problems.

 Notes contain additional information or "reminders" of important information you should know.

<Caution> Cautions alert you to potentially dangerous consequences of a procedure or practice, especially if it could result in serious or even disastrous results, such as loss or corruption of data.

 Q&A

What are Q&A notes?

Cast in the form of questions and answers, these notes provide you with advice on ways to avoid or solve common problems.

Plain English, please!

These notes explain the meanings of technical terms or computer jargon.

Throughout this book, we'll use a comma to separate the parts of a pull-down menu command. For example, to start a new document, you'll choose File, New. That means "Pull down the File menu, and choose New from the list."

And if you see two keys separated by a plus sign, such as Ctrl+X, that means to press and hold the first key, press the second key, then release both keys.

Sidebars are interesting nuggets of information

Sidebars provide interesting, nonessential reading, side-alley trips you can take when you're not at the computer or when you just want some relief from "doing stuff." Here you may find more technical details, funny stories, personal anecdotes, or interesting background information.

Part I:

Getting Started

1

What Is Microsoft Office?

Microsoft Office programs share common menus and buttons that look remarkably similar. When you learn to use one application, you've got a big head start on learning the others.

In this chapter:

- What is Office, what can it do for me, and why should I care?
- Which version of Office is right for me?
- How do I start up Office (and shut it down safely)?
- How do I know which version of Office I have?
- What do the individual Office applications do?

Every time I turn on my PC, I remember that scene in the classic horror film *Frankenstein*. You know the one: Igor pulls the switch, the monster begins to twitch, Dr. Frankenstein's eyes light up, and he exclaims, *"It's alive!"*

The trouble with Frankenstein's monster, of course, is that the parts didn't match up very well. Arms and legs from here, a heart from there, and a brain from who-knows-where. It's no wonder the poor beast couldn't put one foot in front of another without scaring the poor townspeople.

Sometimes it seems like the average computer has the same problem. You pick up a word processor from here, a spreadsheet program from there, a cool chart-making program from somewhere else, and your productivity grinds to a halt. The problem? All those programs were never designed to work together, so you get hopelessly lost every time you switch from one to another.

Fortunately, there's a solution: Microsoft Office. In one box, you get all the business software you need. The programs look alike, work alike, and talk to one another in exactly the same language.

Gee... do you suppose if Dr. Frankenstein had had a copy of Office, the movie would have had a happy ending?

A shelfful of software

There's a lot more to Office than just a bunch of programs in the same box. As the name suggests, there are three powerful business applications inside it that handle words, numbers, and images with style and grace.

But the real appeal of Office is the glue that ties all those applications together. All the programs share common menus and rows of buttons that look remarkably similar. When you learn how to use one application, you've got a big head start on learning the others. You even get an easy-to-use control center that lets you start and stop the individual programs, or get detailed instructions and hands-on help just by clicking a mouse button.

66 *Plain English, please!*

What's the difference between a **program** and an **application**? Nothing, really. Computer experts use the terms interchangeably. Applications are usually big programs that do a wide variety of tasks. Tiny programs that do just one thing are sometimes called **applets**. 99

In this book, I'll show you how to use all the pieces of Microsoft Office—individually and together—to become more productive with your PC. You'll learn how to create great-looking letters and reports, crunch numbers faster than the most dedicated bean-counter, and tie it all together in presentations that'll win the hearts and minds of customers and co-workers alike.

If you wanted, you could buy a bunch of programs and try to glue them together yourself. But you'd wind up with the same headache you'd get if you tried to put together a killer audio/video system using a bunch of individual components. To play a video, you press Start; but to listen to a cassette, you have to press Play. The VCR's Eject button is on the right, but the CD's

Open/Close button is on the left. And have you ever looked at the back of a stereo amplifier and tried to figure out which wire goes where?

Whether you're working with a PC or a home theater, the glue that ties the components together is the most important part. When your computer's programs look and act the same way, it's less confusing for you to switch back and forth. It's also easier to install and upgrade.

Which version of Microsoft Office is right for me?

There are three distinct versions of Office.

Standard edition

For most people, this is the right choice. You get a word processor, a spread-sheet, and a graphics program that lets you create colorful slide shows on your PC. You also get a handful of little programs that help you create graphs, organization charts, and other useful, snazzy additions to business documents. And it costs a lot less than the individual pieces would cost on their own.

Professional edition

Just like the Standard edition, but with the addition of a powerful data management program called Access. Not for everyone, but useful for experts and computer users who don't mind thinking like computer programmers.

CD-ROM edition

Both Office editions come on floppy diskettes, and the Professional Edition also comes on CD-ROM. If you don't have a CD-ROM drive, this is a great reason to get one. With the CD-ROM edition, you get the entire Microsoft Bookshelf, which is a collection of seven complete reference books, including an encyclopedia and *The World Almanac*.

 **<Caution>** What if you don't have enough space on your hard drive to install Office? Don't even think about running it directly from the CD-ROM. You'll wait minutes to complete even the simplest tasks. Better to buy a new hard drive, or try doubling your disk's storage capacity with one of the utilities found in MS-DOS 6.2 or in other products.

How do I start up Office (and shut it down safely)?

How do you start up Office and all the Office programs? That depends. If you've been using Windows for awhile, and you're used to starting programs from the Windows Program Manager, you can keep using that method. But Office also lets you replace Program Manager with the Microsoft Office Manager, a cool control center that's never more than a mouse click away. Take your choice.

Program Manager

When you (or someone else) installed Microsoft Office, it created its own Program Manager group and stuffed it full of icons (see fig. 1.1). To start any of the Office programs, just double-click on the appropriate icon. (If the Microsoft Office Program Manager group is minimized, you might need to double-click on it before you can see the icons inside.)

Fig. 1.1
You can start each of the Microsoft Office programs by double-clicking its Program Manager icon.

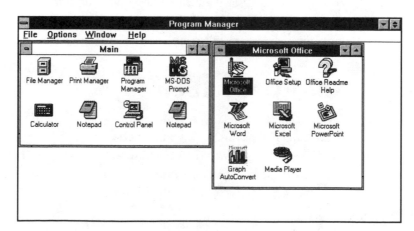

Microsoft Office Manager (in the StartUp group)

There's an easier way to start up Office programs, though. Use the Microsoft Office Manager (MOM), a small toolbar that has buttons for every one of the Office programs. When you ran the Office installation program, the MOM icon should have landed in your Program Manager StartUp group so that MOM starts automatically (and you see the MOM toolbar) every time you start Windows. For more details on how to use the Microsoft Office Manager, see Chapter 5.

 **<*Caution*>**

Always close the Office programs and exit Windows before you turn off your PC. If you don't, you run the risk of losing data, and maybe even making such a mess out of Windows that it won't start up properly. Why take chances? To shut down the right way, click the Microsoft Office button on the MOM toolbar, then choose Exit.

How do I know which version of Microsoft Office I have?

 The easy way is to click the Microsoft Office button . Choose About Microsoft Office from the menu that appears. You'll see a screen like the one in figure 1.2, which unmistakably details the version number.

Fig. 1.2
Which version of Office is installed on your PC? Click the Microsoft Office button—the one at the far right of the Microsoft Office Manager—and then choose About Microsoft Office from the pull-down menu.

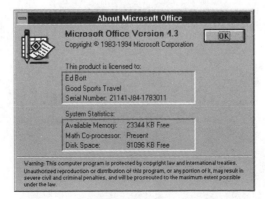

Meet the Office applications

So what's inside the Office package? Plenty. But before I get to that, let me ask a fundamental question: What kind of person are you? No, this isn't some kind of psychological test. There's no right or wrong way to work. It's really a lot simpler than that: how you work will help define which of the big three Office programs you're most likely to call home.

What do those version numbers really mean?

Right now, my PC has more numbers on it than a roulette table. Microsoft Office Version 4.3, it says when I start up. Inside, there's Word 6.0c, Excel 5.0c, and PowerPoint 4.0c. Of course, all those programs are running with the help of MS-DOS 6.22 and Microsoft Windows 3.11.

Why the different numbers? Because each program has to compete with other programs from other companies, each with its own numbering scheme. When one company announces a new version 6, all its competitors have to follow suit. It just won't do for Word to have a lower number than its archrival, WordPerfect.

The numbers to the left of the decimal point are **major releases**, filled with hot new gee-whiz features. The numbers to the right of the decimal point identify **minor upgrades**, new versions with just a few little changes—nothing to write home about. And what about those little letters at the far right? Each one represents a **bug fix**—a new edition of the program that Microsoft published to correct problems that people had complained about in the previous version.

Frankly, the whole notion of labeling software with version numbers is a relic of the Dark Ages, when the only people who used computers were absolute nerds. You know the kind. They survive on Twinkies and Jolt cola and are only dimly aware of the outside world.

Can you imagine how confusing life would be if these people had been responsible for making some of the other products we take for granted every day? You might be driving a Cadillac Seville, version 7.0b. Your kids would be begging you to take them to MacDonald's for a Big Mac 4.25 and a Classic Coke (version 2.0). And you'd probably drive there on Interstate 10.11.

Fortunately, version numbers are a dying species, like Hula Hoops and Pet Rocks. The next version of Windows won't be version 4.0; instead, it'll be called Windows 95, after the year in which it's introduced. If future versions of Office follow the same pattern, they'll be called Office 95, Office 96, and so on. And we'll all have an easier time figuring out which version is the latest and greatest.

In the Office package you get ...

- **Big applications**

Word is a powerful word processor that lets you quickly create everything from simple memos to slick newsletters and brochures. We'll cover Word in detail in Part II.

Excel does for numbers what Word does for nouns and verbs. Anyone who lives or dies by the numbers probably will live in Excel—at least at the office. Use Excel to create budgets and financial reports, turn numbers into easy-to-follow charts and graphs, perform "What If?" analyses of just about any question, and sort through lists in seconds. Read all about using Excel in Part III.

PowerPoint lets you create a professional-looking presentation, complete with snazzy graphics and step-by-step bulleted lists of arguments. Best of all, you can turn a Word document into a presentation with just one click. If your work depends on convincing other people that your products, ideas, and dreams are right for them, you'll love PowerPoint. Read more about PowerPoint in Part IV.

Access (Office Professional Edition only) is a powerful data management program that's mostly for programmers. If someone in your office has created an Access program, you may need this to run it.

- **A bunch of little applications**

Let's see, there's **Graph**, which lets you enter a few numbers and quickly turn them into a chart. **Organization Chart** helps you find your place on the corporate ladder (give yourself a promotion and see how it feels). **Equation Editor** is pretty boring, unless you're a professor of mathematics. **WordArt** lets you twist letters and numbers into creative shapes you can use for logos and headlines. There's even a **ClipArt Gallery** that lets you browse through a few hundred drawings in search of the perfect illustration for your newsletter or presentation. We'll look at these "applets" in more detail in Part V.

- **Some great help aids**

  Office (and the Office applications) are stuffed with helpful hints and step-by-step instructions for getting work done. **Wizards** walk you step-by-step through complex tasks. **Cue Cards** offer detailed instructions that stay right in front of your face while you work. **Previews and demos** let you watch while the program itself demonstrates how to accomplish a difficult task. We'll look at all the Help options later in this section.

- **A license to use Microsoft Mail**

  You don't actually get the **Mail** *program*—just a piece of paper that says you can use Mail if it's already installed on your network. Your network administrator will be glad to know that, but for you and me it's pretty irrelevant.

- **And, of course, MOM.**

  The **Microsoft Office Manager**, that is. MOM is the starting point for all the Office applications. If you like it enough, you can use it to run your entire PC. We'll look at MOM in detail in Chapter 5.

Common Office Features: Menus, Toolbars, and More

In this chapter:

- What can I do with the main menus?

- How can I see a shorter list of choices?

- What are those rows of buttons for?

- How can I tell what a button does?

The three big Office programs are designed like a Holiday Inn. No surprises.

Everyone knows that "Where am I?" feeling you get when you spend the night away from home. You wake up in the middle of the night but can't find the light switch. So you grope around in the dark and bash your shin against the coffee table. Ouch!

One way to avoid bumps and bruises is to stay in a Holiday Inn, where the motto is "No surprises." Every room is laid out exactly the same, so whether you're in Topeka or Timbuktu, you'll know where that coffee table is.

Word, Excel, and PowerPoint, the three big Office programs, are designed just the same as a Holiday Inn—no surprises. When you learn your way around one, you've learned the basic layout of the others, too. When you switch programs, the menus are right where you expect them to be, and buttons that do similar things have identical pictures.

The applications in Office don't always work *exactly* alike. But they get close most of the time. In this chapter, we'll look at the stuff you'll use most often: menus, toolbars, and the Office help system.

What's on the menu?

No matter where you are in Office, you have a choice of menus when you want to do something. Some stay right in front of you all the time; others remain hidden until you ask them to pop up.

Try the main menu first

Every Office program has nine pull-down menus that you can use to do nearly anything. Each of the menus on the menu bar is identified by a single word, and they're arranged in a neat row just below the title bar, as shown in figure 2.1. No surprises—eight of the nine choices are absolutely identical in each program. When you want to save your work, for example, you'll always use the File menu.

Because each program handles a different kind of data, the choices that appear when you pull down menus with the same name will vary slightly from program to program. And every program has one choice that's reserved for that program alone.

Here's a sampling of some of the options available under each menu choice:

- **File.** Save your work; find files you've saved previously; send work to the printer.

- **Edit.** Move, copy, and delete stuff; search for words and phrases.

- **View.** Look at whatever you're working with in different ways—zoom in for a super close-up view, for example. Also the place you go to show or hide toolbars.

- **Insert.** Add special information (like today's date or page number) to whatever you're working on. Also lets you add objects, such as a picture or a graph.

Fig. 2.1

No matter which Office program you use, the top menu choices always appear in the same place. That means you always know just where to go to get any job done.

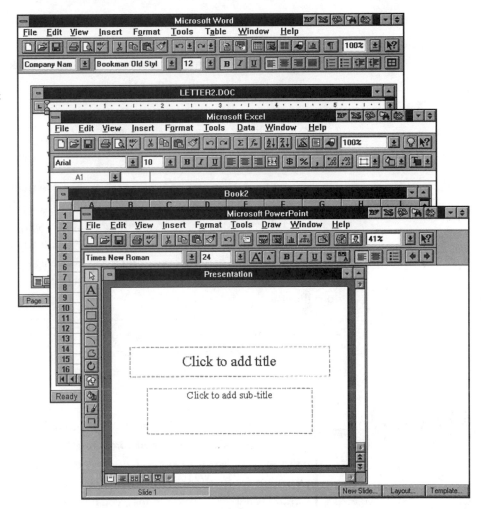

- **Format.** Make your work look more attractive by changing the type-face, page size, colors and shading, and more.

- **Tools.** Do specialized tasks like checking for spelling mistakes. This is also the place where you can change program options, like where your data files are automatically stored.

- **Table/Data/Draw.** The only "uncommon" menu choices. Here's where you go to work with Word tables, Excel lists, and PowerPoint drawings.

- **Window.** Switch from one document window to another, or rearrange the windows that are already open.

- **Help.** All sorts of information that can get you back to work when you're not sure what to do next.

Check the shortcut menus for quick advice

Throughout the Office programs, you're rarely more than one mouse click away from a special **shortcut menu**. It's like having a personal Office assistant following along one step behind you. You snap your fingers—well, actually, you click the right mouse button—and you get a short, easy-to-read list of options. Best of all, whoever puts together these shortcut menus must be psychic, because they contain only the things you're most likely to want to do right now.

Any time you want to do something and you're not sure how to do it, it's a good idea to press the right mouse button. There's an excellent chance that the choice you're looking for is right there (see fig. 2.2 for examples of these shortcut menus).

 **{Note}**

When people talk about the right mouse button, they really mean the button that *isn't* the main one. On most computers, that's the right button. Left-handers (or anyone who just prefers to roll the mouse around with that hand) can switch the functions of the left and right mouse buttons using the Windows Control Panel. If you've done that, you'll have to mentally swap the directions when reading this book.

Fig. 2.2
Click the right mouse button to pop up one of these handy shortcut menus. For the three main Office applications, the menus start the same, but change a little to reflect the different things each program lets you do.

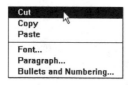

Word

Excel

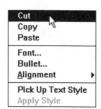

PowerPoint

Or skip the menus and use keyboard shortcuts instead

Menus sometimes get in the way of productivity. Let's say you're working on a long, complicated, important report. Because you don't want a power failure to wipe out your work, you save what you've done every 10 minutes. (Very wise of you.) You *could* take your hand off the keyboard, grab the mouse, pull down the File menu, and click Save? Or you could just press Ctrl+S, which does exactly the same thing in one smooth motion.

There are literally thousands of keyboard shortcuts in the Office programs. No one expects you to memorize them all, but there are a few special keyboard shortcuts for activities you do over and over again. Use them regularly, and you can save enough mouse clicks to maybe go home 10 minutes early one day a week. These ten shortcuts, listed in table 2.1, are really worth knowing about, because they work the same in all the Office applications. In some cases, they're easy to remember because the command Save starts with the same letter as the shortcut (Ctrl+S).

Table 2.1 Top ten keyboard shortcuts

Keyboard shortcut	What does the shortcut do?
Alt+F4 or Ctrl+F4	Close a program window or close a document window, respectively.
Ctrl+C or Ctrl+X or Ctrl+V	Cut, copy, or paste whatever the mouse is pointing at.
Ctrl+Z	Oops! Undo whatever I just did!
Ctrl+B	Make it **bold**.
Ctrl+I	Make it *italic*.
Ctrl+S	Save whatever I'm working on right now.
Ctrl+N	Start a new document/worksheet/presentation using default formats.
Ctrl+F6	Show me the next window.
Ctrl+F	I want to find some text in the current document.
Ctrl+A	Select all (the whole document/worksheet/presentation I'm working with).

Toolbars: one-click shortcuts

Everywhere you turn in Microsoft Office, you run into long rows of buttons just waiting to be clicked. Fortunately, these button collections, called **toolbars**, share the same pictures and descriptions. So whichever program you're working with, the toolbars all look pretty much the same, and they're organized in similar ways, too. When you learn how one toolbar works, you've got a big head start on all the Office programs.

(Tip)

> Toolbars start out in a neat row along the top of the screen, but you can move them around if you'd prefer to see them elsewhere. Just use the mouse to "grab" a portion of the toolbar where there are no buttons, and drag the entire toolbar. If you move it to a side or the bottom of the program window, the toolbar will snap into position along that edge. If you move it somewhere other than an edge, the toolbar turns into a window that floats over whatever you're working on.

Standard toolbar

If you're like most people, you have a few phone numbers that you dial over and over again. To save time, you can program them into your telephone's speed dialer. The **Standard toolbar**, shown in figure 2.3, works the same way, offering one-button shortcuts for the things you're most likely to do every time you start up Office, like opening and saving files.

Fig. 2.3
In Microsoft Office programs, the Standard toolbar at the top of the window works just like the speed dialer on your telephone. Each button acts as a shortcut for one of the menu choices you make most often.

Here are some of the most useful buttons on the Standard toolbar:

Toolbar button	What does the button do?
	Create a new file, open a saved file, save the file I'm working with now.
	Cut whatever I'm pointing at now, make a copy of it, or paste whatever I just copied into the spot I'm pointing at now.
	Send this job to the printer, please.
	Fix those ~~embarassing~~ ~~embarassing~~ annoying misspelled words.
	Oops! Undo whatever I just did!

Formatting toolbar

The other toolbar, right under the Standard one, works the same way. Should you have to pull down a bunch of menus and click through a maze of dialog boxes to do common things? Of course not. It's much easier to just click a button on the **Formatting toolbar** (see fig. 2.4).

Fig. 2.4

Use the buttons on the Formatting toolbar to make your words and numbers look bigger, bolder, and better.

Here are some of the most useful buttons on the Formatting toolbar:

Toolbar button	What does the button do?
Arial ↓	Change to a different font, please.
10 ↓	I'd like these letters to be bigger or smaller, please.
B *I* <u>U</u>	Make it **bold**, *italic*, or <u>underlined</u>.
≡ ≡ ≡	Please center these words on the page (or push them to the left or to the right).

Other toolbars

Each Office program has at least five toolbars, plus the two greatest-hits collections we've already talked about. Most of these buttons handle special jobs you don't do that often, like drawing or charting, or working with databases. When you first start up Office, they're out of sight.

 Q&A

I can't see any toolbars at all! Where did they go? How do I get them back?

They're not gone, they're just hidden. When you can't see the regular toolbars, you can't pop up the Toolbars menu by clicking the right mouse button. Instead, pull down the View menu, and choose the Toolbars option. Check the Standard and Formatting boxes to bring back the default toolbars.

You *could* put all seven toolbars on the screen at the same time, but you won't like the results. Too many toolbars cover up the space you need to work in, as if you'd backed up a dump truck full of buttons and spilled them all over your PC's monitor.

You're better off popping up the other toolbars only when you need them. To show one of these hidden toolbars (like Excel's floating set of Drawing tools, shown in fig. 2.5), point to one of the toolbars you can see, and then click the right mouse button. On the list that pops up, click the name of the toolbar you want to show. When you're finished using the toolbar, right-click on it, then click its name on the shortcut menu to make it disappear.

Fig. 2.5
This is the Drawing toolbar from Excel, one of many extra toolbars that can come in handy for special jobs.

 (Tip)

How can you tell whether a toolbar is hidden or visible? Look for a checkmark next to the toolbar's name on the shortcut menu.

What does that button do?

If you're not sure what the picture on that button is supposed to mean, just point the mouse at the button and leave the arrow there for a few seconds. After a brief pause, you'll see a little yellow label called a **ToolTip** (see fig. 2.6), that pops up to tell you, in English, what the button does.

Fig. 2.6
When you're not sure what a button's for, let the mouse pointer rest over it. After a few seconds, one of these ToolTips will pop up to tell you in plain English.

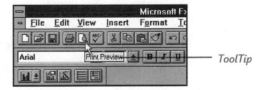

ToolTip

Other look-alike stuff

Besides menus and toolbars, there are a few other parts of the individual Office programs that look and act alike.

- **Summary information** includes titles, author names, and descriptions of what's inside a document, worksheet, or presentation. You can add or update this information any time you save a file, then use it to find files later.

- **Status bars** include tidbits like today's data and time, the current page number, and whether the CAPS LOCK button is on.

- **Rulers** help you position words, tabs, pictures, and margins exactly where you want them.

Have it your way: rearranging toolbars

For most people, the toolbars that come with Office are good enough just the way they are. But if they're not arranged exactly the way you prefer to work, give your toolbars a makeover. You can take buttons off a toolbar, add new ones, rearrange the buttons, even reposition each toolbar off the screen.

To delete a button: If you use a button so rarely that it's more of a distraction than a helper, take it off the toolbar. Point to the toolbar, click the right mouse button, and choose Customize from the shortcut menu. With the Customize dialog box on the screen, point to the button you want to zap, click the left mouse button and hold it down, then drag the button off the toolbar. As soon as you let go of the button, poof—it's gone!

To add a new button: Use the same technique to call up the Customize dialog box, but this time drag a button from the dialog box onto the toolbar. Buttons are arranged into categories, so you may need to hunt a bit to find the right one. If you're not sure what a button really does, click on it and you'll see a description.

To rearrange toolbar buttons: Pull up the Customize dialog box, then click and drag the buttons to the positions you prefer. To add a thin space between buttons, leave an imaginary gap between the buttons you want separated. To put two buttons *thisclosetogether*, drop one right onto the side of another.

When you're through adding and zapping buttons, press the Close button.

Lost? Get Help Fast with a Single Click

If you're lost and confused, and you don't know which questions to ask... let Office offer a helping hand.

In this chapter:

- How can I find out what those strange terms mean?
- I'm lost! How do I figure out where to go next?
- I want someone to walk me through a tough job. Can a Wizard help?
- I used to use WordPerfect and 1-2-3. How does Office work?

The Microsoft Office is a big, sprawling placc, so it's not surprising that occasionally you get a little turned around—or completely lost.

If you get lost and confused in Office, there are plenty of places that are set up specifically to offer help. If you're puzzled by the meaning of an unfamiliar term, click a button and get a quick definition. When you know where you want to go, but you're not exactly sure how to get there, click the same button, and the Office helpers will pop up a detailed set of directions that stay on the screen while you work.

For really tough jobs, the kind that no one except a full-fledged computer genius can figure out, there are even Office guides (called **wizards**) that ask you a few questions and then walk you through the process.

What does that word mean?

Sometimes an Office program uses a computer term that just doesn't make sense. It's even worse when you know exactly what you want to do, but you can't find the right word on any of the pull-down menus. Well, as Yogi Berra used to say, "You could look it up."

When you're using an Office program, it's easy to get quick answers to most questions. Just pull down the <u>H</u>elp menu and click on the choice labeled <u>S</u>earch for Help On. You'll see a scrolling list that looks like the one in figure 3.1.

Fig. 3.1

To search through the help topics for any Office program, just start typing. As you type, Office will "jump" through the list to the next matching topic.

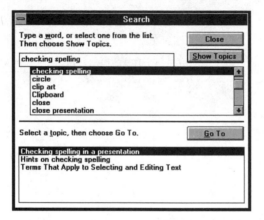

To find the word you're looking for, just start typing in the box. As you type, you'll "jump" to the first word in the list that matches the letters you've typed so far. When you find what you're looking for, click the word or phrase in the list, then click the <u>S</u>how Topics button to see all the available help options. Pick a topic, click the <u>G</u>o To button, and you're in business.

Why are some words in different colors?

Help isn't always immediately helpful. Sometimes it raises more questions, like "What in the heck is a *pivot table*, anyway?" If you're lucky, these not-so-helpful screens will contain special "hot spots," like the ones in figure 3.2, that you can click on for extra help.

Fig. 3.2

Any time you see this index finger, you can click for extra help. Buttons jump to related parts of the help system, while under-lined words have handy pop-up definitions hidden underneath.

In an airport, you'll find all sorts of helpful devices: signs, video kiosks, and maps, for example. As long as you know how to use them, you'll do just fine. When you ask Office for help, you can expect to see the same kind of elements over and over. Like these:

- **Buttons**. Let you jump to another related topic in the help program. (Some buttons, like the one in figure 3.2, look more like icons. How do you know when a picture is really a button? Watch the mouse pointer. If it turns into that familiar index finger, the icon is really a button in disguise.)

- **Underlined text**. Signifies a glossary entry. Click the word to see a quick definition. Click anywhere to make the pop-up box go away.

- **Colored text**. Acts just like a button to let you "jump" somewhere else. Just click the colored text to get more information. To get back where you started, click the button labeled Back.

When the mouse pointer turns into the shape of a pointing finger, that's your cue that you can click to get more information.

What am I supposed to do now?

Sooner or later, it happens to everyone: you're standing on a street corner, holding a map in one hand and scratching your head with the other. You know where you are, and you know where you want to go. You're just not sure which direction you're facing. Do you turn left or right?

When you're standing on a street corner, the easy way to get help is to ask a passerby for directions. When you find yourself confused at a crossroads in one of the Office programs, it's even easier to ask for directions: simply click the Help button.

As soon as you click the Help button, the mouse pointer turns into an arrow with a question mark attached to it. Now you can point to a menu or a toolbar, and when you click the mouse button, you'll jump straight into the help screen that explains what you can do with whatever you pointed to.

 (Tip)

> The Help button on the standard toolbar doesn't work when a dialog box is on the screen. If there's no button labeled Help, press F1, the universal help key. Most likely you'll pop into a help screen that can get you unstuck in a hurry.

Walk me through this process, please

Sometimes it's not enough to simply find your way around a strange place. If you've ever tried to buy a subway ticket in New York City, you know exactly what I mean. Where are you going? One-way or round-trip? Are you a student or a senior citizen? If you don't know which questions to ask...well, you're standing there scratching your head again, aren't you?

But what if you have the world's most helpful ticket-dispensing machine? You push the Start button, it asks you a few questions, and it sells you the ticket you need. That's the basic principle behind the wizards found throughout the Office programs. When you need to perform one of several common tasks, you call on the wizard, who asks you a few simple questions and gets things going for you.

Here are some of the Office wizards you might turn to when you need a little help getting a tricky job done:

- **Excel.** Includes wizards for turning numbers into charts and creating complex mathematical functions.

- **Word.** Wizards let you create common documents, like letters, calendars, and meeting agendas; there's also a wizard for adding a table to a document.

- **PowerPoint.** There are two wizards: the AutoContent Wizard helps you kick-start a presentation, while the Pick a Look Wizard (shown in fig. 3.3) makes it a snap to change the background, typeface, and other visual elements in a presentation.

Fig. 3.3
Why memorize a bunch of trivial details? The PowerPoint Pick a Look Wizard, like its counterparts in Word and Excel, asks you a series of questions, then does all the work for you.

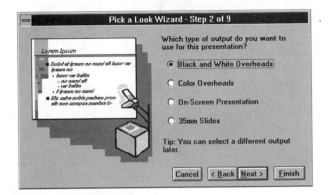

I have a *big* job to do

Wizards are fine for simple jobs, but they run out of steam fast when a job gets complicated. Let's say you've made it from New York to Los Angeles, where no one's ever heard of a subway. You decide to rent a car, and now you need to get from the airport to the Disneyland hotel. Fortunately, there's an information kiosk right there at the Hertz counter. You point to your hotel's name, and quick as a flash it prints out a detailed set of directions. Now, you've got a "cheat sheet" you can use as you drive down the unfamiliar freeways.

Cue Cards work the same way. When you want to do something complicated, like customize the Office toolbar, just pop up a Cue Card. Like our Hertz driving instructions, the Cue Cards stay there as long as we need them. Unlike Wizards, Cue Cards let you do the work yourself by following the step-by-step instructions (see fig. 3.4).

You won't find Cue Cards in all the Office programs. At least for now, they're only available in the Microsoft Office Manager, PowerPoint, and Access (if you have the Office Professional edition). To find Cue Cards, look on the Help menu.

Fig. 3.4

Cue Cards let you do complicated jobs by following step-by-step instructions. Don't look for Cue Cards in Word or Excel, though—for now, they're only available in a few places.

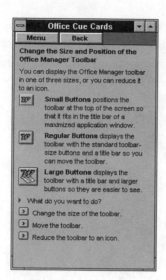

?Q&A

> *That Cue Card told me exactly what to do, but now it won't get out of the way. What gives?*
>
> Cue Cards are supposed to stay "on top," but they can block the part of the program you're trying to work with. If the Cue Card is small enough, you can move it out of the way by pointing to its title bar and dragging it. If that doesn't work, click the Minimize button (the down arrow in the upper right corner) to shrink the Cue Card into an icon. When you're ready to use it again, double-click to restore it.

Show me how this program works

Some people aren't content with guided tours or detailed directions. They want a practice run, with someone else behind the wheel, before they head off into unfamiliar territory.

If that's you, no problem. Office is chock-full of demos and examples that you can watch—once or repeatedly—before you try a new task on your own. Word and Excel together offer dozens of demos. Click the Examples and Demos button, as seen in figure 3.5.

Fig. 3.5

Click on the Examples and Demos button and let Word or Excel take over your mouse and keyboard (temporarily).

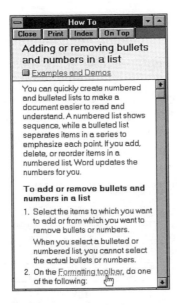

Office pops up a screen (like the one in fig. 3.6) that explains how your chosen topic works. If you want Word to perform each step in the process for you, just click the Demo button. The effect is a little like a poltergeist has taken over your mouse and keyboard. But once you get past the spooky special effects, it's a good way to learn.

Fig. 3.6

You get a step-by-step demonstration of ways to do any of several dozen useful tasks.

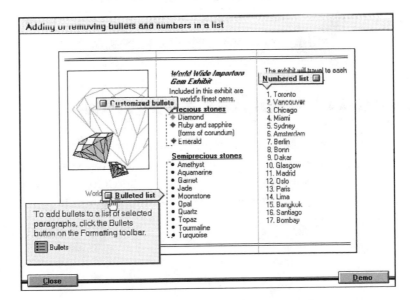

I'm just curious. Surprise me!

Excel's Tip Wizard actually helps you learn how to use the program.

The Tip Wizard button, which looks like a light bulb, turns yellow when it sees you do something that it knows you can do faster or more easily. Click on the button to show the Tip Wizard box (shown in fig. 3.7), and the light bulb turns white again.

Fig. 3.7
Excel's Tip Wizard watches over your shoulder as you work, suggesting shortcuts and tricks.

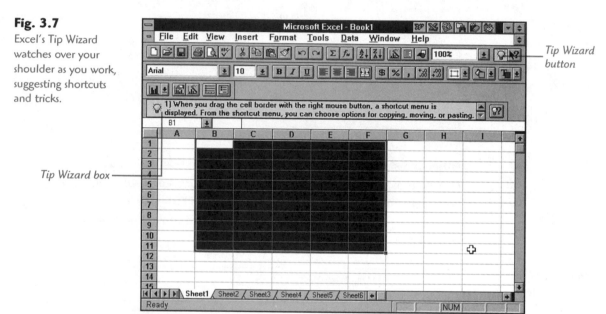

Tip Wizard button

Tip Wizard box

I'm used to another program

If you spent years learning to use WordPerfect or 1-2-3, and you just switched to Office, you're probably feeling a little disoriented right now. It's a little like the feeling you get when you first slide into a rental car—none of the buttons, knobs, or levers are where you expect them to be.

How can you make the switch easier? By turning on the built-in help for both programs.

If you know WordPerfect, pull down Word's Help menu and click on the WordPerfect Help choice. Now you can pick a WordPerfect command in one window and see step-by-step instructions for doing the same thing in Word.

1-2-3 users can get the same kind of help by clicking Excel's Help menu and choosing Lotus 1-2-3.

4

Saving Your Work (and Finding It Again)

What happens if you don't bother organizing your files? Eventually you'll spend so much time looking for stuff that you won't have time to get any real work done!

In this chapter:

- How do I create a new file?
- What should I call my file?
- Why did Windows beep when I gave my file a name?
- I want to work with the file I put away yesterday!
- Hey, where did that file go?

Imagine what a mess you'd have on your hands if you simply threw every scrap of paper in your office into the nearest file cabinet without bothering to label it. Junk mail, annual reports, confidential memos, paycheck stubs—just toss 'em into whichever drawer is open, and keep doing the same thing until the cabinet is full. Eventually you'll spend so much time looking for old pieces of paper that you won't have time to get any real work done.

If you're not careful, the same thing will happen inside your PC. Your computer lets you save your work, so you can pick up tomorrow where you left off today. You can even reuse old data files—changing a few words here and a few numbers there to do an hour's worth of work in just a few minutes.

But you can't reuse your work if you don't save it first. And you can't save any time if you can't find those saved files. In this chapter, I'll tell you secrets for saving files so you can find them *fast*.

How do I keep my files organized?

When we talk about a file, we're not referring to a sheet of paper inside a manila folder—we're talking about a data file stored on a disk inside your computer. Fortunately, these electronic files are as easy to organize as stacks of paper. To make it easier to find files fast, you can collect them in groups and store each group in its own folder, or directory.

What's a file?

As far as your computer is concerned, a **file** is just a collection of information. If it were a file on your desktop, it might contain a piece of paper or a Polaroid picture. On your computer, a file can hold almost anything—a memo, a report, a budget, or a bunch of charts and graphs. If you have a multimedia PC, a file can even hold a recording of Clint Eastwood saying "Go ahead, make my day."

Every file on your computer has a name, and your computer's operating system keeps track of details like how big it is and when you last saved it.

What's a directory?

What would happen if you took every piece of paper in your office and just threw it into a huge cardboard box? You'd never be able to find anything, right? So, to organize your paper files, you use file folders: one for sales reports; another for complaint letters; another for canceled checks.

Directories help you organize your computer files in much the same way. You start with the **root directory**, a special folder that doesn't have a name. Inside that folder, you can create more directories to store groups of files. Most people have directories called DOS and WINDOWS, where all the operating system files are stored. If you used the default installation, your Office files wound up in three separate subdirectories under a directory called MSOFFICE.

Directories have names (no more than eight characters allowed, plus an optional extension of three characters or fewer) and creation dates, just like files. When a directory is stored inside of another directory, it's called a **subdirectory**. On my computer, I've created a directory called DATA, and inside that directory I've created a bunch of subdirectories, like BOOKS and LETTERS and TRAVEL—one for each project or group of related files I'm working on. If you're the sort of person who likes to sort your socks by color, you can put folders inside of folders inside of still more folders until you wind up with a long file name that looks like this: C:\DATA\LETTERS\COMPLAIN\1995\LETTER23.DOC.

Why should I care?

Organizing your working files probably doesn't seem like such a big deal now. But just wait till a year from now, when you've created a few hundred (or a few thousand!) working files with the Office programs. Even a basic filing system will make it a lot easier for you to sort through all those letters and reports later.

How do I create a new file?

Whenever you start one of the Office programs, you begin with a brand new, squeaky-clean document (or spreadsheet or presentation). You don't need to do anything else to start working. You don't even need to worry about what to call it—Office gives it a generic name like Book1 or Document1 until you get around to giving it a more meaningful name.

 After you've started an Office program, it's easy to create more new documents. Just click on the top choice in the File menu: New. Or click the New button (the one that looks like a blank sheet of paper).

 If you're in too much of a hurry to reach for the mouse, you can always press Ctrl+N to open a new document. This keyboard shortcut works the same in Word, Excel, and PowerPoint, and it's easy to remember: "N is for new."

What should I call my file?

Eventually, you'll want to save your file, usually on the hard disk inside your PC. To do so, you'll need to pick a file name that follows the rules for DOS. These rules are pretty strict, and if you don't follow them to the letter, DOS will yell at Windows and Windows will beep at you, then pop up a stern message like the one in figure 4.1. As much as you might *want* to call your new Word document "My really important, highly confidential memo," you'll have to settle for something a lot shorter, like IMPTMEMO.DOC.

Fig. 4.1
If you type a file name that breaks one of the DOS rules, you'll see an error message like this one.

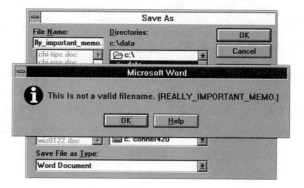

How do I know if my file name is legal?

A legal file name has to follow these rules:

- You're allowed up to eight characters, although you don't have to use them all. You can create a one-character file name if you'd like.

- Every file name can also have an **extension** of up to three characters. Common extensions for Word documents, for example are DOC (short for *document*) and TXT (for *text*).

- File names may use any of the letters from A to Z and numbers from 0 to 9.

- The following special characters are allowed in a file name:
  _ ^ $ ~ ! # % & - @

- You can use brackets ([]), curly braces ({}), single quotation marks, apostrophes, and parentheses as parts of the name.

- You may *not* use the plus sign (+), equal sign (=), vertical-line character (|), or double quotation mark ("). Spaces, commas, slashes (/), and backslashes (\) are also prohibited.

- You can use a period only for separating the eight-letter file name from the three-letter extension.

Why should I worry about file extensions?

File extensions may seem a little silly—what can you do with three characters, after all?—but they actually serve a purpose. Windows uses a file's extension to create an **association** between your file and the program that created it. When you use these associations, you can start up your program and automatically load a document just by double-clicking on the file's name in the Windows File Manager.

①(Tip)

If you just type the file name, without adding a period or an extension, the Office programs will automatically add the right extension for you.

Enough already! I just want to save this file!

Once you've chosen a legal file name, the only remaining task is to tell Office to give that name to whatever you're working on right now. Pull down the File menu and choose Save. You'll see a dialog box like the one in figure 4.2.

①(Tip)

You can't create a directory from inside a File dialog box. To save your new document in a new directory, you'll have to click on the MOM toolbar's Office button and start up the Windows File Manager. Choose File, Create Directory, switch back to Office, and try again.

Fig. 4.2
Whenever you want to save your work, you'll use a dialog box like this one.

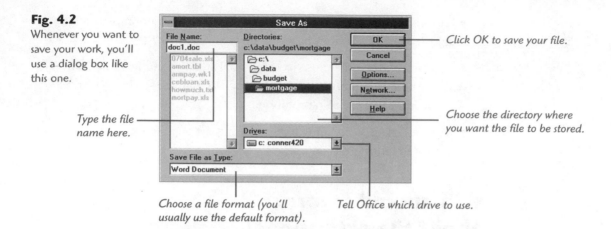

Type the file name here.

Choose the directory where you want the file to be stored.

Click OK to save your file.

Choose a file format (you'll usually use the default format).

Tell Office which drive to use.

What are all those options for?

Whenever you save a file in Word or Excel, the dialog box includes a button called Options. Click that button, and you'll see *another* dialog box, like the one shown in figure 4.3.

Fig. 4.3
More decisions! If you press the Options button when you try to save a file in Word (top) or Excel (bottom), you can ask Office to handle your document with a little extra care.

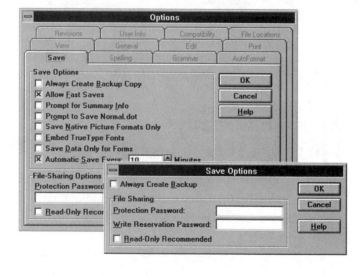

These options let you do three useful things:

- If there's something important in your original file that you might want to look at again, use the **Always Create Backup** option to make a copy of the original version every time you open a file.

- Instead of tying a string around your finger, use the **Automatic Save** option to tell Word (but not Excel) to save your work every so often, because you tend to forget. Until you tell Word to stop, it will automatically save every document you work on, at whatever interval you choose.

- Use the **Protection Password** option to lock up your document or worksheet tighter than James Bond's little black book. Unless someone else knows the secret word, he or she can't look at your Top Secret words or numbers.

 **<Caution>** If you forget your password, you can kiss your data goodbye. There's no way to figure out the password except by trying every possible combination of letters and numbers—and that would take hundreds of years! If your data's important, write down the password and put it in a safe place, like your wallet.

Should I add summary information to my files?

Summary information helps you figure out what's really inside a file. "Draft presentation for Super Bowl promotion" means a lot more than SBPROMO1.PPT, wouldn't you say?

You can't do anything about those silly eight-letter names, but you can give your documents a real title, and even add some comments, when you use the Summary Info boxes (see fig. 4.4). These little details work exactly the same in every Office program. Best of all, you can use these extra details—like keywords and comments—to search for a lost file later.

Fig. 4.4
What's inside
SBPROMO1.PPT? The
Summary Info box lets
you add plain-English
labels and comments
to your documents,
presentations, and
worksheets.

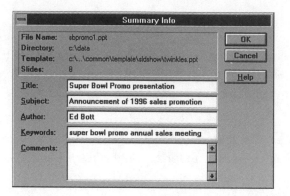

How to be a highly effective Office user

Everyone has a junk drawer—that one catchall drawer where you plop stuff that's too valuable to throw out.

If your entire work area is one big junk drawer, this section's not for you. But if you're even slightly organized, these tips can help you keep your important stuff from landing in your computer's junk drawer.

- It's a bad idea to store your data files in the same place as your program files. Create a separate directory for your data, and store all your working files there. You can name the directory DATA, DOCS, FILES, WORK, PROJECTS, STUFF, or whatever works for you.

- Use subdirectories to keep groups of related documents organized. Inside your DATA directory, for example, you might create subdirectories for LETTERS and MEMOS. Or you might create separate directories for each person who uses the computer.

- Use a consistent file-naming strategy. It doesn't matter what you do, as long as it makes sense to you. For example, you might use the letters LTR to start every file name that refers to a letter, so that LTR0921B.DOC is the second letter you wrote on September 21st. (See why Summary Info is so handy?)

- Begin a new document with its title. Word and Excel pick up the first line of your document and plop it into the Title section of the Summary Info box for you.

I want to work with a file I saved earlier

Opening a file is easy. Just pull down the File menu and choose Open, then pick the name of the file from the list in the File Open dialog box. If you can't find the file, you may need to switch to a different directory or enter a different extension.

Where did that file go?

Imagine how tired you'd get if every time you wanted to put a folder in a file cabinet, you had to go down to the lobby, switch to another elevator and travel up two floors, then walk all the way down a long hall. But that's what Office makes you do every time you try to open or save a file. By default, whenever you use the File Open or File Save dialog boxes, Office highlights the directory where your program files are stored. And that's a terrible place to put the files you work with every day.

You'll be much more productive if you keep your files in a clean, well-organized place that you can get to in one or two steps. Once you've set aside this special place for your files, you can tell Office to take you straight to that directory every time you open or save a file.

Fortunately, it's relatively easy to set up the Office programs so they always take you to the same place when you save your data files (and look for them again). You may need to move up or down the directory tree to find the right folder, but at least you start in nearly the right place. Unfortunately, this is one area where the three big Office programs definitely do not work alike.

> ❝ **Plain English, please!**
>
> When you first set up Office, it makes all sorts of assumptions about where you want to store files and how you want each program to look. These assumptions are called **defaults**. The default program directory, for example, is MSOFFICE, and the default MOM toolbar uses tiny buttons. If you don't like one of these assumptions, it's MOM's default. ❞

Setting up default file locations

Setting default file locations for Word, Excel, and PowerPoint involves three slightly different sets of steps to get the job done.

To tell **Word** where you prefer to store your data files, choose Tools, Options, and click on the File Locations tab. Click on the first line (the one that begins with the word Documents), and click on the Modify button (see fig. 4.5). Type in a directory name, or browse around the list of directories until you find the right one, then click OK.

Fig. 4.5
Use the Options dialog box to tell Word where you want it to take you first whenever you open or save a file.

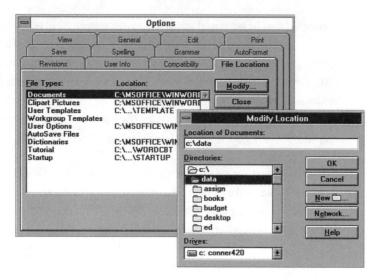

With **Excel**, you also click Tools, Options, but then you choose the General tab, as shown in figure 4.6. In the box labeled Default File Location, type the full path of the directory where you want your data files. No browsing allowed, unfortunately.

Fig. 4.6
To set up a default file location for your Excel workbooks, you have to know the exact directory name, complete with colons and slashes. Yeccch!

> **Options**
>
> | Custom Lists | Chart | Color | Module General | Module Format |
> | View | Calculation | Edit | Transition | **General** |
>
> ─ Reference Style ─   ─ Menus ─
> ⦿ A1   ○ R1C1   ☒ Recently Used File List
> ☐ Microsoft Excel 4.0 Menus
>
> ☐ Ignore Other Applications   ☐ Reset TipWizard
> ☒ Prompt for Summary Info
>
> Sheets in New Workbook: 16
>
> Standard Font: Arial   Size: 10
>
> Default File Location: c:\data
> Alternate Startup File Location:
> User Name: Ed Bott
>
> [OK] [Cancel] [Help]

PowerPoint doesn't have a directory option under its Tools menu, so you'll have to try a different approach. Click on the Microsoft Office button on the MOM toolbar, and choose Customize from the menu. Click the Toolbar tab, select the entry for Microsoft PowerPoint in the list on the left, and click the Edit button. Now you can add the name of your data folder in the box labeled Working Directory (as shown in fig. 4.7). Click OK, make sure there's an × next to the PowerPoint entry, click OK again, and you're done.

Fig. 4.7
To start in the same place whenever you open or save your PowerPoint files, use the MOM toolbar's Customize command to enter a default directory for PowerPoint.

> **Edit Program Item**
>
> Description: Microsoft PowerPoint
>
> Registered Location: C:\msoffice\...\powerpnt.exe
>
> Parameters:
>
> Working Directory: c:\data
>
> [OK] [Cancel] [Browse...] [Help]

{Note} See Chapter 5 for more information about searching for files using the Microsoft Office Manager.

How do I move or rename a file after I've created it?

Most of the Office programs have some simple (or not so simple) ways to work with files, but the easiest way is to click the Microsoft Office button and start up the Windows File Manager. From there, you can move a file, copy it, create a directory, rename a file, or erase it without any fuss.

5

MOM (the Microsoft Office Manager) Knows Best

MOM runs a full-service information kiosk in the lobby of our Office building. The MOM help system offers everything you need.

In the lobby of my office building, there's a security guard on duty 24 hours a day. Most of the time, people just walk right past his station; he might as well be invisible. So, is he useless? Not on your life.

That guard eyes everyone who walks in and out of the building. Whenever anyone asks, he gives directions to a passing visitor. And even though the building directory is never up-to-date, he knows exactly where to find any person, place, or business in the whole building.

The Microsoft Office has an equally unobtrusive caretaker that you'll see every time you start your computer. It's called the **Microsoft Office Manager**, and most of the time it sits quietly on the title bar of whatever program you're running right now. Is it useful? Absolutely. In fact, if you use the Office programs regularly, it's more flexible and easier to get to than the Windows Program Manager.

Who (or what) is MOM?

MOM is the nickname for the Microsoft Office Manager. Think of it as the lobby of your own three-story Office building. You'll almost always stop here when you visit with the Office programs.

In the MOM lobby, there's a pull-down menu of Office programs and services that works just like the directory-under-glass you'll find in real office buildings. If you already know where you want to go, the row of buttons in the top right-hand corner of your screen works just like the buttons in an elevator (see fig. 5.1 for an explanation of what these buttons do).

Click here to start up
individual Office programs.

Fig. 5.1
"Next stop, Microsoft Word..." The buttons on the MOM toolbar work just like elevator buttons to shuttle you straight to the individual Office programs.

Click here to pull down
the Office menu.

Click here to
search for a file.

By default, the tiny buttons sit right on the title bar of all your maximized applications. They're exactly the same height as a typical title bar, so they blend right in, as you can see in figure 5.2. (If your program isn't maximized, the toolbar just sits in the upper right corner of the screen.)

⊛ {Note} _____ | Don't worry if your toolbar doesn't look exactly like the one shown here. As we'll see later, it's easy to add buttons and move them around.

Fig. 5.2
Tiny, aren't they? The MOM toolbar buttons are exactly the same height as the title bar of a typical Windows program, so they blend right in.

MOM toolbar
buttons

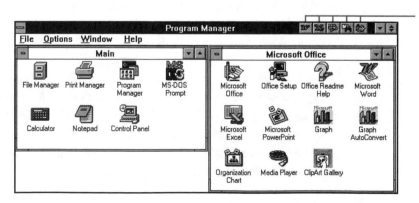

Q&A ___

> *Microsoft Office doesn't start when I start Windows. I have to double-click the Microsoft Office button every time. Can't I just load Office automatically?*
>
> Sure. The Office installation program should have done this, but something must have happened on your computer. Switch to Program Manager, select the Microsoft Office button in the Microsoft Office group, and hold down the Ctrl key while you drag it into your Program Manager's StartUp group. The next time you start Windows, the MOM toolbar will be there waiting.

Can I get directions from MOM?

MOM runs a full-service information kiosk in the lobby of our Office building. Come back here any time you're not sure what to do next. The MOM help system offers everything from quick explanations of technical terms to detailed instructions on how to get the different tenants (Word, Excel, and PowerPoint) to work together better.

To ask Office for help, click the Microsoft Office button at the far right, then choose Help or Cue Cards from the pull-down menu that appears. (The menu should look like the one in fig. 5.3.)

Fig. 5.3

Click on the Microsoft Office button (the one at the far right) to pick from a menu of available programs and Office services.

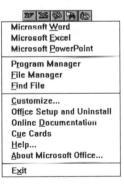

For more details about what's inside Office Help, look in Chapter 3.

I can't find a file! Where do I look?

Office has a search team that can hunt down a lost file on your hard disk a lot faster than you can. Just choose Find File from the Microsoft Office menu (or click the Find File button on the toolbar) to get to the dialog box shown in figure 5.4. If you've used Find File already, you'll see a different dialog box. Click the Search button to get to this dialog box.

Fig. 5.4

Office lets you search anywhere on your computer for files. You can look for a lost file using part of its name, or tell Office to look for a word or phrase that you know is in the file.

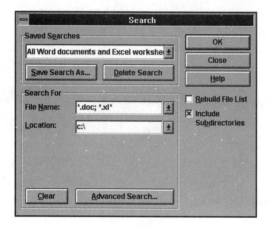

Using the Search dialog box is a four-step process:

1 Tell Office what to look for. Enter a name in the File Name box, as shown in figure 5.4. You can search for two or more names if you separate them with semicolons. Use an asterisk (*) to fill in for any characters you're not sure about: **sb*.***, for example, will find SBPROMO.DOC and SBCOSTS.XLS.

2 Tell Office where to look. In our example, we've specified C:\, our hard drive. If you want to poke through an entire directory or even your whole hard disk, make sure the Include Subdirectories check box has an × in it.

3 Give Office any extra details. You don't have to do this, but it can improve the likelihood that you'll find the one file you're looking for. Click the Advanced Search button and follow the instructions to narrow down the range of dates, or give Office a word or phrase to search for.

4 Click the OK button to start the search.

When Office has finished nosing around, you'll see a list of files that match the criteria you defined earlier. As figure 5.5 shows, you can peek inside files without actually starting up one of the big Office programs.

Fig. 5.5

Whatever files your search turns up appear in this window. You can peek into the file, or you can ask Office to show you summary information about all the files in the list.

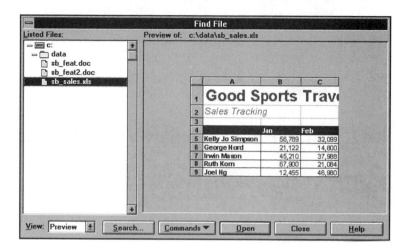

⏺**Q&A**

Find File didn't show me the file I'm looking for. What do I do now?

First, click the Advanced Search button and check all the settings to make sure you haven't accidentally narrowed the range of dates or specified summary text. Check the name you're looking for carefully; Find File is extremely fussy about spelling. If you're looking in a directory that has lots of subdirectories in it, make sure the Include Subdirectories box is checked.

Using MOM to move around

The whole idea behind MOM is to give you a simple shortcut to your Office programs. Going through the Windows Program Manager can be a big hassle—you have to find Program Manager first, and then you have to find the Microsoft Office group. By contrast, clicking the MOM buttons is easy because they're always right there in the top right corner of the screen.

What does *that* button do?

If you're not sure what a button does, let the mouse pointer sit on top of the button for a few seconds. A ToolTip, like the one in figure 5.6, will pop up like one of the name tags that people wear at conventions.

Fig. 5.6
"Hi! My name is Microsoft Word." Pop-up ToolTips are plain-English labels that explain what you can do with the button you're pointing at.

What do I do with all those buttons?

The MOM toolbar lets you quickly start up a couple of programs and switch back and forth between them:

- **To start an Office program...** Just click the button with the program's icon on it.

- **To switch from one program to another...** Click the same button you use to start the program. Office is smart enough to know that the program is already running, so it just switches you there.

- **To find a file...** Click the button with the icon that looks like a folder and a pair of binoculars.

- **To see the Microsoft Office menu...** Click the button at the far right of the toolbar.

What's the pull-down menu for?

Some people like buttons. Some people don't. If you prefer to pick choices from a list of English names, go right ahead and use the menu. Also, a few of the Office services (like Cue Cards) are only available from here.

Changing the way MOM looks

Like just about everything in Windows, MOM can be customized. If it doesn't work quite the way you want, you can change it with a few mouse clicks.

I want bigger buttons!

For someone with the eyesight of a hawk, those little buttons are probably just fine. But if you find yourself squinting to see which icon is which, it's easy to make the buttons bigger.

Just choose Customize from the Office menu and click on the index tab labeled View. Pick Regular Buttons or Large Buttons to change the button size and to rearrange the toolbar into a box that floats on your screen.

If you choose Regular Buttons or Large Buttons, the MOM toolbar won't fit in your Windows title bars any more. The floating toolbar may cover up some of the data you're working with. If this bothers you, click in the check box labeled Toolbar Is Always Visible to remove the ×. Now MOM will duck out of sight any time you're working. To make it reappear, press Ctrl+Esc and choose Microsoft Office from the Task List.

I want more buttons!

If you regularly use another program in addition to the ones that come with Office, you can add it to your MOM toolbar. Click the Office button and choose Customize, then click the Toolbar tab on the dialog box that pops up. You have these options:

- **To add a Microsoft program...** Find its name in the scrolling list, then click in the check box next to it. Make sure you see an ×.

- **To add another program...** If it's a standard Windows program, look for its name in the list. (It's easy to add the Windows Calculator to the toolbar, for example, as you can see in fig. 5.7.) If the program isn't on the list, click the Add button, and fill in the Description (optional),

Command Line, and Working Directory (optional). Office will use what you type in the Description box for the ToolTip that appears when you point at the button. In the command-line box, type the complete path and file name for the program. If you're not sure, use the Browse button to find it. (Figure 5.8 shows what the expanded toolbar looks like.)

Fig. 5.7

Want to add other programs to the MOM toolbar? No problem. Just click to put an × in the check box next to the program's name.

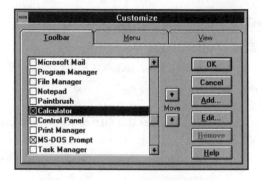

- **To take a button off the toolbar...** Click in the check box next to its name and make sure the × is removed.

Fig. 5.8

The MOM toolbar, after adding new buttons for the Windows Calculator and the MS–DOS prompt.

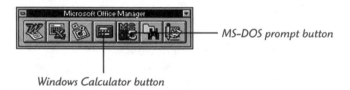

MS–DOS prompt button

Windows Calculator button

I want to rearrange the buttons

That's what the up and down arrows (above and below the word Move) in the Customize dialog box are for. Items on the top of the list appear at the left, while items further down the list appear to the right. To move the Find File button to the far left, just click on its name in the list, and then press the up arrow until its name is above the entry for Microsoft Word.

 **{Note}**

Don't be surprised if the entry for Microsoft Word floats into different positions on the Office menu without any warning. There's a minor (and harmless) bug in MOM that causes this eerie behavior. Use the Customize menu to move it back where it belongs.

Part II:
Using Word

6 Creating a New Document

In this chapter:

- Where do I begin?
- Can Word templates and wizards really do my work for me?
- I need to delete this text
- How do I move around in a document—fast?
- I'm ready to save my work

Word can't make you smarter or more creative, but it's filled with all sorts of clever tricks that can at least get you started.

Any writer will tell you the hardest part of her job is coming up with that first sentence. Staring at a blank screen can be the most frustrating experience on earth, especially when the clock is ticking and the deadline is approaching.

Word can't make you smarter, or more creative, or more clever. After all, it's just a word processor. But it's filled with all sorts of clever tricks that can at least get you started. If you're really lucky, you'll run into one of the Word wizards, who can do part of your work for you.

And once you've broken through the creative logjam, Word can make your documents look downright irresistible, with colorful graphics, bold type, and eye-catching layouts that say, "Read me!"

We'll get to the business of making your words look good a little later. And eventually, you'll see how to use Word with the other Office programs to make powerful documents filled with facts and figures. But first, let's figure out how to get that first sentence onto the screen.

What's in a Word window?

The Word screen may look crowded, but everything you see is there for a reason—to help you turn words and pictures into great-looking, easy-to-read documents.

Standard toolbar
One-click buttons for the things you do all the time with Word, like open a file, save your work, or undo something you accidentally (oops!) did.

Title bar
The name of the program; if you've maximized your document, its name will show up here, too.

MOM toolbar
Use these buttons to start up other Office programs (or jump to them, if they're already running).

Menu bar
All your choices are lined up underneath these nine menu choices. Any time you're not sure how to do something, look here.

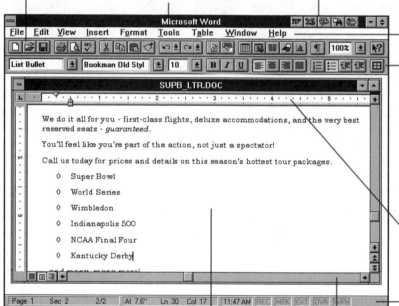

Formatting toolbar
More buttons. This set lets you change the appearance of the words in your document.

Rulers
Help you see where your words and pictures will land on the printed page. If you find them distracting, you can always hide them.

Status bar
Look here for information about the current document ("What page is this?") and your computer ("What time does my computer think it is?").

Other toolbars (hidden)
Word has lots more toolbars, but they only pop up when you need them. Right-click on any toolbar to see the list of available toolbars.

Document window
Every letter, memo, report, and brochure you work on gets its own window. You can open as many windows as you like. If the document is not maximized, it gets its own title bar, showing its file name.

Scroll bar
Use these sliders and arrows to see the parts of your document that don't fit in the window you're looking at now.

Where do I begin?

Ready, fire, aim! Oops—that's not the right order, is it? But some people are so anxious to get results that they forget the most important part of the writing process: What am I trying to say? Who's my audience?

Before you pick a paper size and start pounding on the keys, ask those two big questions first. Then answer these little questions:

- How formal do I need to be?

- Is there a wizard or a template that can get me started?

- Do I need to use any graphics or tables?

OK, I'm ready to start writing

Word assumes you want to get straight to work, but it has no idea what you want to do. So when you first start the program, it hands you the computer equivalent of a blank sheet of paper, as if to say, "Get to work!"

Now, that's fine if you just want to scribble out a bunch of notes. But most of the time, you're going to be producing some kind of familiar business document. A letter, maybe a memo, or even (if you're feeling particularly ambitious) a newsletter to send to all your customers or coworkers.

You'd be a lot more productive if you didn't have to start every one of those jobs from scratch, right? Well, you don't have to. Word includes more than 25 ready-made documents to get you started. They're called **templates,** and if you use them regularly, you can save a few minutes—or even a few hours— on each document you create.

Do it yourself with templates

Have you ever tried to create a work of art using a paint-by-the-numbers kit? You smear a little blue in the spots labeled "B," some red in the spots marked with an "R," and before you know it, you're looking at a pleasant little seascape.

Word templates work the same way. Instead of starting with a blank sheet of paper, Word creates each new document by copying a blueprint that contains text and graphics, lines and boxes, fancy fonts, and maybe even colors. As you replace the template's text and graphics with your own words and pictures, your letter or report slowly takes shape—a lot faster than if you had had to do it all. (See fig. 6.1 for a partial list of the available templates.)

Fig. 6.1

Pick a template, any template. When you choose File, New, Word pops up a list of predefined templates so you can get a running start with your new document.

⊗\<Caution\> Templates are stored in special files that end with the letters DOT. Be extremely careful with these files! If you open the original template file by mistake (instead of creating a new document based on it), any changes you make will be saved in the template. From then on, every document you create using that template will include all those changes, whether you want them or not.

Chances are, there's a Word template for most of the documents you produce every day. You can make your own templates, too, by tinkering with one of the built-in templates or by starting from scratch.

Here are some of the most useful built-in templates:

- **Take care of business.** Use the Invoice and Purchord (purchase order) templates.

- **Write letters, memos, and reports.** Take your choice of three different formats for each (Memo1, Memo2, and Memo3, for example).

- **Spread the news.** Try the Brochure and Press release templates (Brochur1, Presrel1, Presrel2, and Presrel3).

- **Make payday simpler.** Weektime helps you create a weekly time sheet.

(Tip)

> Press Ctrl+N (or click the New button) to create a new document based on the Normal template, which looks just like a blank sheet of paper. Choose File, New from the pull-down menus if you want to use a different template.

Let Word do the work with wizards

For some jobs, even filling in the blanks on a paint-by-the-numbers canvas is too much work. You'll get better results if you hire a professional painter to do the work for you. Word has a few of those experts for hire: they're called **wizards**.

The concept behind a wizard is simple. He asks you some questions, and then, based on your answers, he does all the work, leaving you with a filled-in document. The first time you use a wizard, he might ask a lot of questions, filling in things like your name and address; most wizards have a good memory, though, and the next time you use them they'll skip those questions and just ask a few questions that pertain to the job at hand.

All in all, there are 10 Word wizards. Here's what some of them can do for you:

- **Letter Wizard.** Gets you started with business and personal letters, and even includes 15 "canned" letters you can use in various business situations, like one you can use to demand payment for a bounced check.

- **Memo Wizard.** Helps you put together a complete interoffice memo, using one of three different looks.

- **Agenda Wizard.** Do your meetings last too long? Maybe one of these no-nonsense agenda forms can help.

- **Résumé Wizard.** If you're looking for a new job, this wizard can help—it walks you, step-by-step, through the process of creating a sharp-looking résumé.

- **Newsletter Wizard.** Helps you make like William Randolph Hearst, turning out professional-looking publishing projects with almost no work (see fig. 6.2).

Fig. 6.2

Wizards, like this one for making professional-looking newsletters, ask you a bunch of questions and then do your work for you. (Don't you wish there was a Do the Laundry Wizard?)

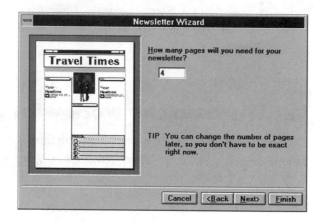

I just want to start writing

Enough already! After all, the whole point of a word processor is to help you write. So let's start writing.

On a fresh document

Most of the time, you'll want to pick an appropriate spot on your document to start working. If you used the Normal template, you don't have a choice: you just start at the top. If you used another template, click where you want your words to appear, and then start typing.

> *Don't* hit the Enter key when you come to the end of a line. Word knows you've run out of room and will **wrap** your words automatically to the next line. Press the Enter key only when you want to start a new paragraph.

Using a template

Some templates, like the Invoice template shown in figure 6.3, contain "generic" text that you have to replace before you can use the document. You don't want your customers making their checks payable to "Your Company Name," do you?

Fig. 6.3

Templates help you get started. Use the mouse to highlight the "generic" text—it will disappear as soon as you start typing.

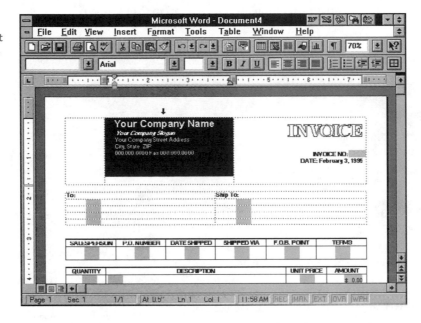

Fortunately, Word makes it easy to replace text. Just use the mouse to select the words you want to replace, and then start typing. As soon as you type the first letter, the template text will vanish and is replaced by your new, more relevant words.

⊗<Caution> When you first start Word, you enter text in Insert mode—that is, everything you type "pushes" the text that's already there out of the way. If you hit the Insert key by accident, you'll switch into Overtype mode, where every letter you type gobbles up the one to the right of the insertion point. (If the OVR indicator on the status bar is black instead of gray, you're in Overtype mode.) If you press the Insert key by accident, be prepared to use Word's Undo feature to get your old text back.

What happens when I get to the end of the page?

When you're writing, you probably won't even notice you've reached the end of a page. That's OK. Just as Word knows when you've come to the end of a line, it also knows when a page is full and a new page needs to begin. (We'll cover this topic in more detail in Chapter 8.)

What's normal?

Word makes a bunch of assumptions whenever you start a new document. For example, it assumes that you speak English, so it uses the U.S. version of the built-in dictionary and thesaurus (we'll get to them in Chapter 9). It also assumes that you use standard 8 1/2" × 11" paper most of the time, so every new document is formatted to go on plain old letter paper.

These built-in choices, taken together, make up the default document. They're stored in a special document template called NORMAL.DOT.

Here's what's inside NORMAL.DOT:

- A default typeface and size for the words in your document. Unless you change the default typeface, every Normal document you create starts out in 10 point Times New Roman.

- A default paper size and orientation. In the United States, you get letter-sized paper in portrait mode.

- Standard margins (1.25 inches on each side, and 1 inch on the top and bottom) and single line spacing.

- All the toolbars and styles you see on the screen. (Yes, you can change them, and when you do, the changes are stored in a template.)

- Special tricks like **macros** (miniature programs written in a special language called WordBasic) and custom menus.

Why does this stuff matter? Well, if you decide that you'd really like your Normal documents to start out in a larger typeface, or you want different top and bottom margins, you'll have to change NORMAL.DOT. Fortunately, that's pretty easy to do. The Format Font and Page Setup dialog boxes both have buttons labeled Default. After you've reset the fonts and margins to your liking, push the Default button to tell Word that you want your preferences saved in NORMAL.DOT.

Now, whenever you start up a new document based on the Normal template, you'll get what *you* want.

Deleting text

OK, so maybe every word you write isn't deathless prose. If you want to get rid of some of those words you just typed, Word gives you lots of different ways to do it:

- [◆Backspace] zaps the character to the left.

- [Del] zaps the character to the right.

- [Ctrl]+[◆Backspace] cuts the word to the left.

- [Ctrl]+[Del] cuts the word to the right.

- [Ctrl]+[X] cuts whatever's highlighted and puts it on the Clipboard.

For more information about how the Windows Clipboard works, see Chapter 2.

Moving around in a document

Are you a fluid writer? Do you get caught up in the rhythm of it all and suddenly find yourself on page 20, with no idea what you wrote before page 5? Word has all sorts of shortcuts for moving around in a document.

The easy way, of course, is just to point the mouse at one of the scroll bars and slide up or down until you hit the spot you want to see. But the keyboard shortcuts are more precise:

- [Home] and [End] move to the beginning and end of the line you're on right now.

- [PgUp] and [PgDn] move up and down one full window.

- [Ctrl]+[Home] and [Ctrl]+[End] skip to the very top and very bottom of the document.

- [◆Shift]+[F5] is one of the coolest Word shortcut keys of all. It remembers the last three places you did something, and jumps to those three places, one after another. This trick comes in very handy if you've scrolled through a long document and you want to hop back to where you started.

- **Go To** (Ctrl+G) lets you tell Word to hop to a specific page number. You can also pop up the Go To dialog box shown in figure 6.4 by double-clicking on the status bar.

Fig. 6.4

The fast way to jump around in a big document. Double-click on the page numbers in the status bar to pop up this Go To box.

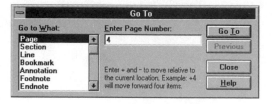

How do I adjust the margins?

You can leave extra room on either side, or the top or bottom of your page, which is useful if you want to add comments in the right margin, for example. You can also trim the margins to pack more words on the page, although that option may sacrifice readability. You can't set the margins to zero, though, because every printer has an unprintable area that Windows won't let you use.

To adjust the margins, choose File, Page Setup, and then click on the Margins tab (see fig. 6.5). You can set margins for all four edges, as well as the **gutter**—that's the inside of the page when you're printing on both sides of the paper. You can also change margins and even paper size in the middle of a document. Just pick This Point Forward from the drop-down list labeled Apply To.

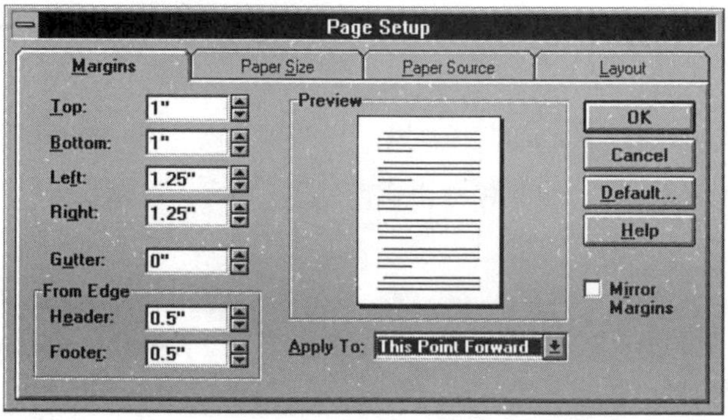

Fig. 6.5

Click on the Margins tab in the Page Setup dialog box to adjust the amount of white space around your pages.

How do I change paper size?

Most of the time, you'll want to print your work on plain letter paper. But what happens when you want to use legal-size paper? Or when you want to work with your text going from side to side along the wide edge of the paper? That's where Word's Page Setup dialog box comes in handy.

Choose File, Page Setup to pop up the dialog box shown in figure 6.6.

Fig. 6.6

Choose File, Page Setup to change paper sizes and switch from Portrait (letter) to Landscape (wide) orientation. This is also the place to tell Word how much space to leave on the edges of each sheet of paper.

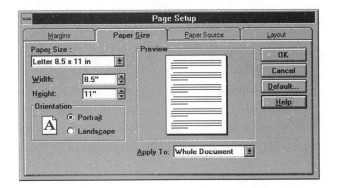

Using this dialog box, you can do just about anything that has to do with your paper:

- Change the amount of white space (the **margins**) on the top, bottom, left, and right edges of the paper.

- Switch to legal-size paper or the European-standard A5 format, or set up Word to use a special paper size. (You want to print on Christmas card stock, 5" × 8"? Word can handle it...)

- Tell Word to use a different tray on your printer. That can come in handy if you have letterhead in one tray and plain paper in another.

Saving a new document

If you've been writing for more than 20 minutes, it's time to take a break. For one thing, it'll keep your shoulders from cramping up and your wrists from developing repetitive stress disorders. For another, it'll give you a chance to save the work you've done so far.

 Make it a habit to save your work regularly. There's no feeling quite as sicken-
ing as the one you get when the power fails and your PC dies after you've
been working for hours without saving. Remember: until you use the Save
command, your work can disappear at a moment's notice!

Saving your Word document is a simple, three-step process:

1 Press Ctrl+S (or click the Save button on the standard toolbar).

2 Enter a name of eight characters or fewer in the File Name text box,
and click OK.

 Word automatically tacks the .DOC file extension onto your eight-character
file name unless you specify something different. You can use other extensions,
but I strongly recommend you use .DOC at the end of every file: Windows
knows that a DOC file is a Word file, and it automatically starts up Word when
you double-click on a file with that extension.

3 Fill out the summary info, if you want to. Choose File, Summary Info to
pop up the dialog box shown in figure 6.7.

Fig. 6.7
Don't forget to fill in
this Summary Info box.
It might seem like a
hassle now, but you'll
thank yourself later,
when you're trying to
pull this one document
out of the hundreds on
your hard drive.

Summary Info	
File Name:	TRAVTMS1.DOC
Directory:	C:\DATA
Title:	Travel Times, Volume 1 No. 1
Subject:	Super Bowl promotion
Author:	Ed Bott
Keywords:	Super Bowl promotion Miami football
Comments:	The first edition of our newsletter

OK · Cancel · Statistics... · Help

There. You're done. That wasn't so hard, was it?

7
Opening, Organizing, and Editing Documents

Word makes it easy to add a new thought, change a word, replace one phrase with another, and move sentences and paragraphs around just by dragging them with the mouse.

In this chapter:

- What's the best way to open a document?
- What's the best view for writing? For editing? For organizing my thoughts?
- How can I move text from one place to another without hassle?
- Using Word to replace one word with another
- Oops! Using Undo to recover from mistakes

Great works of art take time. First, you sketch out the big picture with broad strokes. Then you take a finer brush and fill in the details. Finally, you go over the entire canvas with a magnifying glass, touching up those tiny flaws and making every square inch as close to perfect as you can get it.

If that sounds like a lot of work, you're right. Hey—do you think Rembrandt painted his masterpieces in an afternoon?

Really great writing takes time, too. If you've worked on a big report, you know that nothing ever gets done in one easy session. A paint-by-the-numbers Word template can get you started fast, but then you'll need all your concentration to find just the right thoughts and just the right words. And you'll probably want to move those words around so your message hits its audience with as much impact as possible.

There's no Writer's Block Wizard yet. Word can't do much to help you get your first thoughts on the screen. But once you've gotten started, Word makes it easy to add a new thought, change a word, replace one phrase with another, and move sentences and paragraphs around just by dragging them with the mouse.

Opening a document

What do you do when you want to pick up where you left off yesterday? (Or, for that matter, last month?) First, you have to find the file you were working on. Um, you *did* save it, didn't you?

I want to pick up where I left off yesterday

When you leave the office every night, you probably straighten up your desk. (Well, just a little, right?) At the very least, you take the papers you didn't finish today and stack them up in a neat pile so you can get right to work when you get in tomorrow morning.

You can do the same with the Word files you work on every day. Just look at the bottom of Word's File menu for a list of the files you worked on most recently (see fig. 7.1 for an example). To open any of the files on the list, just click the file's name.

> By default, Word keeps track of the four files you worked on most recently, but you can boost that number to as many as nine. Choose Tools, Options, and click on the General tab. Make sure there's a check mark in the box to the left of the Recently Used Files List entry, and use the little arrows to adjust the number in the box to the right.

Fig. 7.1
This one's a real time-saver: Word keeps track of the four files you worked on most recently. You can reopen any of the files just by clicking its name in the menu.

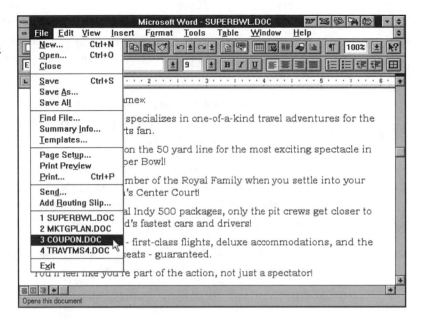

I know the file's out there *somewhere*

You say your boss *finally* got around to reviewing the first draft you wrote two weeks ago, and now you have to make a lot of little changes and a few big ones? No problem. As long as you can remember roughly what you named your document and where you stored it, it's easy to find it again. Just follow these steps:

1 Choose File, Open (or click the Open button) to display the Open dialog box shown in figure 7.2.

Fig. 7.2
The Open dialog box lets you choose the file you want to work with, no matter where it's located.

File name ⎯

Type of file ⎯

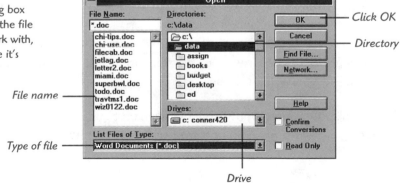

Click OK

Directory

Drive

2 Tell Word which **drive** you want to look on. Most of the time, this will be drive C. To look on your network drive or a floppy disk, click the little arrow underneath the Dri<u>v</u>es label and choose from the drop-down list.

3 Tell Word which **directory** to look in. If you can't find the right directory, double-click the folder icon at the top of the list and work your way down, one level at a time.

4 Tell Word what **type of file** to look for. Most of the time it assumes you'll want to look for files that end in DOC. If your file ends in a different combination of letters, choose All Files (*.*) from this list, and click the OK button to update the list.

5 Highlight the **file name** on the list. (If there are a lot of files, you'll need to click the down arrow to see names at the bottom of the list).

6 **Click OK** to load your file and start working.

I know my document's in this directory, but it's not in the list. What's going on?

Sometimes, Word shows only a few of the documents in a directory—those ending in the extension DOC, for example. To force it to show all the files, choose All Files (*.*) from the drop-down list under the List Files of <u>T</u>ype label. Click the OK button again to see every file in the directory.

I can't remember what that file's called

If you haven't the foggiest notion what you named a file or where you stashed it on your computer's hard disk, don't worry. Just give Word's File Finder some scraps of information about the file and let it go to work. It can sniff through your PC with as much determination as a bloodhound and bring back everything that matches.

Word's File Finder is powerful, but it's hard to use. Still, it's a lot better than trying to re-create your report from memory, isn't it?

Hang onto the bloodhound's leash and follow these steps to find your missing file:

1 Choose File, Find File. As long as Preview is selected in the View box at the lower left, you can click on a document's name in the list on the left and see what's inside in the Preview of window on the right, as shown in figure 7.3.

Fig. 7.3
Use Word's File Finder feature to preview a document before you open it. You can peek inside any Word or Excel file from here.

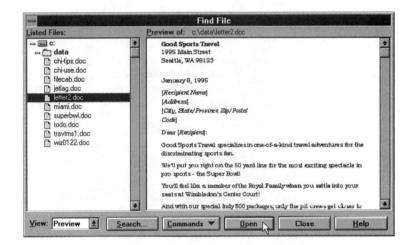

2 If your document isn't on this list, click the Search button to pop up the dialog box shown in figure 7.4. Tell Windows the file name you're looking for (use *.* if you're not sure what the name is) and where to look.

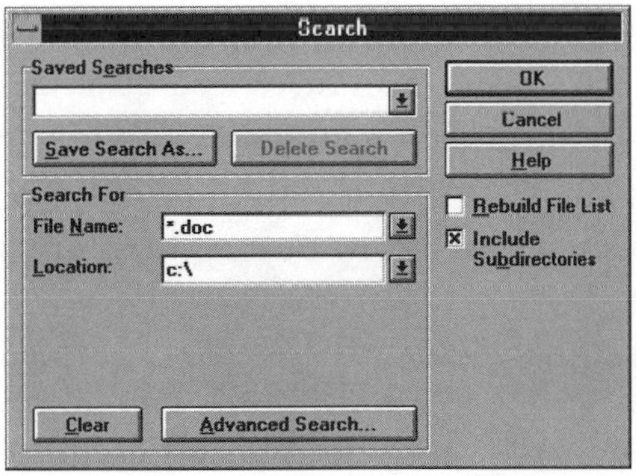

Fig. 7.4
This example will find every Word document in every directory on the main hard disk.

3 If the list is too long, or you still can't find the file, there's one more option. As long as you can remember a distinctive phrase in your document, Word can find it for you. Choose All Files (*.*) from the File Name box, and then click the Advanced Search button. Click the tab labeled Summary, and type the phrase you remember in the box labeled Containing Text, as shown in figure 7.5. Click OK here and in the next dialog box. Word will find every matching file.

Fig. 7.5
As long as you can remember a distinctive phrase in your document, Word can find it for you.

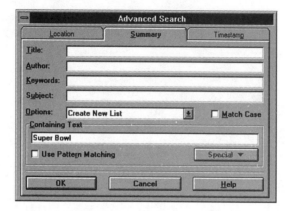

4 When you finally track down the document you've been searching for, click the Open button to start working with it.

I use Word, but my boss uses WordPerfect

Word uses its own special language to store details about your document. WordPerfect (the other popular word processor in a lot of offices) uses a completely different language. Fortunately, Word has a crew of translators on hand to make sure your WordPerfect documents will look OK. If Word recognizes the WordPerfect document, it will just open it.

⑦Q&A

Sometimes my Word documents lose a few details in the translation to WordPerfect. What can I do?

If you regularly exchange documents with a colleague who uses WordPerfect (or any other word processor), choose File, Save As, and pick Rich Text Format from the Save File As Type list. Word will add the RTF extension to your file name. Rich Text Format is a widely accepted standard for formatted documents, so the translation might go more smoothly there.

Three ways to look at any document

Are you writing? Trying to make your document look great? Organizing your thoughts? Word has a special view for each step in the writing process, as shown in figures 7.6, 7.7, and 7.8.

Fig. 7.6

Normal view is the one most people will use, most of the time. You get to see all the words and use the entire screen, without any wasted space. Perfect for quickly typing a first draft.

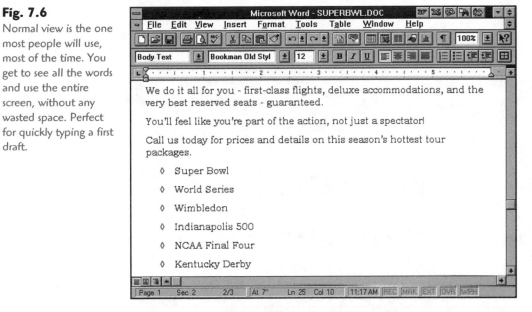

Fig. 7.7

Use Page Layout view to see exactly what your final printed pages will look like. You can see the edges of the "paper," and you get an extra vertical ruler to help you find your place on the page.

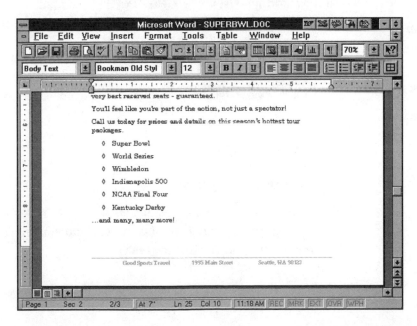

Fig. 7.8
Outline view lets you
look at how your
document is put
together. Use the
Outlining toolbar to
collapse and expand
each chunk of
heading-and-text
with just one click.

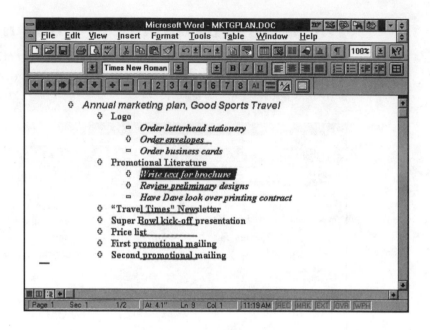

Finding the right point of view

Every great artist knows how to get the ideal perspective on a landscape. Just
hold out your thumb at arm's length, then close one eye, squint, and look real
serious. Fortunately, it's a lot easier to find the right point of view when
you're working with Word. It all depends on what you're trying to do.

{Note}

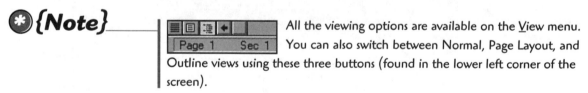

All the viewing options are available on the <u>V</u>iew menu.
You can also switch between Normal, Page Layout, and
Outline views using these three buttons (found in the lower left corner of the
screen).

I just want to type

Word starts out in Normal view, which is perfect for those times when you
just want to get the words out of your head and you aren't ready to think
about how they'll look when they're printed.

I want to see *exactly* what each page will look like

That's what Page Layout view is for. You can see how much space you have on each side of the page. As you scroll through your document, you can even see the edges at the top and bottom of each page. If you've put page numbers or a title on the page, those pieces will show up here, too.

I need to organize my thoughts first

Outline view is perfect for making sure your thoughts are well organized. Use this view to shrink your document to just its main points and to see details under each main heading, then switch to Normal or Page Layout view to write and edit. The Outlining toolbar helps you collapse and expand each section.

> It's incredibly easy to edit your work in Outline view. Click the little box in front of each paragraph and hold down the mouse button. See how the pointer changes to a four-headed arrow? Now you can drag the entire paragraph up or down, anywhere in your document, with one smooth motion.

Arrrgghh! This screen is too cluttered!

For anyone who finds all those toolbars and rulers too distracting, there's Full Screen view (see fig. 7.9). In this view, all you typically see is the page and one lonely icon that you click on to switch back to the regular Word screen. (You can also get back to your previous view by pressing the Escape key.)

> What happens to the menus when you're in full-screen mode? Nothing. They're still there, hidden just above the upper edge of the screen. You can still use them, as long as you know the first letter of the menu you want to use. So if you want to print the page you're working on, you can press Alt+F to bring down the File menu. Once it's visible, use the arrow keys to move left and right and see all the other menus, too.

Fig. 7.9
Bye-bye, menus and
toolbars. Choose Full
Screen view if you
want to work with
as few distractions
as possible.

What about Master Document view?

If you have a bunch of small documents that you want to tie into one large one, you might be tempted to try Master Document view. Ugh. Don't even *think* about it. It's a great idea, but it's very complicated, and it doesn't always work the way it's supposed to. You might even lose all your work.

If you must use it, be sure you have backup copies of all your work. And don't say I didn't warn you....

I want to make the text look a little bigger

What do you do if the words on the screen are a little too small to read easily? Just get a little closer. If you've ever used a camera with a zoom lens, you know exactly how Word's Zoom features works. Choose View, Zoom to display the Zoom dialog box shown in figure 7.10. Click on 200% for an extreme close-up. Try Whole Page to step way, way back. Choose Page Width to expand the text so it's as large as possible without running off the edge of the screen.

①(Tip) The Zoom control on the Standard toolbar lets you quickly switch between different magnification levels.

`70%` ⬇

Bugs! (It's not you, it's the program!)

Fifty years ago, at the dawn of the Information Age, a computer that could barely add 2+2 took up more space than a two-bedroom house. The transistor hadn't even been invented yet, much less the integrated circuit, so this computer was filled with vacuum tubes (remember them?) and huge metal switches. To program it, a team of scientists literally crawled through the room flipping switches on and off.

This massive electronic calculator worked flawlessly, churning out numbers onto paper tape, day after day after day. Until one day, that is, when it decided that 2+2 actually equaled 5 (or maybe 22—the exact details are a little sketchy today). The puzzled scientists crawled through the room, checking every switch, and finally discovered that a cockroach had lodged itself inside one of the switches, causing it to short-circuit. The cockroach died, but it gave its name to a new term for computer users: the **bug**.

Today, computer users still have to live with bugs. And they're a lot harder to find than that original bug, because you can't see them.

Word, like all the programs in the Microsoft Office, is a marvelous piece of work. But that doesn't mean it's perfect. Yes, Word has bugs. So do Excel and PowerPoint, and Windows itself, for that matter.

Sometimes you follow the instructions to the letter, and whatever you were trying to do just plain doesn't happen. You try it again, and again it doesn't work. You double-check the steps and try it again, and still the program doesn't do what you expect it to do. Have you found a bug? Probably.

What should you do when you think you've found a bug?

- First, call Microsoft (or send a fax), describe the problem in detail, and ask whether you've found a bug.

- If you have, ask whether there's a new version of Word (or whatever program caused the problem). Sometimes the bug has been fixed, and Microsoft can send you a disk to solve the problem.

- If there's no easy fix, ask the technical-support representative if there's a workaround. Sometimes they can suggest a procedure that will do what you want to do while sidestepping that nasty bug.

And count your blessings. After all, to track down computer bugs in the 1990s, you don't have to crawl around on your hands and knees searching for cockroaches.

Fig. 7.10
Zoom! Choose <u>V</u>iew,
<u>Z</u>oom to get a closer
look at your work.

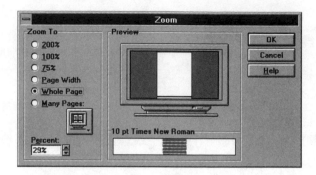

Selecting text

The hardest part of editing your work is just moving words around. Before you can rearrange your text, you have to select it. It's easiest to use the mouse, but if you're comfortable with the keyboard, there are some shortcuts there, too.

With the mouse

Word has built-in mouse shortcuts that let you select chunks of text with simple mouse movements.

- To select **a word**... point to the word and double-click.

- To select **an entire sentence**... hold down the Ctrl key, point to the sentence, and click.

- To select **an entire paragraph** ... move the mouse pointer to the left margin until it turns into an arrow, position it alongside the paragraph, and double-click.

- To select **the whole document**... move the mouse pointer to the left margin until it turns into an arrow, and then triple-click.

With the keyboard

If you're a touch typist, its aggravating to have to take your fingers off the keyboard, find the mouse, click to select a block, then move back to the keys. For you, there's a special keyboard technique that lets you select a word, a sentence, a paragraph, or the whole document. Just put the cursor where you want it and press the F8 key to turn on **extension mode**. That's a fancy term for a simple effect.

Once you've pressed F8, you can press any key to extend the selection—so if you press the period key, for example, Word will extend the selection to the next period, which is usually the end of the sentence.

Keep pressing F8 to extend the selection more. Press it twice to select a whole word, three times for a sentence, four times for a paragraph, and five times to select the whole document. If you get tired of extension mode, press the Escape key to turn it off. To "unselect" your selection, move any of the cursor keys.

 **<Caution>** Be careful when you have a block of text selected! If you inadvertently hit any key, including the space bar, whatever you type will replace whatever you selected. You can bring it back with Undo, but it's alarming to see everything disappear unexpectedly.

Moving words around

OK, the boss says the report you've been working on for three weeks is nearly perfect. All you have to do is take that paragraph at the end of page 2 and put it at the top of page 4, then move a few sentences around on page 6. "That's easy for him to say," you say. It's even easier for you to do. Depending on how far you want to move the text, you have two choices: you can use the Windows Clipboard, or you can use the drag-and-drop feature.

Using the Windows Clipboard

The Clipboard is the best way to cut text from one place and move it to another when you can't see both locations on a single screen. To move a paragraph from one page to another, follow these steps:

1 Select the text and press Ctrl+X, or click the Cut button on the Standard toolbar (the little scissors).

2 Use the scroll bars or the arrow keys to find the place where you want to move the text. Click on the exact spot where you want the beginning of the text to appear.

3 Press Ctrl+V, or click the Paste button on the Standard toolbar.

Dragging-and-dropping

For simple moves, like shifting a word from one end of a sentence to the other, or transposing two sentences in the same paragraph, the easiest way is just to **drag** the text from the old spot to the new one. The technique is simple: select the chunk of text you want to move, and then hold down the left mouse key as you drag it to its new home. It's easy to tell when you're about to move something, because the pointer changes shape, as shown in figure 7.11.

Don't worry about being too precise when you **drop** the text. Word uses a trick called Smart Copy and Paste that puts the right number of spaces on either side of a word or a sentence. It isn't perfect, but most of the time it does just what it's supposed to.

You can use also use drag-and-drop to make a copy of a chunk of text. Highlight the text you want to copy, then hold down the Ctrl key as you drag the text. You'll know you're about to copy instead of move, because a tiny plus sign will appear alongside the pointer.

Fig. 7.11

The easy way to drag a word or a sentence a short distance: just drag it from its old site and drop it in the new one.

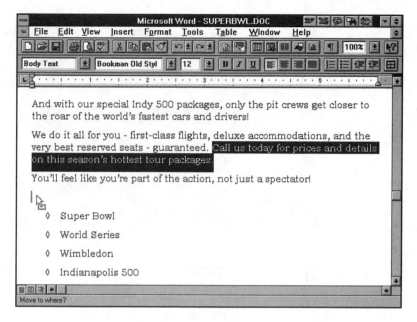

Where's that word?

Finding your way around a one-page memo is easy, but when you're editing a 50-page report, finding the exact spot you're looking for can give you a bad case of eyestrain. You'll get a headache and sore wrists to match if you have to edit a phrase that appears 20 or 30 times throughout your report. Fortunately, Word has an easier way.

Finding text

To find a chunk of text anywhere in your document, just press Ctrl+F (or choose Edit, Find) to pop up the dialog box shown in figure 7.12. Type the text to search for, and click on the Find Next button. Keep clicking that button to find every place in the document where the text you're looking for appears.

(Tip) _____ It's easy to remember this shortcut. When you think of Ctrl+F, remind yourself that the F stands for *Find*.

Fig. 7.12
The Find dialog box lets you search for a word or phrase anywhere in your document. If you're not sure of your spelling, give it your best shot and then check the Sounds Like box.

Replacing text

It's one thing to search for a piece of text. It's quite another to do something with it. Let's say you've written a 50-page report covering everything you could possibly want to know about Acme Corp. Then you discover the company's actual name is Acme Industries, Inc. You could search through your document and painstakingly retype the name each time it appears. Or you could pop up the Replace dialog box and let Word do the work.

If the Find dialog box is on the screen, just click the Replace button. Or, to start from scratch, choose Edit, Replace. When you see the dialog box shown in figure 7.13, type the text to search for in the top box and the text to replace it with in the second box.

Choose one of these options, depending on how you want to make the replacements:

- To make the replacement in the current spot, click the Replace button.

- To skip this occurrence and find the next one, click the Find Next button.

- To have Word automatically change every occurrence, click Replace All.

Fig. 7.13
Use the Replace dialog box to automatically substitute one word or phrase for another. You can even include formatting in the find or replace portion, as in this example.

⊗<Caution> Word is smart, but it's not *that* smart. When you tell it to replace one thing with another, it simply looks for the sequence of letters you specified. So if you tell Word to replace *the* with *a,* it'll turn *thermometer* into *armometer* and *bother* into *boar,* because both those words have those three letters in them. To make sure Word finds only entire words, check the Find Whole Words Only box on the Replace dialog box. And keep both eyes open while Word works!

Finding (and replacing) special stuff

Two of the buttons at the bottom of both the Find and Replace dialog boxes let you search for things other than text or numbers. You can use these buttons to search for formatting (like fonts and styles), or special characters like tabs and paragraph marks.

⊗<Caution> If your find doesn't work, check to see whether you've accidentally specified some formatting (the information will appear in the gray area underneath the Find or Replace box. If that happens, click the No Formatting button and try again.

Oops! I didn't mean to do that!

No matter how careful you are, sooner or later your finger will slip and you'll zap a chunk of text that you've been working on for hours. Computers usually work in nanoseconds, but this one feels more like an *oh-no-second*. "Oh no!" you say as you wonder how you're going to reconstruct the document.

Relax. Word's coolest feature of all is the Undo button, that little counter-clockwise arrow smack in the middle of the Standard toolbar. Click it once to undo what you just did. Keep clicking, and it will keep undoing everything you've done, rolling everything back as much as 100 steps. If you know you want to undo a lengthy sequence of actions, press the little arrow at the right of the Undo button, then scroll through a list of the steps Word can undo for you (see fig. 7.14). If you click on the 5th step in the list, Word will automatically undo the last five actions in one swift motion.

Fig. 7.14
Don't panic! Word's miraculous Undo key can reverse the effects of one, 50, or even 100 keystrokes and mouse clicks. Now, when you make a mistake, it doesn't have to be permanent.

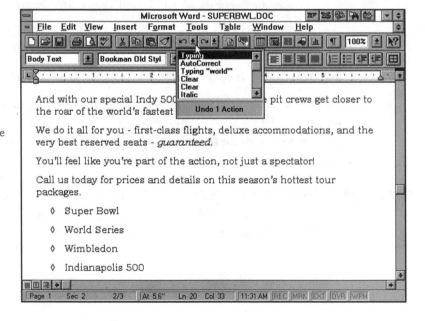

If you've never used Word's Undo button, you'll wonder what all the fuss is about. But the first time Undo saves half a day's worth of your work, you'll be ready to send a dozen roses and a big thank-you note to whoever it was at Microsoft who insisted that it had to be a part of Word.

?Q&A

I deleted a paragraph a while ago and now I want to get it back, but I don't want to lose all the work I've done in the meantime. What do I do?

Save your document under another name, then use the Undo button to roll your document back until you can see the lost paragraph. Copy it to the Clipboard and open the document you just saved. Now you can paste the recovered text into the revised document, and get on with your work.

The Secrets of
Great-Looking Documents

*Word comes with a
huge wardrobe of typo-
graphical accessories
to help you dress your
documents appropriately.*

I can't even imagine what life would be like if my entire wardrobe con-
sisted of nothing but gray flannel suits. I'd fit in just fine at the office,
but I'd look hopelessly out of place at the company picnic. And I'd have a
really hard time relaxing at the beach.

How you dress doesn't just define your comfort level. It also makes a statement about who you are. A gray flannel suit says, "I'm working. Take me
seriously." On the other hand, faded jeans, running shoes, and a well-worn
sweater say, "It's the weekend—let's have some fun!"

Your letters, memos, and reports make a statement about you, too. Think
about it: should a memo to your boss share the same look as an invitation
to a surprise birthday party? Of course not. Your new business plan needs
a nice, conservative, dressed-for-success look; a flyer for next week's big
sale demands a bold, attention-getting look.

Word comes with a huge wardrobe of typographical accessories to help you dress your documents appropriately—for success, to get attention, or just for fun. In this chapter, we'll look at fonts, formats, and styles, the building blocks of great-looking documents.

Plain English, please!

Styles are Word's shortcuts for dressing up text and paragraphs. Instead of picking every attribute off a list or a dialog box, styles save collections of these attributes in a simple name. So a heading style might be bold and centered in a large, easy-to-read typeface.

How can I make my words look more interesting?

Deep down inside, all the letters of the alphabet look pretty much alike—an A looks like an A, a Z is three slashes of Zorro's sword, and the numbers from 1 to 9 are familiar to anyone who's graduated from *Sesame Street*.

But something happens when you dress those old familiar letters up in a brand new font. Each character starts to acquire its own personality. The right font can help your words look strong and forceful, or light and delicate. You can even use a special font called Wingdings to put symbols right in the middle of your memo—like a big, bold ☎ to let everyone know about the new phone number.

What can I do with fonts?

If you stopped two strangers on the street—both roughly the same age and the same size—you might have trouble telling them apart. But put one in a police officer's uniform and the other in a tuxedo, and you'll have no trouble telling the two apart.

Fonts work the same way, as a kind of uniform that the characters on your page wear. When you dress up your text in Times New Roman, it looks like the words in your daily paper: serious and sober. Now change the same words into Britannic Bold: they look more like the headlines in your paper. It's hard to ignore those big, bold letters, isn't it? As you can see in table 8.1, there are big differences between fonts.

Table 8.1   A few typical fonts

What it's called	What it looks like	How it's used
Times New Roman	The quick brown fox	By far the most popular choice for letters and memos. Maybe *too* popular.
Arial	**The quick brown fox**	A good all-around typeface for headlines and text, especially in smaller chunks.
Brittanic Bold	**THE QUICK BROWN FOX**	Big, bold typefaces like this one are best for headlines and labels.
New Berolina	*The quick brown fox*	This old-fashioned typeface is fine for a wedding invitation, but not for a memo.
Wingdings	✳︎〰︎♏︎ ☐◆✋︎♏︎& ♌︎	You're not supposed to be able to read it. Use Wingdings and symbols for special occasions.

Windows gives you five TrueType fonts for starters. Office throws in an extra seven. You can buy more fonts for literally a few dollars apiece. If you want to jazz up your documents, this is one of the best investments you can make.

✱{Note}

Windows uses several kinds of typefaces, but the most popular is called **TrueType**. TrueType fonts are **scalable**, which means that Windows can stretch (or scale) them like a piece of Silly Putty into the exact size you specify. Printer fonts and screen fonts usually come in a limited number of sizes, which means that Windows can only approximate what you ask for. (If you've ever worn a one-size-fits-all baseball cap, you know the problem.) When you want to add new fonts, be sure to choose the TrueType variety. They're guaranteed to work with Word and the other Office programs.

How can I change the fonts in my documents?

When you first start typing, your letters hit the screen in boring old gray flannel. That's fine, as long as you're just trying to capture those thoughts as they tumble out of your head and onto the screen. But eventually you'll switch gears and start thinking about your document's look and feel. How do you pick the look that's right for the occasion?

If you know exactly which typeface you want to use, the easy way is to use the **font list** on the Formatting toolbar (see fig. 8.1). (Actually, it should be called the **typeface list**, but if you want to know why, you'll have to read the sidebar later in this chapter.) Click on the down arrow at the right side to pop the list into view, then scroll through the list and pick out the name of the typeface you're looking for. Use the **font size list** (just to the right of the font list) to make the font bigger or smaller.

Fig. 8.1
Use the font list on the Formatting toolbar to change the typeface and size of the selected text. The TrueType symbols identify these as TrueType fonts.

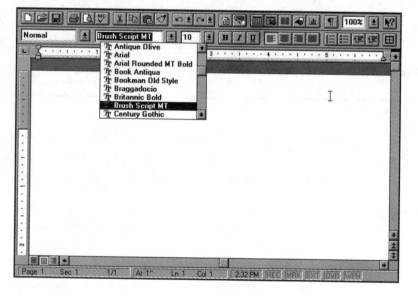

 **{Note}** Before you can change a character's font, you have to select it. If you're not sure how to select text, look at Chapter 7.

What if you're not sure exactly what each font looks like? Then you'll have to work a little harder. Follow these steps to change the look of your text.

1 Select the text you want to change, and then choose F<u>o</u>rmat, <u>F</u>ont. You'll see the Font dialog box shown in figure 8.2.

Fig. 8.2
When you're not sure which font you want, use this dialog box. The Preview panel lets you see what your text will look like before you actually change it.

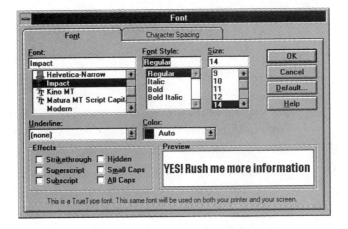

2 Choose a **typeface** from the Font list. For a preview of what your font will look like, see the panel at the bottom of the dialog box.

3 Pick a font **style:** Bold? Italic? Both? Neither? With most typefaces, you get one of these four options.

4 Tell Word **how big** you want the letters to be. For most business documents, use 10 or 12 points for text. Headings can range from 14 points to 72, depending on whether you're writing a memo or printing a poster. Keep watching the Preview panel to see just how big (or small) your letters will appear.

5 Do you want to see the selection in **color**? Word gives you a choice of 16 colors. (Stay away from green and yellow, which are too bright for most people to read easily.)

{Note} ____ You can format text in bright, bold colors so it jumps off the screen, but you'll need a color printer to see those same colors on paper.

6 Do you want to use any **special effects**? Check the Strikethrough box, for example, and your text will appear with a line through it: ~~like this~~. Most people will never use any of these options.

7 Click **OK** to change the look of the selected text.

(Tip)

Use the buttons on the Formatting toolbar to make a selection bold or italic. You can always restore a chunk of text to boring old Normal style by selecting it, then pressing Ctrl+Spacebar.

Q&A

Someone sent me a document, and the fonts look horrible on my machine. What's wrong?

Your co-worker probably used some fonts that aren't installed on your computer. When that happens, Windows tries to substitute another font for the one your co-worker used. Sometimes it works, but other times the substitution looks downright ugly. You have two choices: buy the font and install it on your computer, or change the text formatting to another font that your PC can recognize.

What's the best way to arrange my words on the page?

So far, we've talked about using fonts to make words and sentences stand out on the page. But all that attention doesn't do much good unless we also arrange the words so they fall in the right place. When your words are all dressed up, give them someplace to go.

Wouldn't that big 36-point headline look better if it were centered between the left and right sides of the page? And how about that important summary on page 4 of your report? If you leave a little space on the right and left, it will stand out from the rest of the text on that page, as surely as if you'd hung a sign on it that says, "Read me, please!"

The most important words in desktop publishing

"I'll take Typographic Trivia for a thousand dollars, Alex."

Quick—hand me the remote control! My eyes glaze over when I hear all the technobabble that goes along with desktop publishing. Do you really have to know all these trivial details to put together a brochure or a company newsletter?

Of course not. Desktop publishing is actually quite simple. In fact, you can forget all about the jargon once you master some basic terms.

Let's start with typefaces and fonts. There's a difference between the two, but most people (including the people who designed Word) confuse the terms most of the time.

To understand the difference, imagine how you'd describe the way I'm dressed right now. (Hey, I said you'd have to use your imagination.) You could say I'm wearing a sweatshirt, but you'd paint a much more detailed picture if you described it as a long-sleeved blue sweatshirt, size 40 regular, with a hood.

That difference in detail is precisely the difference between a typeface and a font.

A **typeface** describes the overall look for a group of letters and numbers and punctuation marks. The **font** name is a much more detailed description of the same chunk of text. It includes not just the typeface, but also its size, weight (regular or bold), and style (such as *italic*).

Typefaces come in all levels of complexity, but they can generally be divided into two broad categories: serif and sans serif. **Serifs** are the little decorative flourishes at the end of some characters in some typefaces. *Sans* is French for *without*, so a **sans serif** face has none of these decorations. Look at the tips of the capital T in the type samples below to see the difference clearly.

This is a SERIF typeface.

This is a SANS SERIF typeface.

Most designers agree that serif typefaces are the best choice for big blocks of text because they're easier to read, while sans serif typefaces are better for headlines and short paragraphs.

And what's all this talk about **points**? Well, for more than 500 years, printers have used this standard unit for measuring the size of a typeface. There are 72 points to an inch, so when you use 12-point type, you can expect that six lines of text will measure one inch from top to bottom.

At 1/72 of an inch, a point doesn't sound like much, but adding just one or two extra points of spacing after each line can make your text a lot easier to read.

Word's Format menu does much more than just let you adjust fonts. It also lets you set off text with extra spacing, stack your words up neatly on top of each other, draw precise lines, and center words on the page.

Using the ruler

When you're ready to start moving things around, it helps to have a ruler handy. The Word ruler on your screen looks a lot like the wooden rulers you used in school. It sits just above your document, and takes all the guesswork out of adjusting margins, tab stops, and other pieces of your printed pages.

The ruler takes up a lot of room on the screen, so you'll probably want to keep it hidden until you need it. To make the ruler visible, choose View, Ruler. Use the same menu to hide it again.

What do all those triangles and doodads on the ruler do, anyway? Look at figure 8.3 for the inside story.

Fig. 8.3

You can skip a lot of formatting dialog boxes if you learn how to drag the little markers around on the ruler.

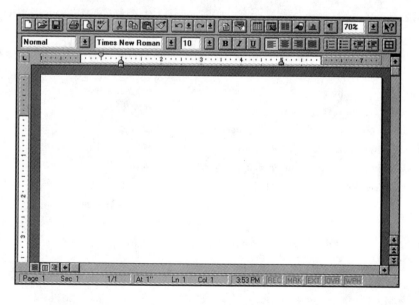

- The **white part of the ruler** shows you the boundaries beyond which you can no longer type on the page. If the page margins are set to the default 1.25 inches on either end, for example, and the selected paper size is 8-1/2" × 11", then each line is a maximum of 6 inches wide.

- The **dark part of the ruler** shows the distance between the edge of the paper and the margins.

- **To adjust the left margin,** aim the mouse pointer between the two triangles at the left of the ruler. When it turns to a two-headed arrow, drag in either direction. As you drag, you'll see a dashed line that extends through your page to help you locate just the right spot for the new margin.

- **To adjust the right margin,** aim the pointer just above the triangle-shaped marker on the right.

- You can use the two-headed arrow to **adjust the width of columns—** the kind in text, as well as the ones found in tables.

- **To indent only the first line of the selected paragraph,** drag the downward-pointing triangle at the top of the ruler's left edge.

- **To indent the remainder of the paragraph,** drag the two upward-pointing triangles at either end of the ruler. When you grab either one and move it toward the center of the ruler, you'll get extra white space on either side without changing the page margins.

- **To indent the entire paragraph,** grab the small box beneath the left-hand indent markers. As you drag this box, both markers above go along for the ride.

Remember, ruler settings apply to the entire paragraph where the insertion point is located. And when you press the Enter key, the ruler settings for the current paragraph continue in the next paragraph.

Adjusting line spacing

Most of the time, you'll use single spacing for your documents. Some kinds of documents, though, are more readable when there's extra space between each line. Double-spacing is especially useful if you expect someone to add comments and corrections to your work. To adjust line spacing, choose Format, Paragraph, then select an option from the Line Spacing drop-down list.

Some people like to press the Enter key twice at the end of each paragraph. Don't! There's a better way to put space between paragraphs. See the Before and After boxes in the Spacing area of the Paragraph dialog box? If you're using a 12-point font and you want to add half a line at the end of each paragraph, for example, enter **6** points in the box labeled After.

Alignment

For every paragraph, you can also choose how it lines up on the page. When should you use the different choices of alignment?

- **Left.** People read from left to right, so this is the most popular choice for text. Every line starts at the same place on the left edge and ends at a different place on the right, depending on how many characters are in the line.

- **Centered.** Use centered text for headlines and very short blocks of text. Don't use it for lengthy passages.

- **Right.** As you type, the text begins at the right edge and each new letter pushes its neighbors to the left so everything lines up perfectly on the right edge. Use this choice only for short captions alongside pictures or boxes.

- **Justified.** When you choose this option, Word sprinkles a little extra space between the words in each line so that every line of your text begins and ends at the same place on the right and left. It's a good choice for text that's arranged into formatted columns, as in a newsletter, but don't use it in memos, because it will make them harder to read.

The four alignment buttons on the Formatting toolbar let you change a paragraph's alignment with a single click. Because this setting applies to the entire paragraph, all you have to do is click anywhere in the paragraph, then click on whichever button you prefer.

I want to start a new page now

When you want to end the current page and force Word to start a new one, you'll need to add a manual page break. It's easy to do: just press Ctrl+Enter. In Normal and Outline views, you'll see a dotted line, complete with the words Page Break, where you added this material.

What you need to know about paragraph marks

See that funny button that looks like a backward P? That's a paragraph mark. Click that button and you'll see a matching symbol everywhere you've pressed the Enter key. You'll also see marks for tabs, spaces, and other formatting characters.

There's nothing complex about a paragraph. Your high school English teacher would tell you a paragraph is a complete thought, but as far as Word is concerned a paragraph is everything that appears in between the two paragraph marks.

A paragraph can be as short as one word, or it can go on for page after page after page (like the average insurance form). How long (or short) should a paragraph be? The best writers use a mix—a few short, a few long. If all your paragraphs are exactly the same length, you'll put your audience to sleep just as surely as if you'd lectured them in a monotone.

When you use Word, there's one more important reason to pay attention to paragraph marks. That's where all your paragraph formatting is stored. If you tell Word you want this paragraph to use the Blippo Bold typeface with triple-line spacing, Word dutifully saves your instructions inside that paragraph mark.

Why does this matter? Because if you copy or move that paragraph mark, you'll also move the styles that go with it. And when you paste it into the middle of another paragraph, there's no telling which style your new paragraph will adopt.

If you're planning to move big chunks of text around, click on the Show/Hide button to see all your paragraph marks. And then make sure you only move a paragraph mark if you also want to move the formatting that goes with it.

How can I save my favorite formats and reuse them?

Let's say you're a big-time producer and you're staging a remake of *Gone With the Wind*, with a cast of thousands.

Every time one of the extras playing a Confederate soldier checks in, you could scurry around to find him a gray uniform, a pair of boots, and a sword. But that would get pretty tiring after a while. Since you know you'll have hundreds of these characters, you can save time and hassle by putting together a special bundle with all the wardrobe pieces a Confederate soldier needs. Now, when each extra checks in, you hand him a big box labeled "Confederate Soldier." Easy, huh?

You can use the same principle to save time and energy with your Word documents. Your letters and memos and reports will use a lot of the same elements—body text, headings, signatures, address blocks, and so on. Instead of formatting each of these elements from scratch when you start a new document, you can use special labels, called **styles**, to keep track of your favorite formats. Now, when you highlight a character, word, or paragraph, all you have to do is tell Word which style to use and it will use all the formatting—fonts, colors, line spacing, everything—that you've assigned to that style.

Word uses two types of styles:

- **Character styles** store collections of information about individual characters—fonts and colors, for example.

- **Paragraph styles** let you collect all the formatting that has to do with paragraphs—alignments, line spacing, tab settings, and so on.

Defining a style from scratch

If you're really brave, you can define a style from the ground up. Choose Format, Style to pop up the Style dialog box shown in figure 8.4. OK, now click the New button, type a name for your style, select a style to base your new style on, click the the Format button, then select Font off the list, and... Hey, wait a minute! This is *way* too much work. Isn't there an easier way?

Fig. 8.4
Creating a style from scratch the hard way. The Style dialog box makes you click button after button after button.

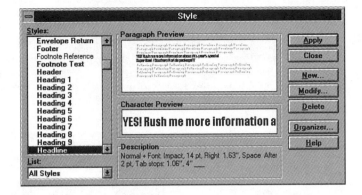

Redefining a style on the run

Of course there's an easier way. If you've dressed up some text exactly the way you want it to appear, it's simple to assign that formatting to any style you want. At the far left of the Formatting toolbar is a pull-down list of available styles (including Normal, Heading 1, Heading 2, and so on). High-light the text you want to use for your style, click in the Style list box, type the name of the style you want to use, and press Enter. If you already have a style by that name, Word will pop up the message box shown in figure 8.5. If not, it will go ahead and create a new style for you. The next time you want to use a style you've created, put your cursor in the paragraph, and choose the style from the Style list box.

Fig. 8.5
The easy way. To create a style by example, click in the Style list box and press enter.

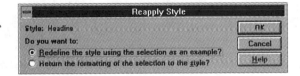

All your styles are saved in the current document, as well as in the NORMAL.DOT file. To make sure the NORMAL.DOT file is saved properly, choose File, Save All.

Painting formats by the numbers

Styles are the most powerful way to copy formatting from one place to another, but there's a quick-and-dirty way, too. Just use the Format Painter button. It's a simple, three-step process:

1 Highlight the text whose format you want to copy.

2 Click the Format Painter button on the Standard toolbar. The mouse pointer will change to a small paintbrush, as shown in figure 8.6.

3 Use the paintbrush to sweep the new format across the text you want to reformat.

Fig. 8.6
Use the Format Painter to copy formatting from one place and paint it onto another block of text.

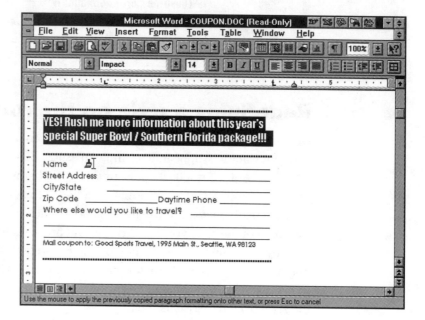

Choosing a style from the Style Gallery

Word comes with a built-in collection of templates, each of which is chock-full of predefined styles. How can you tell what these styles are and how to use them? Simple—just choose Format, Style Gallery to see a close-up view of every template on your system. The three different views in the Style Gallery's Preview window allow you to:

- See examples of how the styles within each template work, so you can modify them to meet your own needs. (Figure 8.7 shows one such example.)

- See each style in a single, alphabetical list.

- Preview what *your* document would look like if you used that style.

Fig. 8.7
Can't figure out what
that template does?
Decipher it with the
Style Gallery.

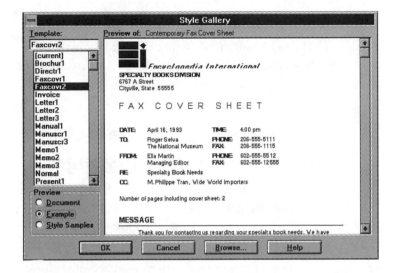

How do I add special symbols to my documents?

Anything that isn't a letter of the alphabet, a number, or a punctuation mark
is called a **symbol**. When you realize how many symbols Word can produce,
you'll use them a lot. Choose Insert, Symbol to pop up the dialog box you see
in figure 8.8.

Fig. 8.8
Hold down the left
mouse button and drag
the mouse pointer
around to see a blown-
up version of each
symbol you have to
choose from.

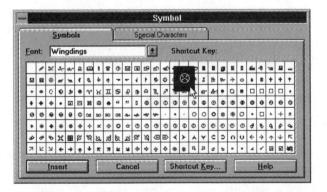

To add a symbol to your document, highlight it in the Symbols box, then
press the Insert button. You can add a bunch of symbols at one time if you
want. After you've inserted a symbol, the Cancel button turns to a Close
button. Click on it to make the box go away.

I need to use a legal symbol

The back half of the Symbol dialog box includes a collection of common business and legal symbols, like trademark and copyright characters. Click on the Special Characters tab to see them.

I need to use a character from a foreign language

If you have to type a word in French or Spanish, where do you get the accents and diacritical marks? ¡No problema! Open the Symbols box, choose (normal text) as the font, and look for your character.

 (Tip)

> There's an even easier way to insert accented characters in Word. Just press Ctrl and the accent character you want to add, then press the letter you want accented. To create an a with an accent (á, for example), press Ctrl+', and then press A. For an n with a tilde above it (ñ), press Ctrl+~,N. Use Ctrl+: for the umlaut symbol found in German words.

I just want to add some cool stuff to my document

If you like cool pictures, you'll love using the Symbols box with the Wingdings font. Take your choice of happy faces, bombs, peace symbol, and a whole lot more.

Can I make these quotation marks look better?

There are two kinds of quotation marks. The normal kind are straight up and down and look the same at the beginning and the end of a quotation. But slick, professionally published documents use curly quotes (like the ones in fig. 8.9), and you can, too. You'll find these symbols in the Special Characters section of the Symbols box.

Fig. 8.9

Smart quotes just plain look better than ordinary quotation marks.

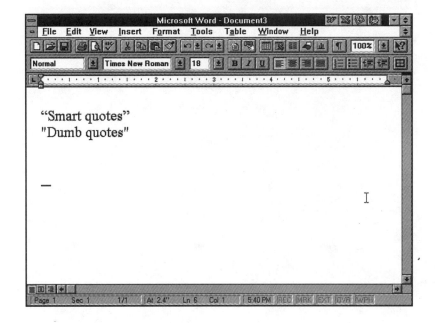

9 Let Word Do Your Work for You

Word has a staff of very hard-working specialists. They take shorthand, they're perfect spellers, they've got a rich vocabulary, and they might even give your writing a little extra zip.

In this chapter:

- I keep typing the same things over and over. Can Word help?

- How do I automatically make my documents look better?

- I can't spell. Can Word double-check my spelling?

- I'm looking for just the right word

- Can Word make me a better writer? (Maybe)

I n every office I've worked in, there's been at least one indispensable person. It's hardly ever the boss, of course. Most of the time it's not even a manager. The truly indispensable co-workers are the folks who do one thing so well that you can't imagine how you'd get through the day if they went away.

You know a few of these heroes. The amazing administrative assistant who can turn a page of shorthand into a complete set of minutes for a meeting. Or the mailroom guy, the only person in the whole building who knows how to unjam the copy machine.

Word has a few indispensable co-workers of its own. They're hard-working specialists, for the most part, who pop up just when they're needed, then vanish. They take shorthand, they're perfect spellers, they've got a rich vocabulary, and they might be able to give your writing a little extra zip.

Let Word do the typing and clicking for you

Why is Word like a pharmacist?

When you've got the sniffles you go see the doctor, who scribbles a few letters ("TID. PDQ.") on a prescription, which you take to the pharmacy. It's a miracle that the pharmacist can even decipher that chicken-scratching, much less translate it into plain English for you ("Take this three times a day, starting right now"). But that's what pharmacists are paid to do.

In the Microsoft Office, Word does something surprisingly similar, thanks to two special features, AutoText and AutoCorrect. You type in a few characters, press a key, and—boom!—Word looks up your shorthand on a list, then furiously types in whatever the two of you agreed on earlier. (No, Word can't figure out a doctor's handwriting. There still isn't a computer that's powerful enough or smart enough to do that.)

Why would you want to use AutoText or AutoCorrect? Because you can save a lot of time and energy by using these shortcuts to insert chunks of text and graphics you use all the time. Here are some examples:

- Expand a set of initials into a **signature**, complete with "Sincerely yours."

- Create shortcuts for **lists of names** you use in memos and reports.

- Insert **boilerplate text**, especially the sort of gobbledygook that lawyers say has to be typed in exactly the right way.

- Spell out **technical terms** and automatically add accents to **foreign words** like *mañana*.

- Automatically correct **frequently misspelled words**.

AutoText and AutoCorrect solve the same problems, but in slightly different ways.

Using AutoCorrect: just start typing

As the name suggests, Word's AutoCorrect automatically corrects mistakes as you type. When you first install Word, it includes entries for some commonly misspelled words. When you type **teh** and then press the space bar (or a period or comma, for that matter), Word checks its list, sees that you meant to type **the**, and changes the text for you. AutoCorrect entries can be up to 31 characters long and can't have any spaces.

Use AutoCorrect to automatically fix common misspellings. It's also good for creating shortcuts for common words and phrases you type regularly. Here's how to use it:

- To **add** an AutoCorrect entry, first highlight the text and/or graphics you want to reuse. Choose Tools, AutoCorrect to display the AutoCorrect dialog box shown in figure 9.1, and then type a shortcut name or the commonly misspelled version of the word in the text box labeled Replace. A good shortcut name for your signature line, for example, might be **sig**.

- To **insert** an AutoCorrect entry in your document, just type the shortcut combination. Word will replace the text as soon as you press the space bar or a punctuation key, such as a period or comma.

- To **delete** an AutoCorrect entry, open the AutoCorrect dialog box, choose it from the scrolling list, then click the Delete button.

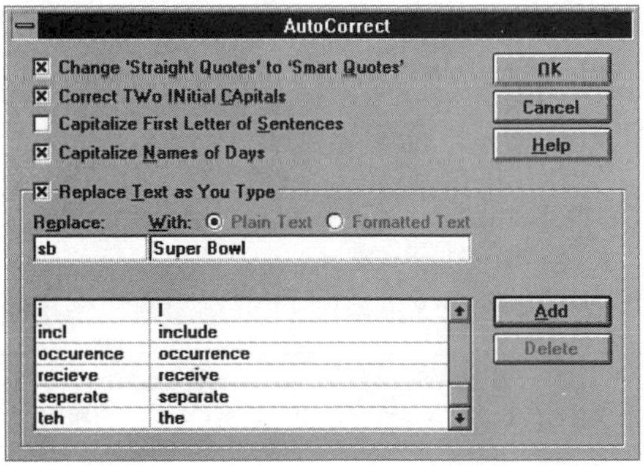

Fig. 9.1

After you highlight the text or graphics you want to reuse, type the misspelled word or shortcut name in the text box at the left. The scroll list shown here includes some common examples.

 **<Caution>** Don't use a real word as the name for an AutoCorrect entry, or you'll be unpleasantly surprised to see the results. For example, when you're working on next year's marketing plan, you might be tempted to redefine the letters **MR** to expand into *Market Research*. You'll change it fast the first time you try to type a letter salutation and accidentally turn "Dear Mr. Clinton" into "Dear Market Research Clinton!"

Q&A ___ *AutoCorrect isn't working. Where do I look?*

Maybe it's turned off. Choose Tools, AutoCorrect, and make sure that there's an × in the box labeled Replace Text as You Type.

Using AutoText: just press F3 and go

What's the difference between AutoCorrect and AutoText? AutoCorrect replaces your text automatically as soon as you hit the space bar. AutoText, on the other hand, doesn't go to work until you specifically request it by pressing the F3 key. AutoText entries can have up to 32 characters, including spaces, in their names. Here's how you use AutoText:

- To **add** an entry to the AutoText list, highlight the text and/or graphics, then choose Edit, AutoText to display the AutoText dialog box shown in figure 9.2. Give the entry a name and press the Add button. (If your entry is a paragraph, make sure you include the entire paragraph in your highlighted selection!)

- To **insert** an AutoText entry into your document, click at the point where you want to add the text, type the name of the AutoText entry (make sure it's at the end of a paragraph or is followed by a space), then press the F3 key. Word looks down its list of AutoText shortcuts until it finds the one you asked for, then pastes it in.

 (Tip) ___ There's an AutoText button on the Standard toolbar, but I don't recommend using it. AutoText is supposed to be a timesaver, so if you really use it, learn the F3 shortcut and keep your hands on the keyboard.

- To **change** an AutoText entry, highlight the new text and/or graphics and choose Edit, AutoText. Highlight the right name on the list, click Add, and answer Yes when Word asks if you want to redefine the entry.

- To **delete** an AutoText entry, just highlight its name and press the Del key.

Fig. 9.2
You decide when to expand an AutoText shortcut into a chunk of formatted text. Just type the name (from the list at the top), press F3, and stand back while Word does the rest.

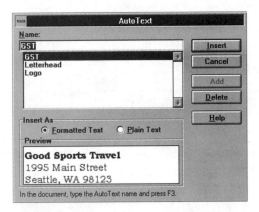

Let Word do the formatting

I call AutoFormat the "Make It Look Good" button. Here's how it's supposed to work.

You type like crazy, not worrying about formatting or other details. When you're done, you toss your file at Word and say, in essence, "Here—clean this up and make it look good."

Sounds great, doesn't it? Too bad it doesn't always work the way you expect it to.

What does AutoFormat do?

When you use AutoFormat, Word works its way through your document from top to bottom, replacing straight quotes with smart quotes, taking out extra spaces and unnecessary paragraph marks, and so on. It also tries to guess which style is best for each block of text. You can tell Word to skip one or more of these steps by choosing Tools, Options. Just click in the dialog box shown in figure 9.3.

Fig. 9.3
AutoFormat tries to make your document look extra-sharp. You can tell Word to skip any of the 10 steps on this list.

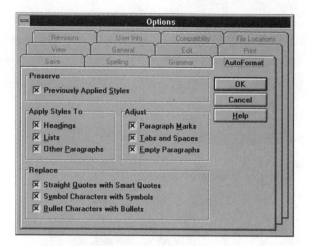

The before-and-after pictures shown in figures 9.4 and 9.5 illustrate the power of the AutoFormat feature.

Fig. 9.4
Don't think—just type! All the words are there in this example, but it doesn't look too impressive, does it?

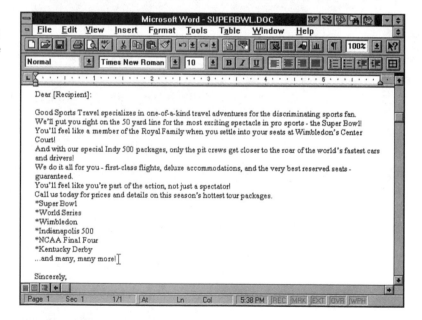

Fig. 9.5
After clicking the
AutoFormat button,
our document looks
better, but it's not
perfect. AutoFormat
added bullets to the
list, but decided to
reformat one paragraph
as a bold heading.

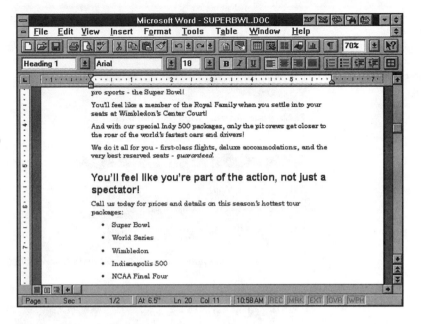

How do I use AutoFormat?

There's a fast way and a thorough way to use AutoFormat:

- Click the AutoFormat button on the Standard toolbar and shazam!
  Word sails through your document, makes all its changes, and puts the
  results on your screen.

> If you don't like what you see after clicking the AutoFormat button, use Undo
> to put things back the way they were. Then try using the menus to run the
> one-step-at-a-time version of AutoFormat.

- When you use the menus (Format, AutoFormat), you go through a
  three-step process, as shown in figures 9.6 through 9.8.

Fig. 9.6
When you use the menus to automatically format your documents, Word lets you say yes or no at every step of the process.

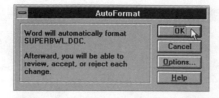

*1. **On your mark...** Word tells you what it's about to do.*

Fig. 9.7
The second step.

*2. **Get set...** Word analyzes your document and prepares its list of changes.*

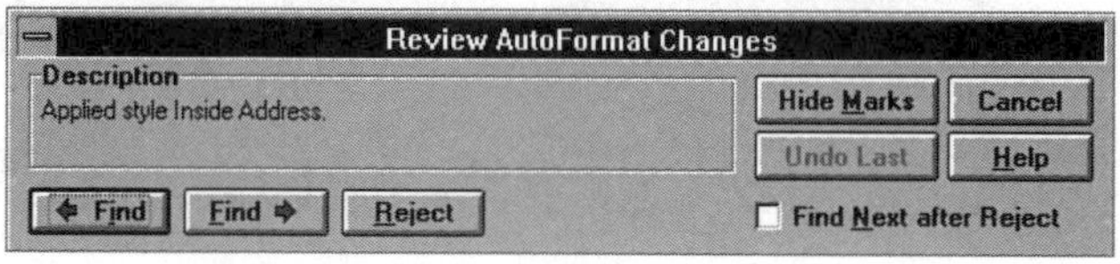

Fig. 9.8
Step three.

*3. **Go!** You go through each suggestion, one at a time, and decide which ones to accept and which to reject.*

Helping AutoFormat work better

The bigger the document, the more likely AutoFormat is to make some mistakes. The most common one is to apply the wrong style tag, turning body text into lists, for example. AutoFormat works best on short documents. It also works well on blocks of text, such as numbered lists and addresses.

Let Word check your spelling

Whoever came up with the idea for a spelling checker deserves a medal. Think about it. All the Office programs share a complete dictionary, and whenever you push the right button, Word (and Excel and PowerPoint) zips through your document searching for embarrassing typographical errors and misspellings. Even if you're the type who can spell *antidisestablishmentarianism* backward and forward, you should use Word's spelling checker regularly.

What the spelling checker can and can't do

Word's spelling checker will only alert you when you use a word that isn't in its dictionary. It can't tell you when you've used the wrong word. So if you type **Supper Bowl** instead of **Super Bowl**, Word will think you meant it. The moral? Spelling checkers are useful, but don't forget to read your document carefully before you pass it around.

How to check your spelling

You can use the spelling checker to look up a word, check a paragraph, or go through your entire document:

- To check the spelling of **one word**, double-click to select the word, then click the Spelling button on the Standard toolbar. If the word is misspelled, a list of suggested alternatives will pop up. If it's correctly spelled, you'll see the message shown in figure 9.9. Um, didn't Word forget to mention that the highlighted word is spelled correctly?

Fig. 9.9
Believe it or not, this message means the word you wanted to check is spelled correctly.

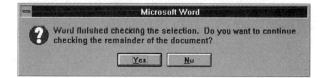

- To check the spelling of **a paragraph or part of a document,** select the text to check, then follow the same procedure.

- To check the spelling of **the whole document,** make sure that no text is selected, then click the Spelling button. When Word finds a word it doesn't recognize, it pops up a dialog box like the one shown in figure 9.10.

Fig. 9.10
When Word finds a word it doesn't recognize, you can change it, ignore it, or add it to your own dictionary.

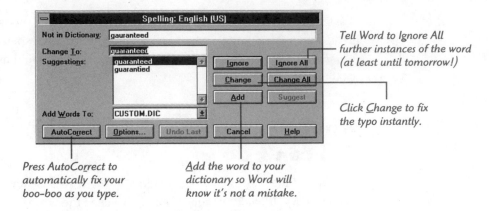

Tell Word to Ignore All further instances of the word *(at least until tomorrow!)*

Click Change to fix the typo instantly.

Press AutoCorrect to automatically fix your boo-boo as you type.

Add the word to your dictionary so Word will know it's not a mistake.

②Q&A

Word's spelling checker keeps finding the same mistakes. Can't it just fix them all?

The best you can do is to add the misspellings to your AutoCorrect list. If you press the AutoCorrect button from the Spelling dialog box, you'll automatically tell Word to substitute the correct spelling when you use this incorrect spelling again.

Let Word suggest the right word

Pick the right words, and your audience will instantly understand your message. Pick the wrong ones, and maybe they'll be left scratching their heads. When the right word is stuck on the tip of your tongue, ask Word's thesaurus for a little help.

To use the thesaurus, click on the word you want to look up (you don't need to select the whole word), then choose Tools, Thesaurus. You'll see a screen like the one in figure 9.11.

Fig. 9.11
Use Word's thesaurus to search for a more appropriate word.

Here's how you use the thesaurus options:

- **To replace the original word,** pick a word from the Replace with Synonym list, and press the Replace button.

- **To look for more options,** click on a word, and press the Look Up button.

- **To exit without making any change,** just click the Cancel button or press Esc.

Making your own dictionary

Using a spelling checker can be as maddening as listening to a leaky faucet. Word is constantly telling you that it's found a word that's not listed in its dictionary. The trouble is, you'll regularly use all sorts of words that aren't in Word's dictionary:

- Proper names, including your name and your company's name.

- Technical terms and jargon unique to your business.

- Slang words and foreign words not found in the standard Office dictionary.

- Words like *I'm* and *you're*, which contain "smart apostrophes."

Drip, drip, drip, drip. Arrrrrghhhh! It's no fun telling Word to ignore all those words, especially in a long document.

The solution? Create your own custom dictionary and use it to give Word an even richer vocabulary. If you look in the directory where Word stores its dictionary and thesaurus (usually C:\WINDOWS\MSAPPS\PROOF), you'll find a file called CUSTOM.DIC. It's easy to guess that that's Word's custom dictionary.

To add a bunch of words to CUSTOM.DIC, you can open the file directly in Word and just type new words into the list, one per line. To add words to the dictionary one at a time, press the Add button any time Word tells you it can't find the word in its standard dictionary.

An even cooler trick is to tell Word to alert you when it sees a certain word, even if that word is in its dictionary. Suppose your boss has told you to avoid using the word "rather" (good advice). Start a new Word document, type the word **rather**, press Enter, and then save the document in the C:\WINDOWS\MSAPPS\PROOF directory, using the name MSSP2_EN.EXC (be sure to use the underline character in the sixth position, and choose Text Only from the Save File As Type box).

By creating this "exclude" file, you tell Word to stop and warn you any time it sees any of the words on the list while performing a spelling check. If you're writing about Dan Rather, you can ignore the warning. But if you've just written "I'm rather concerned..." you'll have a chance to edit the sentence before your boss sees it.

Let Word help make you a better writer. (Really?)

Can Word really make you a better writer? Well, that depends. If you sailed through high-school English with A's and B's, probably not. But if you think that a split infinitive needs whipped cream, nuts, and a cherry on top, keep reading.

What the grammar checker does

There's nothing magical about the grammar checker. It checks your document against more than 40 different rules of grammar and style (see fig. 9.12 for a partial listing) and suggests words you might want to change. You can turn off some or all of its rules, thank goodness, so that Word won't continually harass you about an "error" that you consider an irreplaceable part of your personal style.

Fig. 9.12
Word's grammar checker analyzes your writing against more than 40 separate rules of grammar and style. You decide which rules to follow and which to ignore.

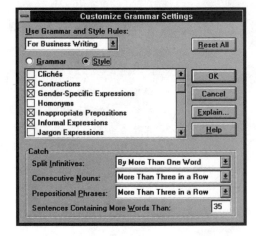

How does the grammar checker work?

Choose <u>T</u>ools, <u>G</u>rammar to start analyzing your document. The grammar checker jumps to the top of the document and works its way down. As it goes, it checks both spelling and grammar simultaneously, one paragraph at a time. Every time it has a question, it stops and offers a suggestion like the one in figure 9.13.

Fig. 9.13
Using Word's grammar checker is like having Mrs. Grundy, your high school English teacher, in your computer. (Sit up straight!)

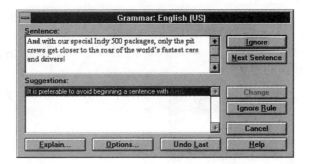

Here's how you use the grammar checker options:

- For each **grammar suggestion**, the grammar checker shows you the sentence and the corresponding rule.

- For a **detailed explanation** of the rule, push the Explain button.

- To **ignore the suggestion** and move on, press the Next Sentence button.

- To **ignore the rule** ("I like to begin sentences with And!"), push the Ignore Rule button.

- If the Change button is visible, you can press to **have Word make the change for you**. Otherwise, just click in the text and start editing. There's no need to close your dialog box until you're all through.

The grammar checker window is like the spell checker window. You can leave it up on the screen while you add a new sentence or make another change. When you're done, press the Start button to resume your grammar (or spelling) check.

Readability? What's that all about?

When you first learn how to read, you struggle over every word. With practice, though, most people get better at it, and most people with a high school education can handle long, complicated sentences with big words.

Word's grammar checker counts up the length of your sentences and the size of your words, and then crunches the data through a couple of special formulas. Eventually, it comes up with a laundry list of statistics like the one in figure 9.14.

Fig. 9.14
When it's through checking your document, Word's grammar checker tells you more than you wanted to know.

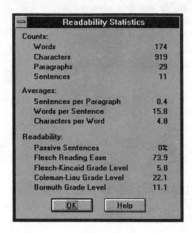

What should you do with all this information? Mostly, I just ignore it. If you must know how your writing rates, look at the Flesch-Kincaid Grade Level, which rates readability along a scale that uses the school grades we all know too well. In the example above, the writing should be understandable by anyone with at least a sixth-grade reading level.

Readability statistics help only if you know your audience. If you're writing for rocket scientists, it's OK to aim high, with big words and long sentences. But for an advertisement that's designed to be read by average people, shoot for a 6th-grade reading level, so that anyone can read and understand your message quickly.

> How many words have you written? There's an easy way to count the words in your entire document. From the main menu, choose Tools, Word Count. If you have a block of text selected, this choice will tell you how many words are in the selection.

10 Lists and Tables

Set off a list with big, bold bullets, and it practically jumps off the page. Or give each item its own row, break the details into separate columns, and you wind up with an easy-to-read, information-packed table.

Everyone uses lists. You don't believe me? Just look around. To-do lists. Packing lists. Laundry lists and grocery lists. The A list. Mr. Blackwell's Best-Dressed List. David Letterman's Top Ten List. The Ten Commandments.

Quite a list, huh?

When you need to communicate with other people, lists are among your most powerful tools. When it's set off from the rest of the text with bold bullet characters, a list practically jumps off the page. And the steady progression of examples adds authority to your arguments. Each new item on the list helps hammer your point home—by the time you reach the end, your conclusion is nearly irresistible.

After a list picks up enough details, though, it becomes too big and complex to be handled by a few bullets. Give each item its own row, break the details into separate columns, and you wind up with an easy-to-read, information-packed table. No matter which format you choose—list or table—Word can handle it for you.

Simple lists: bullets and numbers

Turning plain text into a list is one of the easiest things you can do using Word.

I want to use a bulleted list

 To create a bulleted list on the fly as you type, just click the Bullets button (found on the Formatting toolbar). Type the first item in your list, then press Enter to add another bulleted item. The items in a list can be anything—numbers, words, phrases, whole paragraphs, even graphics. To stop adding bullets and return to normal paragraph style, click the Bullets button again.

To add bullets to a list you've already typed, first highlight the list. Then click the Bullets button to add a simple black dot in front of each item.

I want more interesting bullets

When you first create a bulleted list, Word sets off each item with a big, bold, boring dot. Ho-hum. I prefer more visually interesting bullets. In the Bullets and Numbering dialog box, Word gives you a choice of six predefined bullet types. You can also use practically any symbol as a bullet.

Here's how to use a more interesting symbol to set off each item in a list:

1 Highlight the entire list, then right-click on the highlighted list to open a shortcut menu. Select Bullets and Numbering to pop up the Bullets and Numbering dialog box (see fig. 10.1). You *could* click on one of these choices, but we don't want to settle for anything so mundane. So let's click the <u>M</u>odify button.

Fig. 10.1

When you choose Bullets and Numbering from the shortcut menu, Word offers you these six bullets. Not that interesting, are they?

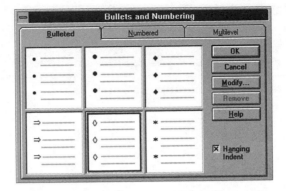

2 In the Modify Bulleted List dialog box that appears (see fig. 10.2), click the button labeled Bullet.

Fig. 10.2

Don't settle for boring old bullets! Choose any symbol you want, and even modify the size, color, and position.

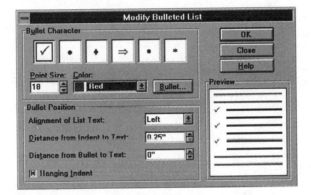

3 Pick a character from the Symbol dialog box. (Change fonts if necessary—this check mark is from the bottom row of the Wingdings font.)

4 Adjust the size, color, and position of the bullet, if necessary. The Preview window shows you how each change will affect the look of your list.

5 When you're satisfied, click OK to change the bullets in your list.

If you do every step correctly, you'll be rewarded with a bulleted list like the one in figure 10.3.

Fig. 10.3

The check marks make effective lead-ins for each item in a bulleted list. Note that we're poised to add another item to the list unless we click the Bullets button again.

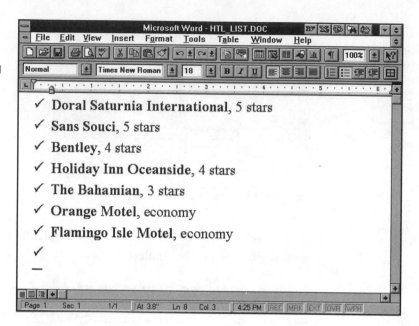

I want to use a numbered list

Sometimes, simple bullets aren't enough. When you're writing step-by-step instructions, for example, you'll want each item to be numbered so your reader can easily follow along.

When you choose the numbering option for your list, Word adds a number to each item. If you add a new item or move items around, Word automatically renumbers the list to keep each item in the proper order.

 To start a numbered list, click the Numbering button on the Formatting toolbar. If you're not happy with the default 1-2-3 format, use the right-mouse shortcut menus to choose from six simple numbering formats that cover numbers, letters, and Roman numerals. If you find these formats a little drab, spice them up!

To customize the number format, click the right mouse button, choose Bullets and Numbering, and then click the Modify button to display the dialog box shown in figure 10.4. Now we can add some more descriptive text to the bare numbers. If you're writing a list of instructions, for example, you can add the word **Step** before each number and a colon afterward, so your readers see Step 1:, Step 2:, and so on, in front of each item.

Fig. 10.4
Replace Word's dull numbering schemes with your own formats. Word will take care of the naming and numbering automatically.

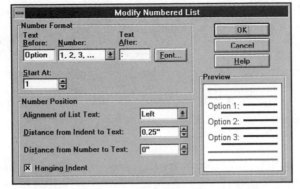

After just a few seconds' worth of fiddling with dialog boxes, you can turn the simple text list into one that outlines options for your readers, as in figure 10.5.

Fig. 10.5
Word automatically adds the word Option before each list entry, then numbers the whole list. If you move an item or add a new one, the numbering adjusts automatically.

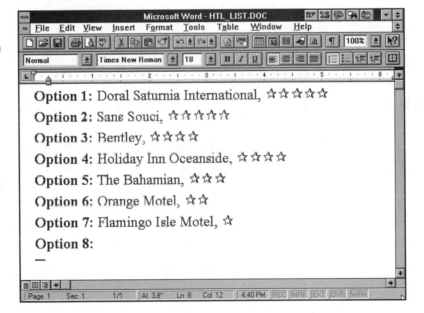

How do I rearrange the entries in my list?

Here's where Word really earns its keep:

- To **reorder list items,** first select the entire item, including the paragraph mark (¶). Then use cut and paste, or just drag the item to its new spot.

- To **add a new list item,** move the insertion point to the very end of the last row in the list, and press Enter.

- To **skip or stop numbering,** click the right mouse button, and choose Skip Numbering or Stop Numbering from the shortcut menu.

- To **restore a list to plain text format,** select the list, and press the Numbering button or the Bullets button.

 Q&A

I tried to move one item in my numbered list, but it didn't work right. The text moved, but the number stayed where it was. What did I do wrong?

¶ To move a bulleted or numbered item properly, you must make sure you've selected the paragraph mark (¶) at the end of the item. (Press the Show/Hide button on the Standard toolbar to make the job easier.) If you don't select the paragraph mark, the bullet formatting stays where it is, and only the text moves.

What can I do with a table?

Word's built-in list formats work great when the lists are simple enough. Apples, peaches, pears, pineapples—no problem. But what happens when you start to add more detail, like a price? Apples, 49¢ a pound; peaches, $1.49...although it's starting to get more complicated, our list can probably still handle it. But what if we add pictures and a description of where each type of fruit is found? Now we've strained our list past the breaking point.

It's time to organize all that information into neat rows and columns. And Word tables are the perfect tool for the job. With the help of tables, you can:

- Align words and numbers into precise columns (with or without borders).

- Put text and graphics together with a minimum of fuss.

- Arrange paragraphs of text side by side.

- Create professional-looking forms.

Word supplies faint grid lines that help you see the outlines of the rows and columns when you're entering text. If you want, you can add borders, shading, and fancy type to make your tables look ultra-sophisticated. And if you've ever struggled to line up columns using tabs, you'll marvel at how much easier it is to work with tables!

How do I add a table?

You can put together a table from scratch, but it's much easier to use one of Word's many wizards to do the job.

Tables made easy: ask the wizard

Word has a template that automates the process of creating a table. Choose File, New, and select Table Wizard from the scrolling list. If you're already in a document, select Table, Insert Table, then click the Wizard button.

Word will open a new document for you and begin asking a series of questions specific to your table (see fig. 10.6). If you tell Word you want 13 columns, for example, it will offer to automatically add the months of the year as column headings.

Fig. 10.6
Let the Table Wizard build a perfectly formatted table for you. As with all the Word wizards, you answer a series of questions, and Word does the work for you.

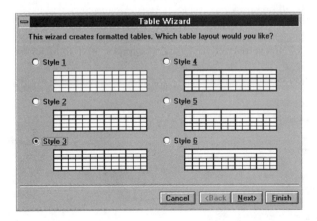

After the Table Wizard has worked its magic, you're offered the chance to choose a look for your table from Word's built-in list of automatic formats. (We'll talk about Table AutoFormat in more detail later in this chapter.)

Word tables at a glance

Heading
You can designate one or more rows to be labels for the columns below. Then, these headings will appear at the top of every page.

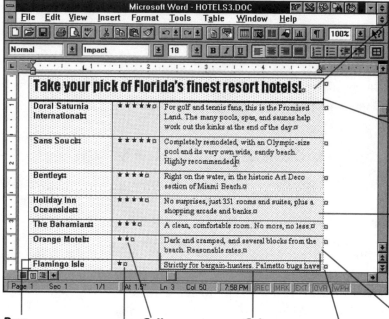

Border
These lines do show up when you print. You can adjust their thickness and location.

Shading
Use shades of gray or colors to help add emphasis to rows and columns.

Gridline
A thin dotted line shows you the edges of each cell while you work. It doesn't show up when you print, and you can turn it off if you want.

Row
Each table can have up to 32,767 rows. (Most tables will be much smaller.)

Cell
The basic unit of a table. Each cell is formed by the inter-section of a **row** and a **column.**

Column
Each table can have up to 31 columns. If you need more, you need to use Excel.

End of cell marker
Cell formatting (such as text alignment) is stored here. To move a cell and its formatting, be sure to select this marker.

End of row marker
To rearrange rows by dragging them around in a table, make sure this marker is selected.

Quick tables

Use the Insert Table button on the Standard toolbar to quickly add an unformatted table to your document. When you click the button, a table grid (like the one in fig. 10.7) drops down from the toolbar. Drag the pointer down and to the right to tell Word how many rows and columns you want in your table.

If you just want to add a few rows and columns to your document, this technique works OK. But for anything complex, use the Table Wizard.

Fig. 10.7
Insert an unformatted table with one click and a little dragging. Be forewarned, though: you'll have plenty of formatting work to do afterward.

Converting text to a table

Let's say you're scanning through a document and you see a block of text that you just know would work better as a table. No problem—select the entire block and click the Insert Table button on the Standard toolbar to instantly surround the text with a table. If the one-button approach doesn't work (the columns are too wide, or there aren't enough rows, for example), click Edit, Undo and try again using the menus: Table, Convert Text to Table. The pull-down menus give you more control over your options.

 To convert a table to text, just do the reverse: Select the entire table and choose Table, Convert Table to Text.

 You can save a table as an AutoText entry, complete with formatting and headings, then insert it into your documents that way. See Chapter 9 for more about the AutoText feature.

How do I work with a table?

Once your information is neatly stashed in a table, you can rearrange it to your heart's content. You can move cells, rows, or columns. You can change the height of a row or the width of a column with a few mouse clicks. You can even have Word reformat your entire table automatically.

Picking out the pieces of the table

Before you can rearrange, resize, or reformat a part of a table, you have to select it. Use the techniques in table 10.1.

Table 10.1   Picking out the pieces of a table

	To select this part of a table...	Do this...
	Cell Contents	Drag the mouse pointer over the text you want to select.
	Cell	Aim the mouse pointer just to the inside left edge of the cell, and click.
	Row	Aim the mouse pointer just to the outside left edge of the first cell in the row, and click.
	Column	Aim the mouse pointer at the top of the column (until it turns into a small down-pointing arrow), and click.
	Multiple rows or columns	Select row or column as detailed previously; hold the mouse button down while dragging to select additional rows or columns.
	Whole table	Choose Table, Select Table.

What can I put in a cell?

Anything you can put in a Word document can also go into a table: text, numbers, symbols, or graphics, for example. You can even add automatic numbering to the items in a row or column of a table; as you move items around, they stay in the right sequence.

Entering and editing data

To begin entering data into a table, just put the insertion point anywhere in the cell and start typing. Don't press Enter unless you want to start a new paragraph—if Word runs out of room, it will wrap the text within the cell. To move to the next cell, press Tab. To move to the previous cell, press Shift+Tab. Use the arrow keys to move up or down, one row at a time.

I know I entered text in this cell, but I can't see it all. What's wrong?

You've run out of room in a row that has been formatted to be an exact size. To fix the problem, choose T<u>a</u>ble, Cell Height and <u>W</u>idth, then reset the row height to Auto. Now, all the rows in your table will adjust in height to accommodate what you type.

Changing column widths and row heights

One way to make a table more readable is to adjust its column widths so that each column takes up just enough room to accommodate the information in it.

The easiest way is to simply use the **mouse** to change the width of a column or the height of a row.

What about the **ruler**? Well, all those little rectangles and triangles and symbols can be dragged around, but it's really hard to remember what they do. If you want to memorize those techniques, be my guest—but I prefer just to drag the edges of the column directly, as shown in figure 10.8.

Fig. 10.8
To make a column wider or narrower, just grab its sides with the mouse pointer until the pointer changes to this shape. You can also use the ruler to rework columns, but the rules are quite complicated.

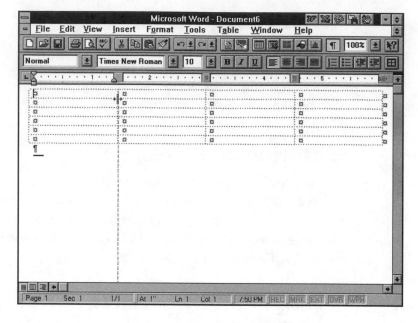

Word includes an option, called **AutoFit,** which automatically adjusts the width of your columns according to what you've already typed in them. If you want to use AutoFit for the entire table, make sure to select at least one cell from each of the rows. Then choose T̲able, Column Height and W̲idth to display the dialog box shown in figure 10.9. Click the A̲utoFit button.

Fig. 10.9
Use the AutoFit button to let Word automatically adjust its columns and rows to the right size.

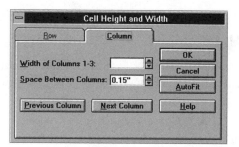

Adding and deleting rows and columns

It's easy to **insert a row** in your table. To add a new row at the bottom of the table, move the insertion point to the end of the last row and press Tab. To insert a row elsewhere, click in the row below the place where you want to insert a new row, click the right mouse button, and choose Insert Rows from the shortcut menu. To insert another row in the same place, just press F4 (Word's do-it-again key).

To **insert a column**, you first have to select a column. Move the mouse pointer to the top of a column until it turns to a small, down-pointing arrow. Click to select the entire column, then right-click and select Insert Columns. Your new column will appear to the left of the one you selected. What if you want to add a column at the right side of the table? You'll have to select the new column and drag it to the end of the table. (Sorry.)

It's a bit tougher to **delete a row or column**. Pressing the Del key clears the contents of the cell, but the cell itself sticks around like a bad cold. The only way to get rid of the cell is to select the entire row or column it sits in, then click the right mouse button and choose Delete Rows (or Delete Columns).

?Q&A

I'm trying to delete some rows from my column, but I can't find the right choices on the menu. Where are they?

All the Word menus—the ones you pull down and the right-mouse-button shortcut variety—can drive you crazy. Why? Because the menus actually change, depending on what you're pointing to. If you want to delete a row or a column, you need to select the row or column first; otherwise, you'll never see the menu choices!

Making great-looking tables

Every table starts out as just a collection of cells, rows, and columns, and nothing stands out from the rest of the table. If you had a talented graphic artist and plenty of time, you could add bold headings, decorative borders, and background shadings to make your table easy to read.

Or you can use Word's built-in design smarts to automatically reorganize your table. This feature, called Table AutoFormat, works so well that even a graphic artist might use it to get started.

Let Word do the work with AutoFormat

Every time you use the Table Wizard, Word offers to reformat your table with one of more than 30 predefined formats. But you don't have to use the Table Wizard to use this feature; you can choose Table AutoFormat from the pull-down menus any time. Just make sure the insertion point is somewhere in the table you want to reformat.

When you use Table AutoFormat, the results are remarkable. They're also much more reliable than the AutoFormat button that Word uses for general documents. Why? Because information is contained in neat rows and columns, it's much easier for Word to figure out how to treat rows, columns, and headings. Look at the before and after pictures below to see what a difference it can make.

Figure 10.10 shows a basic table, with a few symbols and some bold-faced headings, but otherwise minus any pizzazz.

Fig. 10.10

There's nothing wrong with this table, but it's not very interesting or readable, is it?

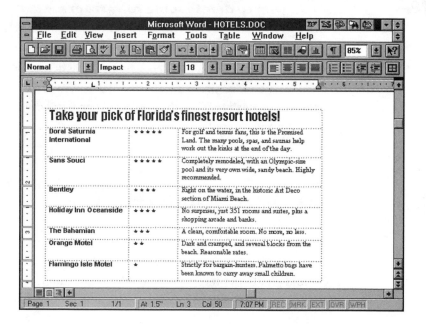

OK, now position the insertion point in the table and choose Table, Table AutoFormat. Take your pick of more than 30 prebuilt designs (see fig. 10.11). Different formats are appropriate for different types of data; for example, there are AutoFormats that work perfectly with lists and others that give you your choice of grids. We'll choose one of the Colorful options.

Fig. 10.11

The Table AutoFormat feature gives you more than 30 different "looks" for your table.

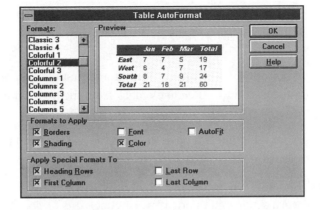

After using Table AutoFormat, we eventually got the look we were after (see fig. 10.12). Because the column widths and fonts were generally OK, we told Table AutoFormat to leave them alone. It added colors, shading, and borders, though, in one smooth motion.

Fig. 10.12

After Table AutoFormat. Our ho-hum table has some life, thanks to shading, borders, and the judicious use of color. (That's a soft yellow in the body and a bright red in the heading.)

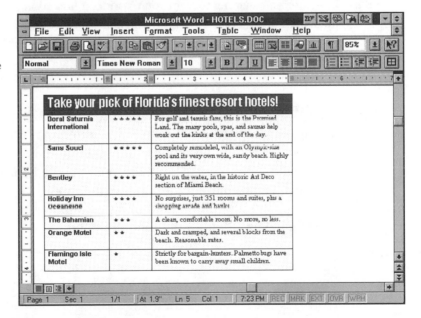

Here are a few tips for using Table AutoFormat effectively:

- Don't be afraid to experiment! If the Table AutoFormat feature doesn't work the first time, choose Edit, Undo AutoFormat (or just press Ctrl+Z), and start over again with different options.

- Text formatting, such as fonts and alignment, can be applied to individual cells, rows, or the entire table. If you're happy with the fonts you've used, uncheck the Font box.

- If your table doesn't have labels in the first column or headings in the first row, remove the check mark from the boxes under Apply Special Formats To.

- If your table doesn't have totals in the last row and the last column, make sure those boxes are unchecked.

- The AutoFit feature doesn't work properly if you've merged cells to form a single cell in one row. Uncheck this option if you have trouble.

How do I make rows and columns stand out?

Use lines and shading to help your readers follow along as they read items in the same row or column. This is especially important when you have wide rows and long columns filled with detail. And column headings should be formatted in bold, easy-to-read fonts so they stand out.

Adding borders

Adding **borders** to a table is simple. First, select the cells, rows, or columns where you want to add borders. If nothing is selected, Word assumes that you want to add borders to the entire table. Choose Format, Borders and Shading to pop up the dialog box shown in figure 10.13.

Fig. 10.13
Use the Borders tab of the Table Borders and Shading dialog box to set border types, add grid lines, and pick line styles and colors.

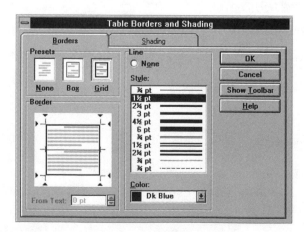

This is the place to turn to when you want to draw thick lines around the outside of the table, thin lines between rows and columns, and colored lines wherever you want them.

1 Choose one of the preset border types. **Bo<u>x</u>** puts lines around the outside of the selection; **<u>Grid</u>** adds lines around every cell in the selection.

2 Choose a **Line St<u>y</u>le** and **<u>C</u>olor** for your borders.

3 To adjust the look of one border (or to remove it completely) click on the line in the box labeled **Bor<u>d</u>er**. If you've done it right, you'll see an arrow at either end of the line you've selected, and all the others will go away.

4 Choose a new **Line St<u>y</u>le** (or check **N<u>o</u>ne**) from the list in the middle of the box. For example, to change the border underneath a row to a thin double line, click on the 3/4 pt double border.

5 Click **OK** to see your changes. If it didn't work, use Undo and try again.

 **<Caution>** Don't confuse table borders with the grid lines you see around your table on the screen. Borders don't print unless you specifically add them by using one of the many table-formatting options!

Adding shading

Adding **shading** is a simple process. Make sure you have first selected the cells, rows, or columns you want to change, then choose F<u>o</u>rmat, <u>B</u>orders and Shading. Click on the <u>S</u>hading tab to bring up the dialog box shown in figure 10.14.

Fig. 10.14
Use the <u>S</u>hading folder of the Borders and Shading dialog box to add foreground and background colors and shading to your tables.

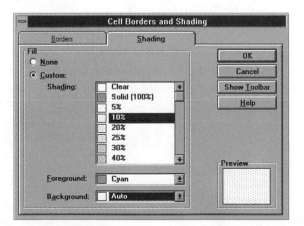

Come here when you want to add a dark background behind bold headings, a light background behind rows and columns, or no background at all for keep-it-simple tables.

1 Pick a **Foreground color** from the drop-down list. This is the color you want to add to your selection.

2 Leave the **Background color** box set to Auto unless you want your table to get really ugly, really fast.

3 Choose the amount of **Shading** you want to apply. For rows and columns where you expect people to be able to read text, start with a value of 10% or, at most, 20%.

4 To remove shading, check the **None** box.

5 Click **OK** to apply your changes to the table.

To quickly add lines and some shading options, try clicking the Borders button on the Formatting toolbar. This displays the Borders toolbar, which gives you one-click access to boxes and grids.

I need bigger headings!

Most of your table will consist of identical arrangements of cells, but sometimes you'll want to make one row a little bit different. You might want your table heading to stretch across the entire first row in big, bold type, for example. Or you might want to add a footnote, in little tiny type, in the last row of a table.

To merge two or more cells into a single cell, first select the cells you want to merge. Then select Table, Merge Cells from the pull-down menu. In figure 10.15, for example, we selected the three cells above Jan, Feb, and Mar, then used this feature to combine them in one centered label, Q1.

Fig. 10.15

The top row of this formatted table once contained 13 cells. Using the Merge Cells option, we've created four larger cells, one for each three–month period.

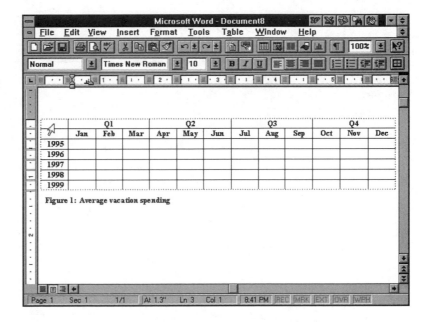

Can I use tables to create a form?

Every business uses forms, whether they want to or not. Purchase orders and invoices. W-2s, W-4s, and 1040s (yikes!). Sign-up sheets and petitions. Every form has two common elements:

- **Label text**, to tell whoever's filling in the form what they're supposed to fill in.

- **Lines and boxes**, so the information goes where it's supposed to go.

Most people create forms using a felt-tipped pen and a ruler. Those who've mastered the art of setting tab stops can probably create a good-looking form that way, although it can take hours of trial-and-error work.

But the best way, by far, to create a form is with the help of Word tables. The weekly time sheet in figure 10.16, for example, looks like it was professionally printed. In reality, though, it consists of four simple Word tables.

The **header** at the top of the page is actually a one-row table consisting of three columns. Because there are no borders, it looks like these three elements (a WordArt logo, some text, and a Word picture) are floating on the page.

The **name block** is also a table, consisting of three rows and two columns. Borders underneath each row help the user fill in the information correctly.

The **time and date block** looks more like a table, doesn't it? In fact, it consists of 9 rows and 6 columns, with borders everywhere except in the lower left corner, where three cells have been merged into one to form an easy-to-spot label. Note the thick border above the section that helps anchor it on the page.

Finally, the **signature block** at the bottom of the page is really a two-row, two-column table with borders underneath each row.

11

Letters by the Dozen

Send personalized copies of your letter to all the people on your mailing list. Or to just a select few. Word even prints the envelopes for you!

In this chapter

- I need to send the same letter to a bunch of people
- How do I manage my mailing lists?
- Word can print envelopes and mailing labels, too?

Imagine that you are Ed McMahon. You need to send a letter to everyone in the country, telling them all that they may have just won $10,000,000. Of course, each one needs to be addressed personally, so they know you took the time to give their letters individual attention. How long do you think it will take you to write all 250 million or so letters?

And since you are Ed McMahon, think about all the people you know! Friends and family, Star Search contestants, magazine subscribers, Dick Clark, Johnny Carson, and other celebrities. Now think about all the trivial bits of information you know about each of these people, like addresses and phone numbers, golf handicaps, favorite foods, and birthdays.

If computers didn't exist, you'd probably be buried under 3×5 index cards, trying to keep track of all this data. But because you have a PC and Microsoft Office, you have no trouble keeping track of all that information.

In fact, you can use a Word feature called **Mail Merge** to write one sweep-stakes letter and then send personalized copies of it to all the people on your list. If you had to do all those letters by hand, you'd wear out your copying machine and get a bad case of writer's cramp! Word does it in seconds. No writer's cramp, no index cards. And it even prints the envelopes for you!

I have a *lot* of letters to write

Okay, so you're not Ed McMahon, but you still do need to do a lot of mass mailings. Let's say you want to send a promotional mailing to some of your best customers. Without a computer, you'd put on a pot of coffee, haul out your little metal box full of index cards, and start copying names and addresses, one by one, into the blank spaces on each copy of your letter. When you were done, you'd have a stack of invitations, each a little different from the others in the stack.

Word does exactly the same thing automatically, using an original letter you compose, plus a table full of names and addresses. And it can do hundreds of letters in the time it would take you or me to do two or three.

Word's Mail Merge Helper isn't called a wizard, but it acts just like one. It does everything but load the paper for you when you want to send a personalized copy of a standard letter to everyone in your address book.

Mail merge in a nutshell

Here's basically what you do (we'll get into specific procedures in a minute):

1 Create your main document (a form letter).

2 Create a data source document.

3 Tell Word to merge your source document into your main document.

Although Microsoft promises that merging is as simple as 1-2-3, that promise is a little misleading. Merging really is a simple process, but you have to backtrack to step 1 before you can go on to step 3. Don't worry! We'll walk you through it.

What's mail merge, and how does it work?

Start with two pieces: a fill-in-the-blanks form letter and a list of names, addresses, and other information. Wind up with a big stack of letters, each personally addressed to one of the people on your list.

Main document
The fill-in-the blanks form letter can contain anything you can put in a letter: words, numbers, charts and graphs, even tables.

Data source document
It's really just a table, where each row is like a single index card that contains all the information about one person, and each column holds data fields.

Title	FirstName	LastName	JobTitle	Company	Address1	City	State	PostalCode	Position
Mr.	David	Jones	Vice President, Informati on Systems	Arlington Manufactu ring Company	4596 East 194th Street	India napoli s	IN	46299	Senior Program mer
Ms.	Jennifer	Norman	Human Resources Manager	Jackson Data Systems	3546 Breezeway Road, Suite 3	Cinci nnati	OH	45555	Systems Analyst
Mr.	Ralph	Thomas	Manager	Applied Systems Corporatio n	2232 Old Route 42 North	Lucas	IN	47888	Program ming Manager

Header row
Contains the names of each field.

Data fields
Match up with the merge field in the main document.

Merge field
When you insert a merge field into a main document, you tell Word to look for a matching piece of information in your data source document.

The result
The result can go to your printer to be printed onto plain paper, or onto envelopes or mailing labels. It can even go into a new document that you can edit further.

I'm ready to start

Before you fire up the Mail Merge Helper, take a few minutes to think about what type of information you need in your form letter. Most often, you'll need to insert names and addresses into the letter, but you also might want to add special information, like a price, a local phone number, or an E-mail address, that will be different for different people in your list. Jot down your list on a scrap of paper, the margin of this book, or your napkin. Keep it handy—you'll need it a bit later.

Got your list? Let's get started!

1 Close any open documents, then choose File, New, and click OK to start with a fresh slate.

2 To start the Mail Merge Helper, choose Tools, Mail Merge. You'll see a dialog box like the one in figure 11.1.

Fig. 11.1
This is the first screen you see when you start Word's Mail Merge Helper.

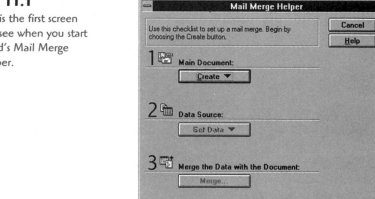

3 In the Mail Merge Helper dialog box, click the Create button under Main Document, then choose Form Letters from the list, like you see in figure 11.2.

Fig. 11.2
We'll do a form letter now and look at labels and envelopes a little later.

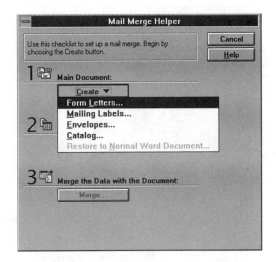

4 In the next dialog box, Word tells you it can work with the document you have open, or it can start a new one. Since our current document is blank, go ahead and click **A**ctive Window. Word then does some background work and returns you to the Mail Merge Helper. If you don't want to use the document you have open right now, click **N**ew Main Document.

{Note} _____ The text boxes in most of the Mail Merge Helper dialog boxes coach you about what to do next. If you get lost, look there first for help. If you're still stuck, ask for help! Choose **H**elp, **E**xamples and Demos, then press the button next to Mail Merge. Word's built-in demonstration of how mail merge works is seriously useful stuff.

Get out that list you jotted down earlier

Now that Word knows which document it will be using as the "blanks" part of the form letter, it's time to create the "fillers" for those blanks:

1 Under Data Source, click the **G**et Data button, and choose **C**reate Data Source. Word opens the Create Data Source dialog box (see fig. 11.3).

Fig. 11.3
This is where you create the fields for your form lettter that will be filled in the individual letters.

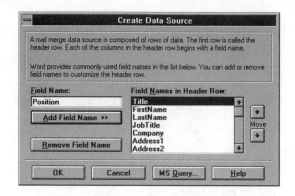

2 The long list at the bottom of the dialog box includes some common fields that Word thinks you might want to use, such as Title (like Mr., Ms., Dr., and so on). If you don't want to keep a field in this list, click on it, then click the Remove Field Name button. If your list is intended to keep track of people interested in vacationing in Florida, for example, you probably don't need to store JobTitle and Company.

3 If you want to add your own field (like the ones you wrote down on that napkin), type it in the Field Name box, then click the Add Field Name button right below it. Depending on what you plan to do with your list, you might choose to track golf handicaps, credit ratings, birthdays, or customer referrals..

{Note} You can't use spaces to name a field in a data source file. So Referred By won't be accepted. Either run the words together or separate them with the underscore character. Both ReferredBy and Referred_By are acceptable names for data fields.

4 The order of the fields doesn't affect the merge, but it can make it easier for you to enter data. (It's easier for your brain to think "Ms., Beth, Lucas, Indianapolis, IN, Scorpio" than "Lucas, Indianapolis, Scorpio, Beth, IN, Ms.") Click on the field you want to move, then click the up or down Move arrows to the right of the list. Word moves the selected field up or down on the list, as you indicate.

5 When you're happy with the list, click OK. Word asks you to give the data source a name. Do it, and click OK again.

6 A message box appears, telling you that your data source contains no
data. No problem—that's what we're getting ready to do next. Click on
Edit Data Source, and read on.

Plugging in your people

When you first create a new data source document, it starts out empty, just
like a stack of blank index cards. Once you fill in the blanks on the "cards,"
you can use your information over and over again.

After you press the Edit Data Source button, Word displays an easy-to-use
data form that works just like an index card. The form should look like the
one in figure 11.4. Use the form to add new **records** (cards) or change the
information in records you've already entered:

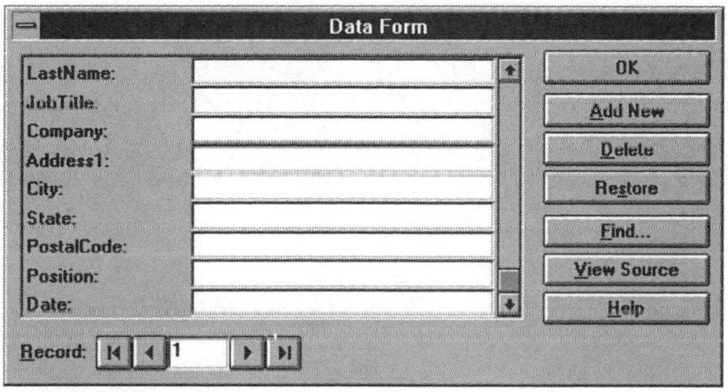

Fig. 11.4
To add new records or
edit existing ones, use
Word's data form.

- To **add another record to your data source document**, just press
  the Add New button, and start typing in the blank data form.

- To **move from one field to another**, use the Tab key. Use Shift+Tab
  to move to the previous field.

- To **move from one record to another** in your data source document,
  use the VCR-style controls on the data form.

- To **change information in your data source document**, simply
  move to the record, click the field you want to change, and make the
  correction.

- To **undo changes you've made** to a record, click the Restore button.

- To **delete a record**, click the Delete button.

 **<Caution>** The Restore button works only if you catch your mistake before you've moved to a new record. Clicking this button won't bring back a record you've deleted, either. Yikes!

When you're finished adding in all your people and their info, click OK. Another message box appears, telling you that your main document contains no merge fields. But, you already knew that, because your main document is still blank. All that is about to change.

Form letters 'R' us

To set up your form letter, click the <u>E</u>dit Main Document button in that message box (it's still there, right? If not, just click <u>E</u>dit under Main Document in the Mail Merge Helper). Word switches back to the blank document and adds the Mail Merge toolbar to your workspace (shown in fig. 11.5). You'll learn more about the buttons on this toolbar shortly.

Fig. 11.5
Use the Mail Merge toolbar to insert merge instructions into a form letter.

Start typing your letter like you would any other letter. When you come to a place where you want to insert a merge field, follow these steps:

1 Make sure the insertion point is in the place you want the merge field to appear.

2 Click the Insert Merge Field button on the Mail Merge toolbar to drop down a list containing all the merge fields in your data source document.

3 Click on the name of the merge field you want to insert in your letter, as we're doing in figure 11.6.

 **<Caution>** Those funny << and >> characters on either side of each merge field are called **chevrons**. They're special codes that Word uses to recognize merge fields.

You wouldn't try to use tape to attach sergeant's stripes to your sleeve—you have to sew them on so they become an integral part of the uniform. Similarly, you can't type or insert the chevrons around the names of your merge fields. You *must* use the Insert Merge Field button, or Word will ignore your instructions and treat your intended field as just another part of the letter.

Fig. 11.6
This field will insert the name of the job title you're applying for.

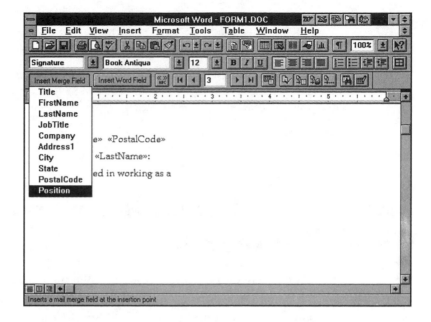

4 Continue typing the rest of your letter, repeating these steps for each additional merge field. When you're done, save the letter. It will look something like figure 11.7.

Fig. 11.7
If these potential employers knew how little individual attention you're putting into these cover letters, they might think twice about hiring you. But they'll never know!

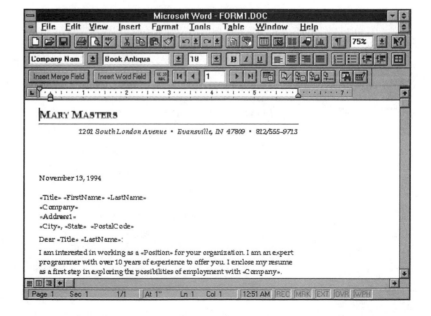

Remember to add spaces and punctuation between merge fields when necessary; for instance, you'll usually want to add a space between first and last names, and a comma and a space between the city and the state. Otherwise, everyone who gets your merge letter will see their names all squished together like this:

        Mr.DavidJones

I want to see what my letter and data will look like together

What if you want a sneak preview of what the finished product will look like? Like the "index cards" in your data source, you can flip through your data source document when you're working with the main document, thanks to Word's Mail Merge toolbar. To switch between the field view and the preview, click the View Merged Data button on the Mail Merge toolbar. Remember, this is just a preview—the merge hasn't actually happened yet.

Use the following buttons on the Mail Merge toolbar to control your view of the data:

 View Merged Data switches between viewing merge fields and showing you what the final letters will look like.

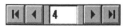 The **Go To Record** buttons let you flip through your data source document to see what your merged letters will look like. (You'll have to push the View Merged Data button to see the results.) If you know exactly which record you want to see, click in the box between the buttons, and type in the record number, and press Enter.

 Takes you back to the Mail Merge Helper dialog box.

 Check for Errors in your main document or data source document. (See <u>H</u>elp for details on this function. You won't use it very often.)

 These buttons allow you to **Merge to New Document**, **Merge to Printer**, or display the Merge dialog box for additional options.

Find Record locates a specific record in your data source document.

 Edit Data Source displays the data form so you can add a new record or change an existing one.

②Q&A

> **I'm seeing all this gibberish about Merge Fields in my main document. What happened?**
>
> Somehow you've turned on the View Field Codes option, and Word is showing you the normally hidden codes it uses to track your merge information. If you have the Show Field Codes option turned on for some reason, then you'll see {MERGEFIELD FirstName} instead of «FirstName». To shoo those bizarre codes back into hiding where they belong, press Alt+F9.

Merging East and West

Okay, you've got your letter and you've got your data. You have a basic idea of how the finished letters will look. The hard part is done! Just a few house-keeping issues, and you're home free.

To get the merge started, make sure you have your main document open, then choose Tools, Mail Merge again. The Merge dialog box opens on your screen, as in figure 11.8.

Fig. 11.8
Almost there!

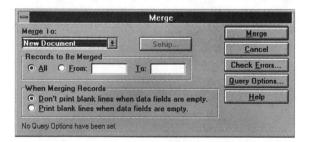

I don't want to mail my letters to *everyone*

You might have hundreds or even thousands of names and addresses in your data source document. When you merge the data source document into a form letter, Word lets you specify a set of conditions to use. For example, you can select only customers who have made purchases in the last 60 days, who live in New York , who *don't* live in Florida, or whose last names begin with H.

To filter out only the records you want, click the Query Options button in the Merge dialog box. You'll get a dialog box that has two tabs: Filter Records and Sort Records. Click Filter Records to bring it to the front (see fig. 11.9). Here you can tell Word what you want to include or exclude in your merge. If you only want to send letters to women who use the title Ms., you'd do this:

Fig. 11.9

Press the Query Options button on the Mail Merge Helper, then tell Word which records you want to include in your mail merge.

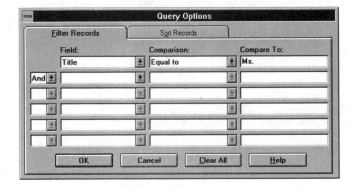

1 Select Title from the Field list.

2 Select the Comparison criteria. These are your typical "equal to," "not equal to," "greater than," and so on. To find an exact match for our example, choose Equal to.

(Tip)

> For details on each of these comparison operators, click Help or press F1.

3 In the Compare To box, enter what you want to find—in this case, enter **Ms.**

4 If you need even more specific search criteria, choose And or Or, and fill in the next row of blanks.

5 When you click OK, Word will take you back to the Merge dialog box.

Are we there yet?

At last, the time has arrived to put it all together. You should be back at the Merge dialog box again. If you click on the Merge To drop-down list, you get three choices (see fig. 11.10):

- **New Document.** Word will put the merged letter into a file, so you can check the results before you print them.

- **Printer.** Be careful about printing big merges straight to the printer. If something goes wrong, you have to start it again. This is handy, however, if your hard drive is almost full and you need to run a bunch of letters.

- **Electronic Mail.** You have to have an E-mail system installed to use this feature. For more help, choose this option, then press F1.

Fig. 11.10
Most of the time, you'll choose New Document.

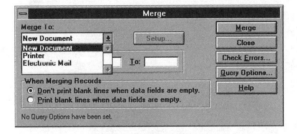

What about these 500 matching envelopes?

Its sad but true: In most American offices, there's a typewriter next to the laser printer. What's it there for? Well, the letter may be perfectly printed, but most people don't know how to make their word processor and their laser printer work with envelopes. So they type the envelopes—or worse, address them by hand.

Fortunately, Word lets you create envelopes and mailing labels automatically. Best of all, it works just as easily with one letter as it does with a hundred. It might take a few tries to get it right the first time, but once you learn Word's envelope secrets, you'll send that old Selectric to the scrap heap.

I want to make mailing labels

Sometimes its more practical to use a mailing label—I don't know of many printers that will address *boxes*, for example! Word can print out sheets of labels to match any of 56 styles of standard Avery mailing labels.

 **{Note}** If you want to create labels for a mass mailing, you'll need to go through the Mail Merge Helper. Go on to the next section.

To create a single label, choose Tools, Envelopes and Labels, then click on the Labels tab (see fig. 11.11). To choose a label format, click the Options button, and select the kind you need from the scrolling list. When you're ready, put the label sheet in the printer, then click Print.

Fig. 11.11
Don't waste them! To print a single label on a sheet that has some labels missing, choose Single Label, and enter the Row and Column numbers of the label you want Word to hit.

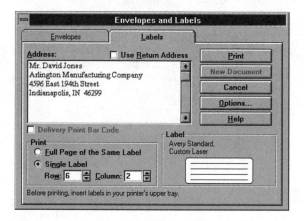

 **<Caution>** Always be wary of what you try to feed your printer. Some printers don't digest used label sheets very well. Some don't even like envelopes. If you're not sure about your printer's recommended diet, check its user manual.

I want to address envelopes for my whole mailing list

Word uses the same tools to address envelopes and labels, whether you're doing one or a hundred. Setting up a data source document to print envelopes is no more difficult than building a form letter.

{Note}

To address a single envelope using your printer, position the insertion point anywhere in your letter, and choose Tools, Envelopes, and Labels to display the Envelopes and Labels dialog box. If necessary, correct the Delivery Address, and then set up the Return Address. Use the Feed icon to change the way Word feeds envelopes into the printer.

Just as with a form letter, you'll use the Mail Merge Helper to handle envelopes. Click the Create button in the Main Document section, then choose Envelopes from the drop-down list.

(Tip)

The procedure for setting up mass-mailing labels is identical, except that you choose Mailing Labels.

Create your data source like last time, then choose Setup Main Document Setup. After you work your way through a series of familiar dialog boxes, you'll come to the heart of the envelope-addressing routine: the dialog box shown in figure 11.12.

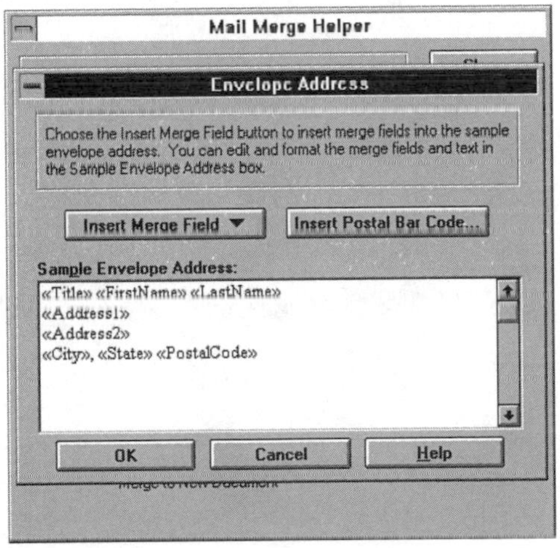

Fig. 11.12
Use your Word data source document to print matching envelopes for every one of your form letters.

Use the Insert Merge Field button to add information to your document, then click Close to return. From this point on, your merge document will work just like a form letter.

⊕(Tip)

How do you change fonts in a mail merge envelope? In the Envelope Address dialog box, highlight the text you want to reformat, and then click the right mouse button. The shortcut menu that pops up includes options for changing fonts and paragraph formatting.

❓Q&A

Our mail service prints our labels out by ZIP code. Can I do this, too, so the letters and labels are in the same order?

Sure! If the order in which the letters are printed is important, you can sort the records before you do the merge. In the Query Options dialog box, click the Sort Records tab to bring that page to the front. You can base the sort on up to three fields. For example, start with the ZIP code. In the Sort By list, choose the PostalCode field. Then choose Ascending, so that 00000 is first and 99999 is last.

12

Fancy Word Stuff

For casual writing, you don't need to dress up your documents. But when you really want to impress your audience, dress your documents in formal wear—the equivalent of a tuxedo or an evening gown.

In this chapter:

- What can I do to keep from getting lost in a long document?
- How can I add the date and time to my document?
- What do I need to know to use Word for desktop publishing?
- Is there a trick to help me move graphics around?
- Can I put a paragraph in a box so it really stands out?
- How can I break my document into columns?

There are documents, and then there are DOCUMENTS.

Most of the time, you'll use Word for everyday documents, like letters and memos. You don't need to dress up for this kind of casual writing—for you and your documents, blue jeans and sneakers will suffice.

But every so often you have to produce something that really matters. A report that's going all the way to the board of directors, say, or a brochure you plan to mail to 500 top customers. When the stakes are that high, it's time to dress your documents in formal wear—the equivalent of a tuxedo or an evening gown.

In this chapter, we'll cover stuff most people never try with Word: desktop publishing, for example, and tricks that help you keep your place, even in a 50-page document.

I'm lost in this long document

You've just sent a week's worth of work to your laser printer, and now you're walking back to your office with an armful of paper. Let's see... there's a 12-page PowerPoint presentation, a stack of spreadsheets, and that 48-page Word report you've been working on for weeks. It took an hour to print all that stuff, but it's finally done. So you walk down the hall, and ... ah-ah-ah-ah-*achoooo!* You sneeze.

The papers go flying in every direction, and when you finally get all the pages picked up, you realize you have no way of telling which page belongs with which document, in which order.

It doesn't *have* to be that way, you know. Each time you create a document, Word reserves a special area at the top and the bottom of each page for a **header** and **footer**—labels that appear on each and every page of your document.

You can put just about anything in a header or footer, but most often you'll use these spaces for things like titles, page numbers, dates, and labels (like "Confidential" or "Draft").

How do I create a header or footer?

There's no need to *insert* a header or footer into your document, because both are already there, just waiting for you to fill them in. To add text to a header or footer, you first have to make them visible. Switch to Normal or Page Layout View, then choose <u>V</u>iew, <u>H</u>eader and Footer (see fig. 12.1).

Fig. 12.1
In Page Layout view, the text of your document appears in gray while you work with the header and footer.

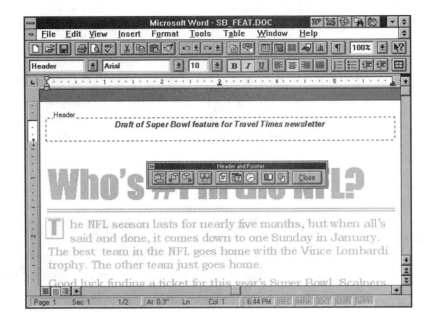

You can type anything you want in a header or footer box. You can also change typefaces and sizes, realign the text, and adjust the space between the header or footer and your text.

While you work, the Header and Footer toolbar floats nearby with all the buttons you need to get around. Here's what the buttons are for:

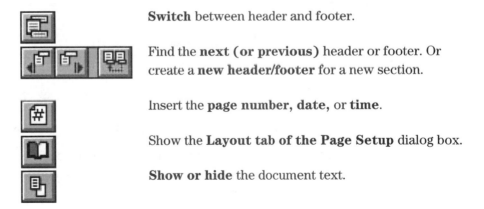

Switch between header and footer.

Find the **next (or previous)** header or footer. Or create a **new header/footer** for a new section.

Insert the **page number, date,** or **time**.

Show the **Layout tab of the Page Setup** dialog box.

Show or hide the document text.

How do I move a header or footer around?

Headers are always at the top of the page; footers are always at the bottom. You can't change those facts, but you *can* change the space between where the header ends and where your document begins. You can also add space between the end of the text on each page and the beginning of the footer.

To reposition and resize headers and footers, use the vertical ruler to the left of either element (see fig. 12.2), as follows:

Fig. 12.2
Use the vertical ruler to change the size and position of a header or footer.

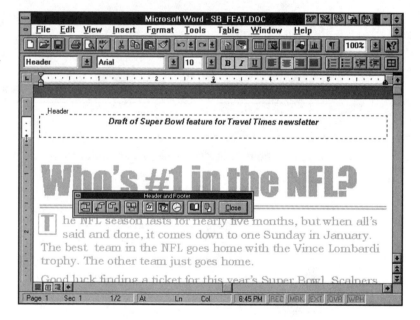

If you can't see the ruler, it's just hiding. Choose View, Ruler to bring it back.

1 Use the Header and Footer toolbar to show the one you want to resize.

2 Click on the top or bottom of the white part of the vertical ruler (called the **margin boundary**) until the pointer changes to a two-headed arrow, as shown in figure 12.2.

3 As you drag the margin boundary up and down, the header or footer will grow or shrink to match.

4 Use the buttons on the Formatting toolbar to change the alignment of your header or footer (centering the text, for example).

Extra-special header and footer tricks

Do you want the exact same header and footer on every page? Maybe not. If you have a fancy title page, you probably won't want to mess it up with a label at the top and bottom of the page. And if you're planning to use both sides of the paper for your printouts, you can set up different headers and footers on left and right pages. If the title of your report is on the right page header, for example, maybe you don't need it on the left page.

Word lets you handle both instances with ease. To pop up the Page Setup dialog box (shown in fig. 12.3), just click the Page Setup button on the Header and Footer toolbar.

Fig. 12.3

The Page Setup dialog box lets you tell Word where you want your headers and footers to appear.

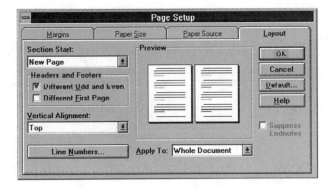

In the dialog box, you can do the following:

- Check the box labeled Different Odd and Even to use different headers or footers on left and right pages.

- Check the box labeled Different First Page to set up a different header or footer for the first page of a document or section.

Use the Header and Footer toolbar to jump back and forth between different headers and footers.

?Q&A

I put page numbers in a footer, but now I don't want them any more. How do I get rid of them?

To zap any part of a header or footer, choose <u>V</u>iew, <u>H</u>eader and Footer. If you're not already in Page Layout view, Word will switch for you. Highlight the page number code (and anything else in the footer that you don't want any more) and press Del. Voilá! No more page numbers.

I just want to add page numbers

You don't have to hassle with headers or fuss with footers if all you want to do is slap some numbers on your pages. Word has a special shortcut for that job. When you choose <u>I</u>nsert, Page N<u>u</u>mbers, Word creates a footer (or a header, if you prefer) in your document, then plops a page number into it. It just takes a few clicks in the dialog boxes shown in figure 12.4.

Fig. 12.4
Choose <u>I</u>nsert, Page N<u>u</u>mbers to quickly plop page numbers into your document.

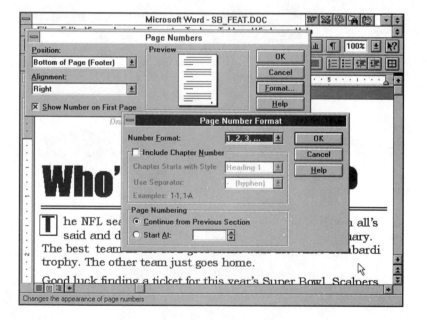

Here's how to tell Word that you want to include page numbers:

1 In the Page Numbers dialog box, tell Word where you want numbers to appear: on the top or bottom of the page.

2 Left? Right? Centered on the page? Tell Word how to align the page numbers. The Preview box will show you where your choice will appear.

3 Click the Format button to display the Page Number Format dialog box, and pick a numeric format. If you're happy with a simple 1,2,3, skip this step.

4 Do you want a number to appear on your first page? (If you have a fancy title page, you probably don't.) Uncheck the Show Number on First Page box to hide the first page number.

5 OK? Then click OK.

⊛ *{Note}*

You'll only see page numbers in Page Layout view or when you use the Print Preview command. In Normal and Outline views, headers and footers are hidden.

❓ *Q&A*

I'm trying to add a page number, but the command on the Insert menu is gray. What's wrong?

Try it again, and this time look in the status bar at the bottom of the screen for an error message from Word. You're probably working in Outline view. The command you want doesn't work unless you're in Normal or Page Layout View.

How can I add today's date?

Let's say you've been polishing the same report for three weeks straight. Every day you print out at least one new version of your work-in-progress, either to read yourself or to send to other people for their comments. How can you tell yesterday's version from today's? One easy way is to add a footer to your document, then insert a code that automatically displays the current date and time every time you open the document.

To add today's date to your document—in a header, in a footer, or just in regular text—choose Insert, Date and Time. You'll see a dialog box like the one in figure 12.5. Pick a format, click OK, and Word will type today's date wherever you've placed the insertion point.

Fig. 12.5
Add today's date and time in any format you like.

That's not exactly what we want, though, is it? If we simply insert today's date, it will never change, and we won't be able to tell one version from another. What we really want is to insert a secret code that tells Word to look up today's date and put that in our footer every time we open the document. This secret code is called a **field**, and it's easy to insert a **date field**—just check the box labeled Insert as Field.

?Q&A

I just printed my report, and the date in my footer is wrong. What do I do?

Make sure your footer contains a date field, and not just text. To check, point to the date and click the right mouse button. Choose Toggle Field Codes from the shortcut menu to see the hidden code; if that menu choice isn't available, try replacing the date with a date field. Highlight the date; choose Insert, Date and Time; and make sure the Insert as Field box is checked.

I want my document to look its best

No, this isn't the Twilight Zone, but we definitely *have* left the comfortable boundaries of Word, the word processor. Now we're heading straight for the heart of Word, the desktop publisher. When you discover this side of Word, you learn that there's a lot more to your documents than just words, numbers, and the occasional table.

Word, the desktop publisher, lets you dress up your memos, reports, and newsletters with pictures, charts, fancy logos, and colorful backgrounds. With the help of special boxes called **frames**, you can pin graphics down on your pages exactly where you want them. Without frames, you might as well try to pound nails through Jell-O.

To use Word for even the simplest desktop publishing chores, you absolutely, positively need to know about frames.

What are frames? And why should I care?

If you've ever tried to park your car at a crowded football stadium, you've seen the basic principle in action. As each car enters the gate, parking attendants wave it into the next space in line, filling up each row completely before starting a new one. Don't even think about parking anywhere else, either, unless you want that big guy in the orange jumpsuit to start screaming at you.

OK, so what happens if you pull into the Shea Stadium parking lot in a semi-truck pulling a big ol' trailer? Oops! That 18-wheeler will never fit into a space designed for a Taurus or a Toyota.

You run into the same kind of problem in Word when you try to park a big chart or a picture alongside ordinary words and numbers. As far as Word is concerned, your picture is just another character. But when it tries to park next to those tiny letters, it leaves an enormous empty space between the current line and the one above.

To set aside space in the stadium parking lot, we could use a bunch of orange safety cones. Anyone who sees them knows that they'll have to go around and park on either side. When you use Word to create a frame, you mark off a section of your page the same way. When Word sees the frame, it knows that that space is reserved, and it rearranges the words and numbers around the outside of the frame.

❋ {Note}

You can put anything in a frame, including tables and text. If you're having trouble positioning a headline on the page, consider putting it in a frame.

Here's what you need to know about frames:

- Whatever you put inside a frame stays inside the frame, no matter where you move it.

- When you add text or another picture inside a frame, it expands to make room for the new stuff.

- You can move a frame anywhere on the page, even outside the margins.

- Text "flows" around objects when they're inside a frame.

- You can spot a frame by the thick dashed line around the outside (see fig. 12.6 for an example).

Fig. 12.6
The thick dashed line around the outside of the picture means it is inside a frame. Grab the dark squares to resize the frame, or drag the whole thing to a new position.

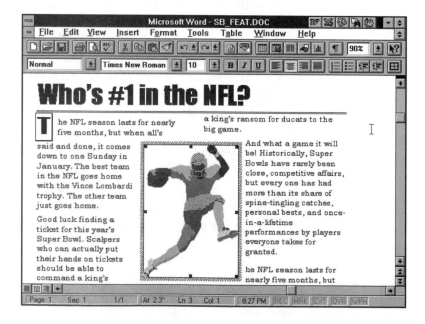

How do I put something in a frame?

The easiest way to create a frame is to wrap it around an object that's already sitting on your page. To put a frame around a picture, for example, first select the picture, then choose Insert, Frame. The frame wraps around the picture as snug as a sheet of Saran Wrap.

You can also create an empty frame and then fill it with a picture, but why go through all that hassle? It's much easier to select an object first, and then wrap a frame around it.

How do I put a frame where I want it?

It's easy to move a frame or change its size—as long as you remember to select it first. When you click anywhere inside the frame, the dashed line around the outside will appear, and the pointer will change to one of the shapes shown in fig. 12.7.

Fig. 12.7
When the pointer changes shape, you can move the frame or resize it.

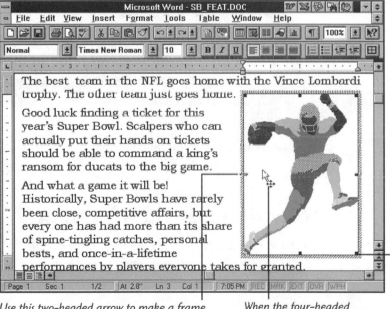

Use this two-headed arrow to make a frame bigger or smaller. Aim at the black sizing handles and pull the sides to resize the frame.

When the four-headed arrow appears alongside the pointer, click and drag the frame to move it anywhere.

Hold down the Shift key and grab one of the sizing handles in the corners to keep from distorting the picture as you stretch the frame. (This technique may take a little practice.)

I want my picture perfectly positioned

Choose Format, Frame to display the Frame dialog box, shown in figure 12.8. Then check out the ways that Word can help rearrange your pages for you.

Fig. 12.8
The Frame dialog box lets you position graphics precisely—and automatically—on the page.

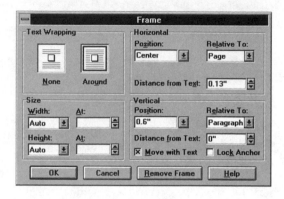

From the Frame dialog box, position the elements on your page as follows:

- Click in the Text Wrapping box to tell Word whether or not you want text to flow around the edges of your framed object.

- Choose a Horizontal and Vertical position for your frame. If you drag the frame to a position, Word will record the exact measurements. If you want Word to do the work, choose a relative position. In figure 12.8, the frame is centered horizontally—that is, between the left and right edges of the paper.

- Leave both the Width and Height set to Auto; that way Word will always make sure that the frame fits perfectly, no matter what's inside.

How do I get rid of a frame?

To remove the frame without losing whatever's inside it, switch to Page Layout view, select the frame, and choose Format, Frame. Then click the Remove Frame button.

To zap the frame and everything inside it, you also have to be in Page Layout view. Select the frame, and press Del.

(Tip) — If you accidentally delete a frame or a graphic, don't worry. Just click the Undo button and it will return.

OK, I want to put a picture inside this report

To add a picture to a Word document, you have two choices: you can take a picture that's already been created in a graphics program and paste it into your document. Or you can draw your own pictures, using Word's built-in tools.

To insert a picture, follow these steps:

1 Choose <u>I</u>nsert, <u>P</u>icture from the pull-down menus. You'll see a dialog box like the one in figure 12.9.

Fig. 12.9
Word lets you sneak a peek at a picture before you insert it into your document.

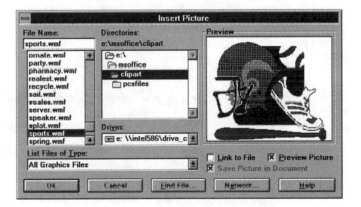

2 Change directories, if necessary, to find the place where your picture files are stored. (Usually these files are stored in C:\MSOFFICE\CLIPART.)

3 Scroll through the list of graphics files until you find the one you want.

4 Check the <u>P</u>review Picture box if you want to take a sneak peek at each picture as you select its name.

5 Check <u>L</u>ink to File, and uncheck the Save Picture in Document box if you don't want to save the picture in a separate file. Leave the <u>L</u>ink to File box blank to add the entire picture to your Word file.

6 Click OK to insert the picture into your document.

✱ {Note} Don't forget to add a frame around each picture as soon as you've added it to your document!

❓ Q&A *I have a picture that I can see in another program, but Word says it doesn't understand the file format. What do I do?*

Use the Windows Clipboard to put it in your document. Open the picture using your graphics program. Select it, and press Ctrl+C to copy it to the Clipboard. Now switch back to Word, put the insertion point in the space where you want to add the picture, and press Ctrl+V. Windows will translate the picture into a format that Word can understand, then paste it into the current document.

I can draw my own pictures? Really?

Well, maybe *you* can, but I can't draw anything more complicated than a stick figure. Give the average five-year-old a box of 64 crayons and he'll be ten times the artist I am.

So please don't ask me for too much advice on adding your own drawings to your Word documents.

To switch into the Microsoft drawing program, choose <u>I</u>nsert, <u>O</u>bject, then choose Microsoft Word 6.0 Picture from the list. To actually start drawing, use the Drawing toolbar (see fig. 12.10).

Fig. 12.10
The Microsoft drawing program starts out with a blank canvas. The Drawing toolbar (at the bottom of the screen) lets you add basic shapes, lines, and chunks of text.

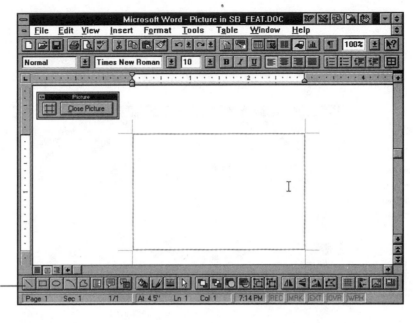

Drawing toolbar —

❋ {Note}_____ You can add charts, pictures, and other graphic items from other programs— including built-in Office programs like ClipArt Gallery and Microsoft Graph. We'll cover this topic in more detail in Chapter 26.

❓ Q&A_____ *My picture is covering up my text. How do I move it around?*

Well, neither one is transparent, so either your picture's going to cover your text, or your text is going to cover your picture. Select the picture, put it in a frame, then move it where you'd like it and let the text wrap around it.

How do I make part of my document really stand out?

You can add borders and shading around any object, whether it's in a frame or not. To add a box around pictures, text, or tables, just choose Format, Borders and Shading. These options are identical to the ones you use with tables.

Let's say you're producing a promotional mailing, and you know that your reader will spend, oh, 3 or 4 seconds looking at your letter, if you're lucky. If you put the most important paragraph in a box, then add a colorful tint over it, the reader can't help noticing it. (See fig. 12.11 for an example.)

Fig. 12.11
Use borders and shading to make a paragraph leap off the page. In this example, we've also made the text bigger and bolder, and indented it all for emphasis.

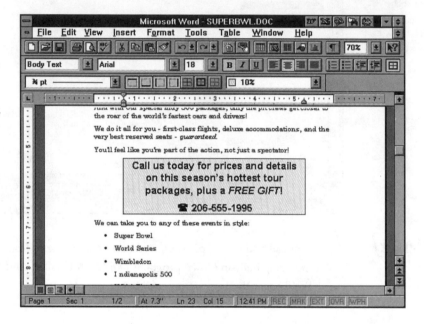

Here are a few things to remember when using borders and shading to highlight text:

- Borders are applied to the entire paragraph. You can't put a box around a word within a paragraph.

- The Borders toolbar pops up automatically when you choose F*o*rmat, *B*orders and Shading. Use the Outside Border button to draw a box automatically. The No Border button removes all lines.

- Use the Line Style box to adjust the line thickness to the size you want.

- When you indent a boxed paragraph, the box automatically resizes to fit.

- Use the Bottom Border button alone to underline the entire paragraph.

- When you select a shading, it fills the entire box.

How do I make this long document easier to read?

When you type a memo, you'll most often let your text run from one side of the page to the other in an unbroken line. For short documents, that works just fine. But long documents are much more readable if you use two or three narrow columns instead of one extremely wide page.

To break your text into columns, follow these steps:

1 Choose Format, Columns. You'll see a dialog box like the one in figure 12.12.

Fig. 12.12
Just point and click to turn your text into newspaper-style columns.

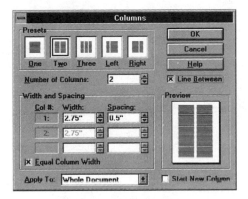

2 Choose one of the preset column layouts—two or three equal columns, or two unequal columns.

3 If you want to draw a line between the columns, check the box labeled Line Between. Preview your page layout in the box at the lower right.

4 To reformat just a section of your document into columns, change Whole Document to This Section or This Point Forward in the Apply To box. Choose Insert, Break, and click on Continuous Section Break to mark the beginning and end of the section.

①(Tip)

Use the Newsletter Wizard to create a blank document already set up for two, three, or four columns. If you don't want the fancy logo or graphics, just delete the first page, and use the second page to start composing your document one column at a time.

13 Putting It on Paper

In this chapter:

- How can I see what I'm about to print?
- How can I cancel a print job in a hurry?
- My letter's one line too long. Can I shrink it just a bit?
- My printer isn't working! What do I do?

When it works, it's magical. When it doesn't, it's a Maalox moment. Let's put the magic back in printing!

If you knew how complicated the process of printing a page really is, you'd swear it couldn't be done.

You type words, insert pictures, arrange numbers into neat rows and columns, and slide boxes around on the imaginary piece of paper sitting on your computer's screen. Word turns your brilliant thoughts into a few million little dots, which it sends off to Windows' Print Manager, which in turn sends them across a wire to your printer, which clanks and whirs and buzzes and spits out something that looks like what you see on the screen.

When it works, it's magical. When it doesn't, it's a Maalox moment. Let's put the magic back in printing, OK?

Before you print, preview!

Some people like surprises. Not me. I especially hate that surprised feeling you get when you pull a 48-page report out of the printer and discover that you forgot to add that chart on page 3. Oops! See you in half an hour.

 Some people just print and pray. Not me. I always, always, always click the Print Preview button before I send those pages to the printer. You should, too. With a single click, you get to see *exactly* what you'll pull out of the printer.

When you flip into the Print Preview screen, everything changes (see fig. 13.1). The Standard and Formatting toolbars vanish, and the tiny Print Preview toolbar appears. The whole idea is to show you your pages—one at a time or all at once—just the way they'd look if you were to lay them out on your desk.

Fig. 13.1
Use Print Preview to see exactly what your document will look like before you send it to the printer.

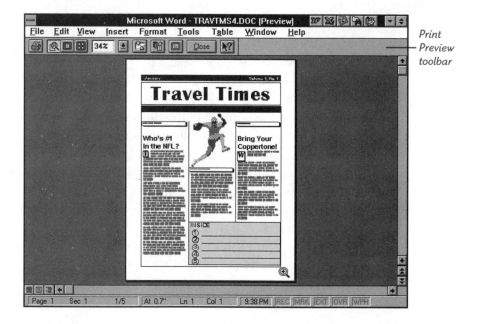

Print Preview toolbar

You can preview one page or an entire document. You can zoom in for a quick look at the details, then step back to see a bunch of pages at once. If there's a mistake, or you just don't like the way one of your pages looks, you can fix it right there. And you have complete control over your document, thanks to the Print Preview toolbar.

Who needs menus? The Print Preview toolbar lets you move around, zoom in, even edit your document in Print Preview mode:

 Print tells your printer to spit out one copy of the document you're looking at—no questions asked.

 When the **Magnifier** button is pressed, the pointer changes to a magnifying glass. Click on a spot you want to see up close. Click anywhere on the page to return to full page (or multiple-page) view. Click the Magnifier button again to change the pointer back to a normal insertion point.

 The **One Page** button fills the window, from top to bottom, with just the page you're looking at right now. Use the Page Up and Page Down keys to move around in the document.

 Tell Word you want to see **Multiple Pages** side-by-side in the preview window. A great view for seeing the big picture, but not for reading text.

 Zoom Control is nearly useless; you'll use the buttons to the left much more often.

 View Ruler hides the ruler when you're not using it, and brings it back again when you need it.

 The **Shrink to Fit** button has nothing to do with Levi's. Use it when your report is running two or three lines long and you want to squeeeeeeeeeze everything into one page less.

 Press the **Full Screen** button to clear nearly everything off the screen except this toolbar and the document you're previewing. (Press it again to get back where you started from.)

 Close sends you back to a normal editing screen.

 When you press this **Help** button, the pointer changes to a matching shape. Point to a part of the screen, click once, and Word will pop up instant Help or a box filled with formatting information.

How many pages can you preview at one time? The answer depends on your computer's hardware, especially the video card and monitor. If you have a Hulk Hogan-size monitor, you might be able to set things up so you can see 50 pages at once. On the average screen, though, you'll only be able to see 18 at one time. And even then, you'll feel like you're looking the wrong way through a telescope (see fig. 13.2).

Fig. 13.2

Click the Multiple Pages button, and drag to select the number of pages you want to preview at once.

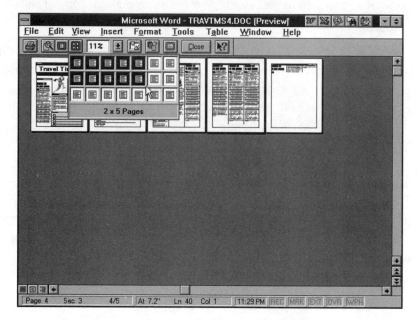

You mean I can edit here?

Yes, you can edit your text here. You can move whole chunks of text, reformat characters or paragraphs, adjust margins, or even insert a graphic. But only if you can actually see what you're doing, which is rarely true when you're using Print Preview.

The only time I use Print Preview's editing mode is when I want to fix a mistake in a big headline or move a graphic from one page to another. To change a word or a sentence, I switch back to Normal or Page Layout view.

Can I get a quick close-up of my page?

When you spread all the pages of your document out on the screen, you get a great sense of the big picture—where graphics are placed and where headlines fall, for example. But what if you want to quickly look at some picky little detail, like what that headline *really* says? There's an easy way to zoom in for a quick look, then pull back to see the big picture again.

Make sure the Magnifier button is pushed in, then click anywhere on a previewed page. The pointer changes to one of the two magnifying glasses you see in figure 13.3.

Fig. 13.3
When the pointer turns to either of these magnifying glasses, you can click (with either button) to zoom in and then back out again.

It *almost* fits. Now what?

Use the Shrink To Fit button. But don't expect miracles, especially if your document is heavily formatted or filled with graphics. Shrink To Fit works best on simple memos and letters, when you want Word to make things just a teeny bit smaller so that last line will tuck itself in on the previous page.

If you don't like what Word does when you push the Shrink To Fit button, just use Undo to put everything back the way it was.

Enough already! I just want to print

All systems go? Then press the Print button. Just like the Print button on the Standard toolbar, this one doesn't stop to ask questions. You get one copy of your entire document using whatever paper type your printer is set to use right now.

If you want to print an extra copy, or print just a few pages, skip the toolbar and head for the menus. When you choose File, Print, the Print dialog box, shown in figure 13.4, displays.

How many copies? Type in a number, or use the little arrows to nudge this number up or down.

*Check the **printer**. Is that the printer you really want to use? (If it isn't, press the Printer button below and pick another one.)*

Fig. 13.4
Don't touch that button! Choose File, Print if you want to print extra copies or set other printing options.

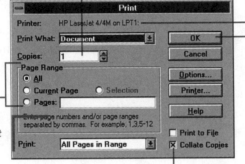

*Click **OK** to send your job to the printer.*

Which pages? Pick just the current page, or a list of pages, or the whole document.

*For more than one set of copies, click here to **collate** each set instead of printing two copies of page 1, two copies of page 2, and so on.*

Q&A_____ ***My pages come out in the wrong order every time I print, with the last page on top and the first page on the bottom. Is this a bug?***

It's not a bug, it's just the way your printer works. Fortunately, Word can work with your printer by sending pages to the printer in reverse order. Choose File, Print, and click the Options button. Make sure there's a check in the box labeled Reverse Print Order. Click OK and try it again.

What's Print Manager, and why should I care?

Windows is like a big corporation filled with middle managers. There's a File Manager, and a Program Manager, and *this* guy, who handles all the print jobs that come from Word and all the other Office programs.

When you send a document to the printer, you're actually sending it to the Windows Print Manager, which will send it off to the printer as quickly as the printer can handle it. Because your programs can send stuff to the printer faster than the printer can print, it's possible for a bunch of print jobs to stack up at your printer like airplanes circling O'Hare Airport.

If you want to see what's happening to a Word document after you sent it to the printer, look on the Windows desktop for the Print Manager icon. Double-click there and poke through the list of documents waiting to be printed. As long as you're here, you can delete a job before it gets to the printer. You can also pause and resume different print jobs from here.

Printing in color

No doubt about it—Word is a colorful program. You can format any piece of text in a color, and throw shades and color patterns behind tables and charts. All that clip art is in color. Even the toolbars are filled with colorful icons.

So what happens when you take your colorful image and send it to the printer? If you're using a standard laser or dot-matrix printer, it's like heading into a '50s sitcom: all black and white.

Today, you have plenty of choices if you want a color printer, with prices that are competitive with those plain black-and-white models. The hottest models these days are called **inkjet printers**; they use a bunch of tiny tubes that splatter drops of colored ink on your paper in precise little patterns.

Should you get a color printer? If all you print out are letters and memos, probably not. Color printers are slow, and each page costs more than an equivalent page from a black-and-white printer.

If you use lots of charts and graphs, then color is a must. When you don't have a color printer, everything gets translated into different shades of gray, and no one will be able to tell the difference between the bars on your graph or the slices in your pie chart.

If you use PowerPoint a lot, I don't need to tell you that color counts. Go ahead—put together a presentation and prove conclusively that you need a new color printer *now*.

 Don't close Print Manager until it's handled all the print jobs in its list. When you close Print Manager, it automatically deletes all the documents that are waiting in line. If you want to put the Print Manager out of the way, use the Minimize button instead.

 Did you just send a bunch of pages to the printer and realize you'd made a mistake? Quick! Double-click the Printer icon on the status bar at the botttom of the screen. If you're fast enough, you might be able to stop the job before it reaches the printer.

It's not working!

Printers have to be way, way up there on the list of Things That Cause Ulcers And High Blood Pressure. The average laser printer is a big, complicated machine, filled with gears and belts and sticky black powders and an *actual laser*. There's an entire volume in the Murphy's Law series dedicated exclusively to printers. So there's no way we can cover every possible thing that can go wrong when you try to print a Word document. But this list covers the most common problems.

I push the Print button and nothing happens

I once spent more than an hour cursing at a laser printer before I noticed that it was, well, uh... OK, it wasn't plugged in. I remember that embarrassing moment vividly every time I run through the following checklist of Incredibly Obvious Printer Boo-Boos:

- Is the printer connected to your PC? (Check the plugs on either end of the connection, just to be sure.)

- Is the printer plugged in and turned on?

- Does Windows know about your printer? Before Word can work with a printer, you have to install a **printer driver**—a small program that lets Windows communicate with your printer. When you use Word's File, Print command, press the Printer button to make sure your printer is set up as the default printer.

- Is the printer out of paper? Is there a paper jam?

- Are there any error messages on the printer's front panel? If there are, try turning the printer on and off to clear its memory and reset it, then try again.

It takes too long to print

Is that really the problem? Or are you frustrated by how long it takes before you can use your computer again? If your pages take too long to come out of the printer, you might just need a faster printer. But if you want to get back to work more quickly, the problem could be Word, which sometimes acts like it can't walk and chew gum at the same time.

When you push the Print button, Word puts all its energy into printing your documents. If you have a lot of pages, you can find yourself waiting a long time. To tell Word you want it to go into walk-and-chew-gum mode, choose File, Print and click the Options button. Put a check mark in the box next to the Background Printing option. From now on, Word will print a little more slowly so that it can continue to pay attention as you work with the next document.

My printouts don't look right

You'll have to be more specific. You mean that what you see doesn't match what you get? The problem might be fonts. Check the font-formatting in your document at the point where it starts looking out-of-kilter. If your printer doesn't support those fonts, you'll have to change the text to another font that your printer can cope with.

? **Q&A**

How can I tell which fonts are OK to use?

When you select a font from the Font List, look for a TT symbol or a tiny printer icon alongside the name. Those two labels point out TrueType fonts and fonts that are built into your printer. If there's no symbol next to the font name, it's a screen font only, and your printer won't know how to handle it.

The Print menu is grayed out!

Windows doesn't know enough about your printer. Word (sensibly) won't allow you to waste time trying to print to a printer until it's properly set up. If you know how to use the Windows Control Panel, you can fix this problem yourself by double-clicking on the Printers icon and adding your printer to the list. If you have no idea what I'm talking about, you'll have to find your local Windows expert and ask for help.

Part III:

Using Excel

14 Creating a New Worksheet

In this chapter:

- What's the difference between a workbook and a worksheet?

- The Excel screen is easy to figure out

- How do I do calculations?

- How do I move around in the worksheet?

- Okay, I'm done now. How do I save my work?

Excel can race through millions of calculations—literally!—while you're still trying to find your desktop calculator's ON switch.

Deep down inside, Excel is just a calculator. Of course, that's like saying the Grand Canyon is just a hole in the ground. Or the space shuttle is just an aircraft. Or Houdini was just a guy who did magic tricks.

Excel can add, subtract, multiply, and divide, and a whole lot more. It can race through millions of calculations—literally—while you're still trying to find your desktop calculator's ON switch. It has the memory of an elephant, the level-headed logic of Mr. Spock, and the specialized knowledge you'd expect from a banker, broker, mathematician, and all-around financial wizard, all rolled into one.

Excel lets you raise a number here or lower a number there to see exactly what would happen under different circumstances. This is called "What if?" analysis, and it's the real reason why a spreadsheet is a million times more powerful than a calculator. What if sales go up 10%? What if we cut the price of potatoes by 20 cents a pound? What if I refinance my mortgage? What if my boss gives me a $10,000 raise next year? What if I win the lottery? (Hey, it could happen...)

The Excel workspace at a glance

This file, GSTEXRP3.XLS, is an Excel **workbook**. Like an accordion file folder, it can hold up to 255 separate worksheets, each in its own separate compartment.

Standard toolbar
Looks a lot like its counterparts in Word and PowerPoint, doesn't it? Open files, save files, cut/copy/ paste—all the most-used Excel features are here.

Formula bar
One of two places where you can enter or edit a cell's contents. (You can also edit directly in the cell.)

Column headings
Column headings are usually letters.

Formatting toolbar
Lets you change the font, alignment, and number format with a single click.

Row headings
Row headings are usually numbers.

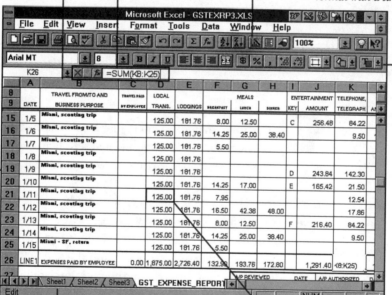

Worksheet tabs
Help you find individual worksheets easily. You can give plain-English names to worksheets, but you can't use spaces.

Cell
Can hold any kind of data—numbers, words, dates, or formulas. Excel analyzes the cell's contents before deciding what to show in the cell.

Where am I?

When you start up Excel (by clicking on its button in MOM or double-clicking its icon in Program Manager), you automatically open a new, blank Excel workbook. Excel gives this workbook the temporary name Book1. (Nobody expects you to use this generic name, of course; you'll get a chance to give your workbook a more meaningful name later.)

 If you start up Excel and immediately open a workbook you've already created and saved, Excel closes the blank Book1 workbook automatically.

What's a workbook?

If you've ever used an accordion file folder, you know how Excel workbooks work. Inside that accordion folder, individual compartments keep all your important papers separated from one another. An Excel workbook starts out with 16 similar compartments, each designed to hold one **worksheet**. Just like the expandable folder, you can make room in a workbook for a lot of worksheets or just a few (any number between 1 and 255). Index **tabs** separate the individual worksheets; put plain-English labels on each tab and then riffle through them quickly to find exactly the worksheet you want.

Excel doesn't get any points for creativity here, either. You start out in Sheet1, and if you look down at the bottom of the window, you'll see tabs for Sheet2, Sheet3, and so on. We'll talk more about those other worksheets later. For now, let's concentrate on the wide-open worksheet in front of us.

OK, what's a worksheet?

Worksheets are where you'll do most work with Excel. Think of each worksheet as a blank sheet of paper crisscrossed with straight lines that set up a precise grid on the page. Each pair of vertical lines defines a column, while each pair of horizontal lines sets up a row. And at the intersection of each row and column is a **cell**, which is a little rectangle where you can store numbers, text, or formulas.

✱ *{Note}_____* ❘ The terms **worksheet** and **spreadsheet** mean the same thing.

Whether an Excel worksheet is empty or full, you should have no trouble finding your way around—just imagine that you're following the map of an *incredibly* orderly city. The rows and columns on an Excel worksheet act just like streets and avenues. Every column (or avenue) has a letter for a name, and every row is like a numbered cross street, as shown in figure 14.1.

Fig. 14.1
Rows, columns, cells.
Welcome to the
incredibly orderly Excel
neighborhood.

Look in the **Name**
box to see which
cell is selected.

Gridlines
separate rows
and columns.

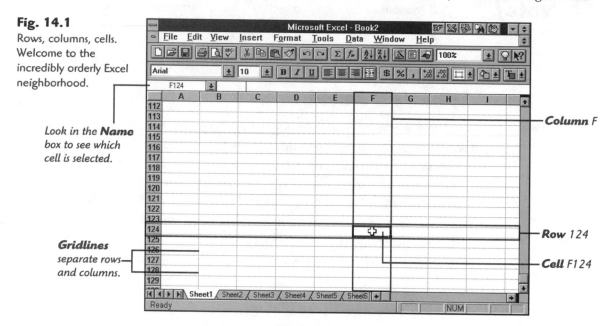

Column F

Row 124

Cell F124

As you cruise along Excel's avenues and cross streets, you move from one cell to another. Because cells are located at the intersection of a row and column, each one has a unique address or **cell reference**, which combines the letter of its column and the number of its row. If you start in the upper left corner, for example, at the intersection of column A and row 1, you're at cell A1. When you move one cell to the right, you land in cell B1. In this neighborhood, getting or giving directions is easy: "F124? Sure, just keep going one block past Avenue E, then hang a right and go 124 blocks. You can't miss it."

Where do I begin?

Before you begin to enter data, think about what you want to do with your worksheet. Do you want to analyze last year's expenses, category-by-category and month-by-month? Then you'll need 12 columns, one for each month of the year, plus one row for each category. If you want to add up your expenses for each month and each category, you'll need an extra row and column to hold the totals. And don't forget to allow one row at the top for the column titles, plus one column on the left to hold the row title.

Most worksheets start out with the simple arrangement of rows and columns. The easiest way to get started is to enter descriptive titles for rows and columns. With that task out of the way, you can then enter your data and create formulas to help you analyze it.

There's no need to worry too much about the structure of your worksheet at this point. It's easy to move cells around and add more rows and columns later.

Just start typing

Once you've formed a mental picture of the basic layout of your worksheet, it's time to start filling in the titles and the data. Typing in a cell is easy: point at the cell, click to select it, and then start typing.

Whatever you type shows up in two places: in the cell and in the **formula bar**, just above the A-B-C headings over your columns. Think of the formula bar as a scratch pad, where you can type anything you like; your characters don't actually go into the cell until you explicitly tell Excel to put them there.

As soon as you begin typing, three small boxes appear to the left of the formula bar (see fig. 14.2).

Click the **Enter box** to put the contents of the formula bar into your worksheet.

Click the **Function Wizard button** to pop up a fill-in-the-blanks form that builds Excel formulas automatically.

Fig. 14.2
When you begin entering data, these three boxes appear to the left of the formula bar.

Click the **Cancel box** to tell Excel, "Oops! Never mind." Excel restores whatever was in the cell before you started typing.

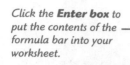

	A	B	C	D	E	F	G	H	I	J	K	
8		TRAVEL FROM/TO AND	TRAVEL PAID	LOCAL			MEALS			ENTERTAINMENT	TELEPHONE,	
9	DATE	BUSINESS PURPOSE	BY EMPLOYEE	TRANS.	LODGINGS	BREAKFAST	LUNCH	DINNER	KEY	AMOUNT	TELEGRAPH	A/
15	1/5	Miami, scouting trip		125.00	181.76	8.00	12.50		C	256.48	84.22	
16	1/6	Miami, scouting trip		125.00	181.76	14.25	25.00	38.40			9.50	
17	1/7	Miami, scouting trip		125.00	181.76	5.50						
18	1/8	Miami, scouting trip		125.00	181.76							
19	1/9	Miami, scouting trip		125.00	181.76				D	243.84	142.30	
20	1/10	Miami, scouting trip		125.00	181.76	14.25	17.00		E	165.42	21.50	
21	1/11	Miami, scouting trip		125.00	181.76	7.95					12.54	
22	1/12	Miami, scouting trip		125.00	181.76	16.50	42.38	48.00			17.86	
23	1/13	Miami, scouting trip		125.00	181.76	8.00	12.50		F	216.40	84.22	
24	1/14	Miami, scouting trip		125.00	181.76	14.25	25.00	38.40			9.50	
25	1/15	Miami - SF, return		125.00	181.76	5.50						
26	LINE1	EXPENSES PAID BY EMPLOYEE	0.00	1,875.00	2,726.40	132.90	193.76	172.80		1,291.40	K8:K25)	

Microsoft Excel - GSTEXRP3.XLS

K26 =SUM(K8:K25)

Sheet1 Sheet2 Sheet3 GST_EXPENSE_REPORT

A/P REVIEWED   DATE   A/P AUTHORIZED

Edit   NUM

(Tip)

If you hit the wrong key while you're typing, press Backspace to fix your mistake.

You can see how easy it is to enter stuff into your worksheet. You'll learn a lot more details about entering and editing in Chapter 15.

(Tip)

If you like using the keyboard better, you can press Esc instead of clicking the Cancel box, and press Enter instead of clicking the Enter box.

Q&A

I've already clicked the Enter box. Now I see a typo I made! How can I fix it?

There are a couple of easy ways to fix mistakes you've already entered:

- If you just need to fix one or two characters, go back to the cell and click on the formula bar, then click at the place you want to change.

- If you screwed up the whole thing and want to start over, just choose Undo from the Edit menu.

OK, I'm through typing. Now what?

Every time you compose something in the formula bar, you're sending a message to one of the cells on your worksheet. When you're through typing, just press Enter to have Excel pick up the message and deliver it to the correct cell reference. Excel the mail carrier first checks the cell reference to see where to go. Unlike the U.S. Postal Service, though, Excel also checks the content of your message to see how to deliver it.

When you enter words or numbers, Excel assumes you're entering a **constant value,** and simply takes your message and stuffs it into the appropriate mailbox. It's just as if you wrote the words "Travel Expenses" on a slip of paper, put D12 on the envelope, and told Excel, "Please put this message in the box at the corner of Avenue D and 12th Street."

If you start your message with an equal sign, though, Excel interprets your message as a formula, and handles it differently. When you type **=SUM(D4:D15)**, and write D16 on the envelope, you're telling Excel, "Please add up all the numbers in all the mailboxes on Avenue D between 4th and 15th Street. Write down the total, and put it in the mailbox at D16."

Here's how to tell the difference between a value and a formula:

- A **value** is information that never changes unless you choose to change it. It might be a number (42), a date (2/1/95), or a snippet of text ("Travel Expenses").

- A **formula** is a combination of values, cell references, mathematical signs (**operators**), and special Excel functions that combine to produce a new value. Formulas can be kindergarten-simple (2+2) or genius-level (if you know what the "one-tailed probability of a chi-squared distribution" is, Excel will calculate it for you).

?Q&A

I typed in a number, but all I see is ######. What's the deal?

Your number is too long to fit in the cell. If you only saw a few digits of the number, you could get horribly confused. So Excel stuffs a bunch of number signs (####) in the cell to tell you there's something there, but you can't see it. You'll have to make the column wider before you can see the number.

How does Excel know what to do next?

Excel follows a simple set of rules to decide what to display in the cell when you press Enter. If you type letters or numbers, you'll see whatever you typed in the cell. If you start by typing an equal sign, though, Excel treats everything else you type as a formula. It stores the formula, but in the cell it shows you the result of its calculation. So if you type **=2+2** and press Enter, you'll see 4 in the cell.

When Excel can't figure out what to do with your formula, it fills in the cell with #NAME? or #REF? or something equally confusing. That's Excel's way of saying, "Huh?"

Table 14.1 gives some examples of stuff you might type into an Excel cell, and tells what Excel does with it.

Table 14.1 What you type and what Excel does with it

Enter these...	Examples...	Excel treats it as...
Numbers only, in any format	42 $999.95 34.8%	Number
Letters & numbers	Travel Expenses 12 #10 envelopes 5% Discount	Text
Anything that looks like a date or time	1/20/95 3:30 AM September 15	Date/Time
Anything beginning with an equal sign	=2+2 =F124*.0825 =SUM(D4:D15)	Formula

② Q&A

I typed something in one cell, and it's spilling over into the next cell. Is that OK?

Yes, it's perfectly normal. Text that doesn't fit in one cell will spill over into the next cell if it's empty. If there's something there, your text will cut off at the border between the two cells. To see all the information in the cell, select it and look in the formula bar. Better yet, make the cell wider. (Look in Chapter 16 for more details on adjusting column widths.)

① (Tip)

Each time you hit Enter, Excel moves down one cell. That's convenient if you're entering a column's worth of data, but it can annoy you if you want to enter data from left to right. Try using the Tab and Shift+Tab keys.

To move up or down a column quickly, use Enter and Shift+Enter, respectively.

How do I do calculations with Excel?

Whenever you want Excel to flex its calculating muscles, you type in a formula. Simple formulas let you add, subtract, multiply, and divide numbers stored in other cells. In your expense worksheet, for example, you might enter all your expenses in one column, and then create a formula that adds all those numbers and puts the total at the bottom of the column. From now on, if you change one of the numbers in the column, the bottom line changes automatically. How's that for cool?

If you plan to use a constant value throughout your worksheet, put that value in a cell near the top of your worksheet. Now you can refer to that cell in other formulas instead of typing the value in multiple places. For example, you might store the current interest rate in cell C4, as shown in figure 14.3. Then, instead of typing that number in every cell that calculates interest and payments, you can just insert a reference to cell C4. In effect, you're telling Excel, "Run over to C4, look up the current interest rate, and use it here." When interest rates change, you just change the contents of C4—all your other calculations will be automatically updated.

Fig. 14.3

Enter a constant value, like the current interest rate, in its own cell. If you refer to that cell in other formulas, you can change one number and automatically update your entire worksheet.

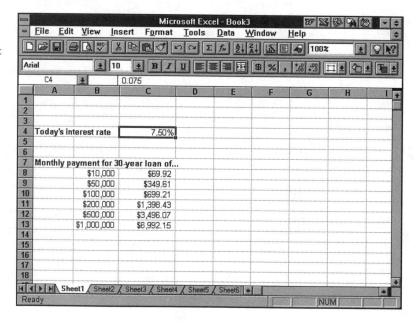

When you enter a formula, you have to follow Excel's rules:

- A formula always begins with an equal sign.

- It can contain constant values, mathematical operators, Excel functions, references to cells and ranges, and even other formulas, in any combination.

- You can use any of these mathematical operators as part of a formula: add (+), subtract (-), multiply (*), divide (/), calculate percentage (%), or increase exponentially (^).

- To control the order of calculation, use parentheses. Excel does multiplication and division before addition and subtraction, so =3+4*5 is 23, while =(3+4)*5 is 35.

 Q&A

> *My calculation didn't work! The cell just says* 2+2 *instead of showing me the result I expected (4). What did I do wrong?*
>
> You left out the equal sign. Excel is maddeningly consistent about this sort of thing. Without the equal sign, Excel treats your formula as simple text.

I need to perform a complicated calculation

Asking Excel to do only simple addition or multiplication is like hiring a Harvard MBA to balance your checkbook. Sure, Excel can add up a column of numbers, but its biggest asset is its repertoire of mathematical, financial, statistical, and logical functions. If you've got a stack of numbers, Excel can crunch them in more than 300 ways, from simple averages to complex trigonometric formulas. An Excel **function** is simply a specialized calculation that Excel has memorized. Every function includes two parts: the **function name** (such as AVERAGE) and any required **arguments.**

Plain English, please!

Arguments? What's all the shouting about? **Arguments** are the various items Excel needs to know to produce the result. An argument might be a word, a number, or the name of another cell. Arguments always appear to the right of the function name, inside parentheses.

The formula =AVERAGE(number1,number2,...), for example, needs at least two numbers to be calculated. You'll need to replace number1, number2, and so on, with something else. Thus, the formula =AVERAGE(5,10) gives you a result of 7.5.

The ellipsis (...) means you can have an unlimited number of arguments in the formula.

Some functions are so simple they don't need any arguments. If you type **NOW( )** in a cell (complete with the empty parentheses), Excel will display today's date in the cell.

The most complicated functions demand that you fill in just the right information. To calculate the monthly payment on a loan, for example, you use the function PMT(rate,nper,pv,fv,type). You have to fill in (in this order) the interest rate, the number of payments, the present value (whatever that is), the future value (whatever *that* is), and the type of loan. But you don't have to memorize these complicated formulas.

Let the wizard handle tricky calculations

Here's a good use for the PMT function:

Let's say you want to know whether you can afford the mortgage payments on a new house. You could call your local bank and throw a whole bunch of "What if?" questions at your loan agent: "What if I put up a bigger down payment? What if I find a more expensive house? What if interest rates go up next month?" You'll spend the entire afternoon on the phone, and at the end of the day you'll have a piece of paper full of scribbled numbers that won't make any sense when you look at them next week. The good news? If you get the loan, you might also get a free toaster.

Or you could use Excel to build a worksheet and ask it all the "What if?" questions. Excel, the mortgage analyst, is open 24 hours a day and never gets tired of answering questions. It might take a few minutes to set up your worksheet, but once that job's done, you can save your work and reuse it any time. No toasters, though.

To start, put together a worksheet like the one in figure 14.4.

Fig. 14.4
This worksheet calculates your monthly mortgage payment.

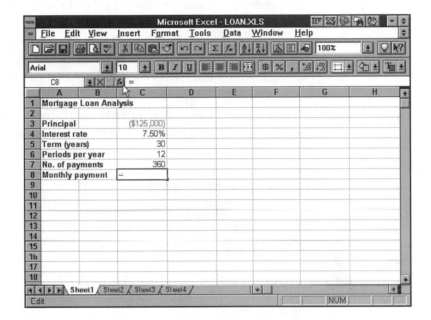

To figure out your monthly mortgage payment, start with this basic worksheet:

1 Remember, if you owe someone money, the starting balance is a negative number. In cell C3, enter a minus sign followed by **$125000**.

2 Type **7.50%** for the interest rate in cell C4; Excel is smart enough to translate the percentage into its decimal equivalent: .075.

⊛ {Note} ⎯⎯⎯⎯ Negative numbers usually are shown in parentheses on your worksheet (and in red if you have a color monitor).

3 Enter the number of years in cell C5 and the number of payments per year in cell C6. For a biweekly mortgage, change the 12 to 26.

4 Type **=C5*C6** in cell C7—Excel will calculate the total number of payments automatically.

5 We'll let Excel walk us through the grunt work of calculating the monthly payment. Type an equal sign (=) in cell C8 and press the Function Wizard button on the left of the formula bar.

When you summon the Function Wizard, you first have to choose from a list of Excel's 319 built-in functions (see fig. 14.5). As you scroll through the list of function categories, the list of function names on the right changes. In this case, we're looking for a financial function (click Financial), and, based on its description in the dialog box, PMT is the most likely candidate (click PMT). (It helps if you know that an annuity and a loan are different versions of the same thing.)

Fig. 14.5

Pick a function, any function. The Function Wizard lets you scroll through lists of functions organized by category.

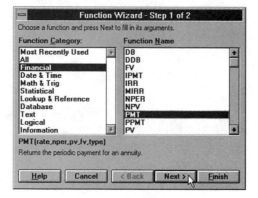

To use the Function Wizard, just press the Next button and fill in the blanks (see fig. 14.6). As you fill in the values or cell references you want in your formula, the Function Wizard automatically plugs those entries into the formula bar. To accept the formula, press Finish; to start over, press the Cancel button.

Fig. 14.6
The Function Wizard
plugs your entries into
the formula bar
automatically.

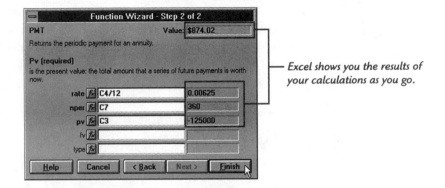

*Excel shows you the results of
your calculations as you go.*

Fill in the Function Wizard's blanks to build your formula automatically. Follow these steps:

1 Click in the entry box next to `rate`, and then click in cell C4 to add that cell reference in the blank. Since we're calculating a monthly payment, we need to divide the annual interest rate by 12, so enter **/12.**

2 If an entry box is labeled in bold, you must fill in a value or a cell reference. The lighter titles (`fv` and `type`) are optional.

3 Click the Finish button to return to the worksheet, then press Enter to accept the formula.

If you're not sure how an Excel function works, click the Help button for a detailed explanation (and usually a helpful tip or two). If you want to keep the Help screen visible while you work, choose Help, Always On Top from the pull-down menus. (You might want to adjust the size of the Help window so you can see your worksheet.) When you're finished with Help, choose File, Exit.

Adding it all up automatically

The one Excel function that you'll use more than any other is SUM. Using this function is just like hitting the Total button on your desktop calculator. In fact, there's even a button on the Standard toolbar that adds up a column or row of numbers automatically. If you don't recognize the AutoSum button, it's probably because you were out sick the day they covered it in high school algebra.

To use the AutoSum button, just select a blank cell beneath a column of numbers (or at the end of a row of numbers), then click the AutoSum button (although it looks like a stylized E, it's actually a Greek sigma). Excel will insert the SUM function with the argument already filled in (see fig. 14.7). Click the Enter box in the formula bar or press Enter to make it official.

Fig. 14.7

Click the AutoSum button to have Excel automatically add up the numbers in the column above.

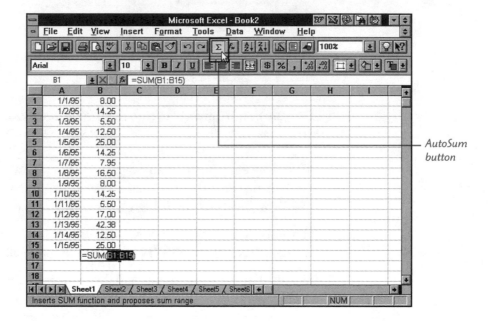

AutoSum button

? Q&A ___

One of my cells has #DIV/0! in it. What's that all about?

Any time you see a cell that begins with the number sign (#), that's Excel telling you that it can't handle your formula. In this case, Excel is scolding you like a high school math teacher, telling you that you can't divide by 0. The formula you entered is still under there; you'll have to fix the problem before Excel will take away the error message.

How do I move around in a worksheet?

As long as your worksheet is just a few rows and columns, it's easy enough to get around by just pointing and clicking or tapping the arrow keys. Sooner or later, though, your worksheet will get so big that it won't fit in a single window. When that happens, refer to table 14.2 to learn how to get around by using just the keyboard.

Formulas and functions

Mr. Spock might raise one of those strange pointed eyebrows if he ever set eyes on Excel. But once he'd had a chance to check it out, there's no question that he'd give his full approval to Excel's **logical** functions.

You don't need to be half-Vulcan to use these functions, either. Right here on Earth, there are countless practical uses for Excel's simplest logical function, called IF.

Let's say you've created an Excel worksheet that automatically calculates monthly invoice statements for your customers. You'd like to reward your best customers with an extra 10-percent discount, and you'd like Excel to apply the discount automatically.

Normally, you'd use the SUM function in the cell where you display the grand total. If you use the IF function instead, you can ask Excel a simple yes-or-no question: did this customer spend more than $1000 this month? Then you provide two sets of instructions—one for Excel to use if the answer is yes, the other if the answer is no.

The IF function uses three arguments: the logical test, the value if true, and the value if false. In our invoice example, assuming that the subtotal was in cell D24, we'd fill in the following formula: **=IF(D24>1000,D24*90%,D24)**. It looks a bit intimidating, but Excel will have no trouble figuring out what to do.

Each of the three arguments is separated by a comma. The first argument, the logical test, asks Excel to look in cell D24 and see whether the number in the cell is greater than 1000 (we could also use <, the less-than symbol; =, an equal sign; or <>, the not-equal sign). If Excel says, "Yes, it's greater than 1000," it uses the second argument and calculates 90% of the subtotal, effectively passing along a 10% discount. Otherwise, it uses the third argument and simply picks up the subtotal from cell D24.

As you become more experienced with Excel functions, you'll find plenty of uses for the IF function. Live long and prosper!

Table 14.2   Getting around with the keyboard

To do this...	Press this...
Move to beginning of row	Home
Move up/down one window	↑/↓
Go to the top left corner of the worksheet	Ctrl + Home
Move to the lower right corner of your worksheet	Ctrl + End
Jump to the next sheet	Ctrl + ↑
Jump to the previous sheet	Ctrl + ↓
Move to a specific cell or named range	F5 (GoTo)
Move from left to right or top to bottom, in a selected range	Tab
Move the opposite direction in a selected range	Shift + Tab

(Tip)

Use the Zoom control on the Standard toolbar to step back and see the "big picture" of your worksheet. Scroll through the worksheet, and select the area of the worksheet you want to see. Then choose View, Zoom and click in the circle labeled Fit Selection. Now you'll see your entire worksheet (although if your worksheet is big enough, you may not be able to read it!).

Q&A

I pressed the End key, but I didn't go to the end of the row the way I expected. What does this key do, anyway?

When you press the End key, you turn on end mode. (Look in the lower right corner of the screen if you don't believe me. See? It says END.) What happens next depends on which key you press next. If you press an arrow key, you'll jump to the next cell that has data or formatting in it. Press Home to jump to the lower right, to the last cell in the block. Or just press Enter to move to the last cell in the current row. End mode is handy when you're jumping back and forth between two adjacent blocks of cells.

Saving a new workbook

After you've built the basic structure of your worksheet and entered some data, it's always a good idea to save it under a descriptive name. If you get interrupted, you can always close the file and come back to it later. Click the Save button, choose the proper directory, and give your workbook file a legal file name. (You don't have to type the .XLS extension. Excel will automatically add that for you.)

If you use Excel to balance your checkbook each month, for example, you might call these files CB-9412, CB-9501, CB-9502, CB-9503, and so on. That way it's easy to tell which month is which, and Excel will list them in order (1994 workbooks before those for 1995).

For more details on how to save and name files, see Chapter 4.

Opening another new workbook

To create another new workbook, press Ctrl+N, or click the New Workbook button. Excel doesn't even try to be imaginative with names—each new workbook gets another generic name, like Book2, Book3, and so on. After the new workbook is open, you're ready to start working again!

15

Working with Worksheets and Workbooks

In this chapter:

- What's a range, and why should I care?

- How do I edit the contents of a cell?

- I need to move stuff from one place to another!

- How can I fill in a list automatically?

- I forgot a column. Show me how to add it

- How can I work smarter with more than one worksheet at once?

Moving to a new neigh-borhood means learning all the shortcuts and finding out where the best Chinese restaurants are. There are lots of hidden treasures to find inside Excel, too!

Whenever I move to a new neighborhood, the first thing I do is drive around. I learn where the good Chinese restaurants are hidden, how late the grocery store stays open, and which houses have big barking dogs. I also learn all the shortcuts that get me where I want to go faster, and I explore the side streets where the really interesting little shops are.

When you first look at an Excel worksheet, you might figure it's a pretty boring place. Rows, columns, cells—what's so complicated about that? Actually, there's a complex world inside that worksheet, and once you learn some simple techniques, you'll discover ways to do everyday work faster. You'll also discover that Excel lets you look at data—words and numbers—in ways you've never considered before.

In this chapter, you learn how to take a simple worksheet design and adjust all the pieces so they match the work you want to do right now. Once you learn your way around, maybe this neighborhood isn't so dull after all.

Opening a saved workbook

Good morning! It's another working day, time for you and Excel to pick up where you left off yesterday.

To open a file you've already created and saved, pull down the File menu first. Excel automatically keeps track of the four files you used most recently, in a list at the bottom of the File menu. If the file's not there, click the Open button and hunt through your data directory until you find it.

Working with more than one cell at a time

When you drive along the streets and avenues in your town, you pass one house after another. Each one's different, but that doesn't stop the postman from thinking of all those houses in logical groups—like that row of brownstones on A Street, or all the addresses in ZIP code 90210, or every house that has a big barking dog.

As you cruise up and down Excel's rows and columns, you can arrange cells into similar groups. When you select two or more cells at the same time, you've selected a **range**. And working with ranges instead of dealing with one cell at a time can cut hours off your workday.

What's a range, and why should I care?

Anything you can do with one cell, you can do with a range. You can, for example, format a range of cells all at once. If you highlight a range and click the Bold button, for example, all the characters in the range will turn to bold-face type. You can even give a range a plain-English name so it's easier to refer to later.

Selections in a range are always rectangular. If your selection is 3 cells deep and 4 cells wide, your range contains 12 cells—there's no way to exclude one of the cells. As you drag the mouse around, the cells turn dark to show you that they're selected.

Excel uses two addresses to identify a range, beginning with the cell in the upper left corner and ending with the cell in the lower right corner of the selection. Excel uses a colon (:) to separate the addresses. In figure 15.1, for example, the selected region is A1:D7. The active cell is outlined in bold and is not highlighted.

Fig. 15.1

Any time you select two or more cells, you've defined a **range**. To use this range in an Excel formula, enter **A1:D7**.

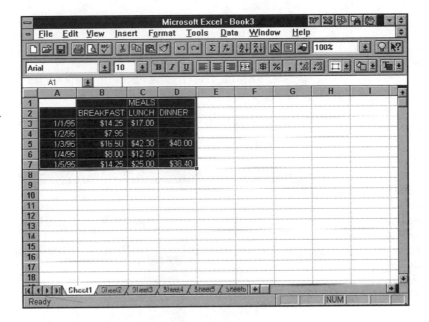

Selecting cells and ranges

Before you can actually do anything in Excel—like format a cell, or delete a row, or move a range from one place to another—you first have to select something. And the easiest way to select stuff in Excel is to use the mouse.

If you want to do something with a single cell, use these techniques:

- To **select the cell**, point and click.

- To **position the insertion point** in the cell, point and double-click.

- To **select characters** in the cell, double-click in the cell, then drag through the characters you want to select.

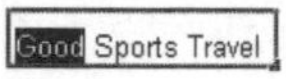

- To **select a word** in the cell, select the cell, then double-click the word. (This also works with cell addresses, formula arguments, and other things that aren't, strictly speaking, words.)

If you want to work with more than one cell, use these techniques:

- To **select a range**, click in the cell at one corner of the range and drag the pointer to the opposite corner.

- To **select a group of unconnected cells**, select the first cell or range, hold down the Ctrl key, and select the next cell or range. Continue holding the Ctrl key down until you've selected all the cells you want.

- To **select an entire row or column,** click on the letter or number in its heading (see fig. 15.2).

- To **select multiple rows or columns**, select the first row or column, and hold down the mouse button while dragging through the rest.

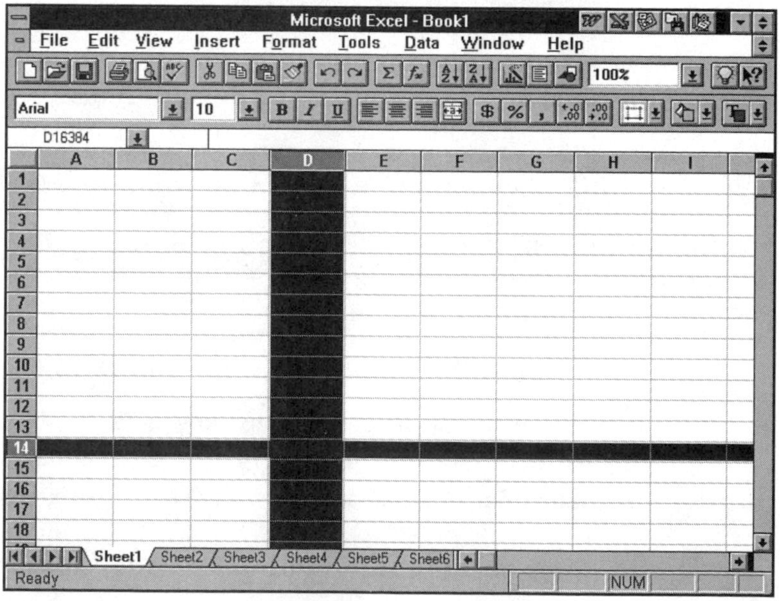

Fig. 15.2

To select an entire row or column, click the letter or number in its heading. Note how the labels (D and 14, in this example) change shading to show they've been selected.

How do I move around in a range?

After you've selected a range, some keys work a little differently. As you're filling in data, the Enter key still moves you down to the next cell, but only within the range. When you reach the bottom of the range, Excel moves the active cell to the top of the next column. To move within the range from right to left, one row at a time, use Tab; Shift+Enter and Shift+Tab move in the opposite direction.

Making worksheets easier to understand

When you mail a letter, what's the most important piece of information on the envelope? To the post office, the address is everything. But as far as you're concerned, it's the name that matters most.

Like the post office, Excel is most concerned about addresses (cell references)—its job is to make sure that all your data ends up in the right cells. So Excel is content to know that the formula that totals up all your annual expenses is located in cell G24. But that connection isn't so obvious to you or me, unless we want to puzzle out what each formula means. Wouldn't it be more convenient if you could simply assign that cell a name like TotalExpenses?

You can. Excel lets you give any cell or group of cells a plain-English name. The effect is just like nailing up a sign that says "The Simpsons" on the mailbox outside G24. Your postman knows where the Simpsons live, just as Excel knows how to track down your cell named TotalExpenses. Now you can use either the boring, Excel-style rows-and-columns address or the plain-English version. If the Simpsons move, they take the sign with them; likewise, if you move TotalExpenses from G24 to F13, the cell name moves with it.

Why should I use names for cells and ranges?

Every important cell on your worksheet—especially the ones where you plan to change data to test different "What if?" scenarios—should have a name, not just a number. On an invoice worksheet, for example, you can name one cell `SalesTaxRate` and another `InvoiceTotal`. Then, in the `TotalAmount` cell, you can replace those confusing cell addresses with the easy-to-understand formula **=InvoiceTotal*SalesTaxRate**.

Here are some very good reasons why you should use range names:

- Names make it easier for you to understand how your worksheet works, especially when you want to reuse a worksheet you created long ago.

- You're less likely to make mistakes as you move cells around, because Excel automatically keeps track of named cells and ranges.

- When you make mistakes, it's easier to find them, because your formulas are written in plain English.

- It's easier to get around because you can jump to different cells or ranges by choosing their names from a list.

OK, what kind of names can I use?

Excel is picky about what you can and can't enter when naming a cell or a range. (Just to make things extra confusing, the rules are completely different from the ones for naming a file or a worksheet tab.) Here are the rules:

- You can use a total of **up to 255 characters,** but it's better to keep them simple.

- The **first character** must be a letter or the underline character. You can't name a cell 1stQuarterSales, but Q1Sales is OK.

- The **remaining characters** can be letters, numbers, periods, or the underline character. No other punctuation marks are allowed.

- **Spaces are forbidden**. So if you try to name a cell Sales Tax Rate, Excel will just beep at you, but Sales_Tax_Rate is OK.

- A cell or range name **cannot look like a cell reference**, so you can't rename a cell Q1 or W2, for example.

How do I name a range?

The easiest way to name a cell or a range is to use the Name box, located just to the left of the Formula bar (see fig. 15.3). Here's how you do it:

1 Select the cell or range you want to name.

2 Click in the Name box to highlight the entire cell address.

3 Type a legal name for the cell or range (remember, you can't start with a number).

4 Press Enter to add the name to the list in your worksheet.

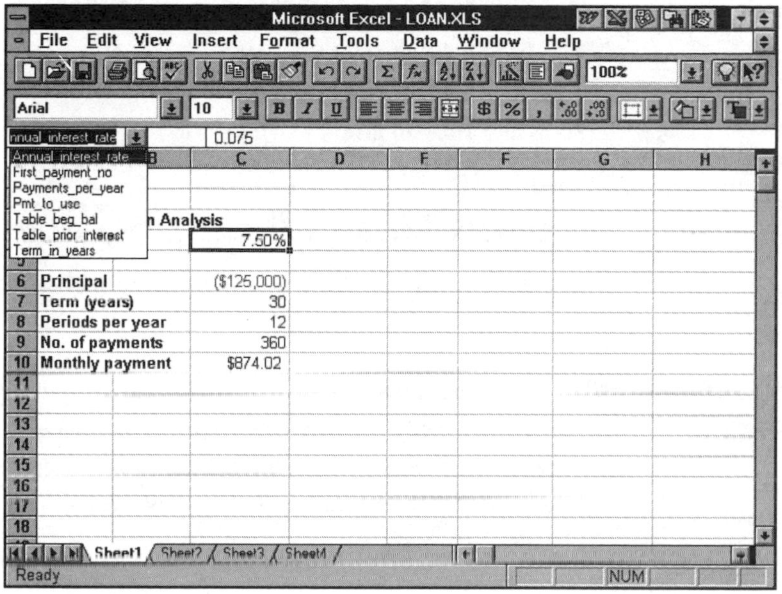

Fig. 15.3

To give a cell or range a plain-English name, just select it, then type the name in this box. Use the drop-down list of range names to jump to named ranges in a worksheet.

Once you've created a range name, you can select the entire range with a couple of mouse clicks. Just choose the range name from the drop-down list and Excel will instantly jump there.

⓵ (Tip)

Use the drop-down list of range names to fill in formulas, as well. Instead of typing in the names, just point to the name in the list and click. Excel will paste the name directly into your formula.

Editing the contents of a cell

Once you've selected an individual cell, it's simple to replace everything in it or just change a few details.

I want to replace everything in a cell

Just select the cell and start typing. The new value will automatically replace the old one.

I want to change part of what's in a cell

Double-click to select the cell, then use the mouse to select the portion you want to replace. When you start typing, the highlighted text will be replaced by whatever you type.

I want this cell empty, now!

Press the Del key, which erases the contents of the current cell. (It's the same as choosing <u>E</u>dit, Cle<u>a</u>r, <u>A</u>ll.)

 **<Caution>** Don't use the space bar to delete the contents of a cell. Excel will think you've put something in the cell, and might miscalculate averages or counts. And don't choose <u>E</u>dit, <u>D</u>elete to clear a cell, either. That menu choice actually removes the entire cell and readjusts the cells on your worksheet like pieces in a jigsaw puzzle.

 Q&A *Aaargghh! I just erased the contents of a cell, and I didn't mean to! Now what do I do?*

 Relax. Take a deep breath. Now press Ctrl+Z or click the Undo button. Most of the time, this will bring back the data you accidentally wiped out.

 Excel has a really lousy memory, so you have to be careful as you work. After you've used Word for a while, you might get used to fiddling around recklessly with documents, knowing that you can always press the Undo button (and keep pressing it) to put things back the way they were. But Excel's Undo button only keeps track of the very last thing you did. If you delete a row, then reformat another cell, you can undo the formatting, but not the deletion.

Moving stuff from one place to another

What happens when you move something from one place to another? Let's say you tell Excel, "Pick up whatever's in G24, and move it to F13." What happens next?

- If there's anything in the destination cell, F13, it'll be wiped out just as surely as if you'd hit the Del key. Zap! Gone. Terminated. Hasta la vista, *baby*.

- If there's a formula in G24, it will adjust itself to reflect the new location. If the original formula in G24 was =SUM(G19:G23), the new copy will change to =SUM(F8:F13). In both cases, the formula SUMs the five cells just above the one it's in. (Confused? See the sidebar, "Understanding cell references," for an explanation.)

- Because you moved the contents of G24 to F13, G24 is now empty. If you had copied G24 instead of moving it, the contents would have remained unchanged.

Can I just drag a cell from one place to another?

If you just want to move a cell a short distance, the easiest way to do it is just to drag the cell (or an entire range, for that matter), and drop it on the new location. Well, it's easy once you get the hang of it. Excel doesn't give you an obvious clue that you've actually grabbed a cell, the way that Word does, but you can watch the status bar. You'll just have to practice until you get it.

When you point at various parts of a cell, you'll see several Excel pointers that are designed to do different things. The trick is learning how to tell these pointers apart (see table 15.1).

Table 15.1   Excel's pointers

When you do this...	You'll see this pointer...	And then you can...
Point anywhere in a cell		Select a cell or a range
Select a cell or range, then point at its border		Move a cell or range by dragging and dropping it
Make a selection, hold down the Ctrl key, then point at its border		Copy a cell or range by dragging and dropping it
Select a cell or range, then aim at the fill handle in the selection's lower right corner		Automatically fill in a series of data (see AutoFill, later in this chapter)
Make a selection, hold down the Ctrl key, then aim at the fill handle		Automatically fill in a different series of data

When you point to the thick border on the edge of a selection, the pointer changes to an arrow. When that happens, you can drag the selection and drop it in a new location. As you drag, you'll see a ghostly reflection of the cell's borders follow the mouse pointer around.

If you hold down the Ctrl key while you drag the selection, the mouse pointer changes to an arrow with a plus sign beside it; that's your only cue that you're about to copy rather than move the contents of the selection.

Frankly, I find this Ctrl+key rigmarole hopelessly confusing, which is why I use the *right* mouse button when I want to drag something from one place to another on a worksheet. When you right-drag a selection and drop it in a new location, a shortcut menu pops up, giving you a chance to tell Excel exactly what you want it to do (see fig. 15.4).

Fig. 15.4
Use the right mouse button to drag a selection from one place to another, and this shortcut Move/ Copy menu will pop up at your destination.

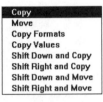

| Copy |
| Move |
| Copy Formats |
| Copy Values |
| Shift Down and Copy |
| Shift Right and Copy |
| Shift Down and Move |
| Shift Right and Move |

(!) (Tip)

When you copy one cell to a range, it fills that whole range. This is an extremely useful technique when you're adding formulas to a highly structured worksheet. To total every column in a budget worksheet, for example, just create the SUM formula under the first column, then copy the formula below all the other columns.

When should I use cut, copy, and paste?

To move or copy a selection outside of the current window, your best bet is to click the right mouse button and pop up Excel's shortcut menu (see fig. 15.5). Don't bother dragging and dropping. If you're even one-tenth the klutz I am, you'll overshoot your target every time.

Fig. 15.5
Don't like to drag-and-drop? Click the right mouse button, then use the shortcut menu to quickly cut or copy a range from one place...

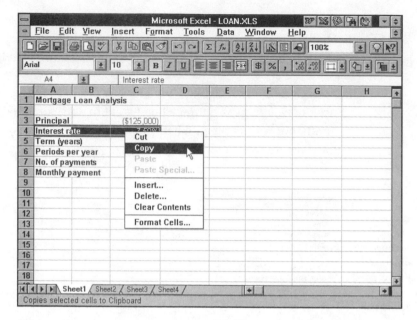

...and paste it in another.

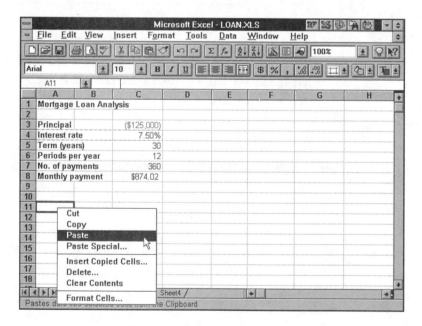

Follow these steps to cut or copy and then paste a range:

1 Point at the selected range, right-click, and choose Cut or Copy from the shortcut menu.

As soon as you click the menu choice, the border around the selection begins to move, like a line of marching ants. (You don't believe me? Just look...)

2 Point to the cell where you want to paste the selection and right-click.

3 Choose Paste to insert the selection. (Or press Esc to chicken out.)

Understanding cell references:
It's all relative (except when it's absolute)

The first time you move or copy a formula, you might be surprised to see that Excel automatically changes any cell references in your formula. Is this a bug? Not at all—it's an example of how Excel uses **relative references** to help you build powerful worksheets without a lot of typing.

What's a relative reference, and why should you care? Imagine you're lost in a strange neighborhood. You stop a passer-by and ask for help in getting to the train station. He might give you directions that relate to where you are right now: "Go three blocks straight ahead, then turn right and go five more blocks. Can't miss it." Or he might use an **absolute reference**: "It's at the corner of Avenue D and 24th Street."

When you copy or move a formula, Excel automatically adjusts cell addresses to reflect their relative position. If you move the formula three rows down and five columns to the right, it adds 3 to each row number and counts 5 letters higher

in the alphabet for each cell address in the new formula. So a reference to D5 changes to I8.

But what happens when you store a scrap of crucial information, like the current interest rate, in one cell? You want your Excel formulas to look in that one cell whenever they need to make an interest-related calculation. In that case, use dollar signs to order Excel to use the cell's absolute address. When you type **$A$4**, Excel treats that as an absolute address, and doesn't adjust it when you move or copy a formula.

You can mix and match relative and absolute addresses in a formula, or even in the same address. For example, $A4 tells Excel to leave the column address at A, but adjust the row address relative to the new location.

When you enter a cell address in the formula bar, you can quickly cycle through relative, mixed, and absolute addresses. Just point anywhere in the address, and press F4 to cycle through all four variations.

 **<Caution>** The Excel version of cut and paste doesn't work like other Windows programs. When you cut something in Excel, you get to paste it somewhere else, and then the Windows Clipboard empties out. Other programs (including Word) leave the stuff you cut in the Clipboard so you can use it again if you want.

Moral: If you want to reuse the same range, use Copy instead of Cut, then delete the original.

Excel's amazing mind-reading trick: AutoFill

Excel can count from 1 to several gazillion. It knows the days of the week and the months of the year, and it knows that Q2 comes after Q1 and before Q3. That's not exactly rocket science. But you can take advantage of Excel's skills with lists to fill in the rest of the months after you type **January**.

This feature is called **AutoFill**, and you can use it to fill in standard lists, series of numbers and dates, or even custom lists (as long as you don't mind teaching Excel what to do the first time). It's a simple mind-reading trick, really, but it'll save you a minute here, and 20 seconds there—before you know it, you'll have saved up an entire coffee break!

How can I fill in a list automatically?

First, you need to learn to recognize Excel's **fill handle**. Select a cell or a range; you'll see a thick border around the entire selection. Look in the lower right corner for a small black square. That's the fill handle. When you aim the mouse pointer at the fill handle, it turns to a thin black cross; at that point you can drag in any direction to start filling in values.

Using AutoFill is like refilling an ice cube tray in your freezer. As you drag (pour the water), the selection gets bigger and includes more cells. When you release the mouse button, Excel fills every cell in the selection with values, as shown in figure 15.6. Which values? That depends on what's in the first cell.

Fig. 15.6

Filling in a series automatically.

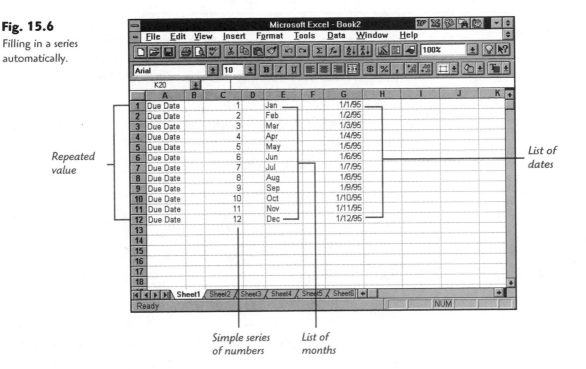

Repeated value

List of dates

Simple series of numbers

List of months

Here's how you create the various kinds of automatic lists:

- To **repeat a value**, type it in the first cell, then grab the fill handle and drag. Your value—the words Due Date, the number 42, whatever—will be repeated in the AutoFill selection.

- To **create a simple series of numbers**, type in a starting number, grab the fill handle, hold down the Ctrl key, and drag the AutoFill pointer. Your list starts with the original number, and increases by 1 throughout the AutoFill selection.

- To **fill in a list of months or days**, type the first entry in the list, in full or abbreviated, and drag the AutoFill handle.

- To **extend a list of dates**, type the first date, in any format, and drag the AutoFill selection.

❶(Tip)

AutoFill is one of the best, most useful Excel features. I could write a whole chapter on it! But since there's no room for that in this book, I highly recommend that you check out Excel's help demonstrations on AutoFill. There are two really good ones.

To get to them, press F1, click on Examples and Demos, click the button next to Entering Data, and choose either of these:

- Filling a Range of Adjacent Cells

- Using AutoFill to Create Trends

Adding (and deleting) cells, rows, and columns

When you first set up a worksheet, you probably won't get the arrangement of rows and columns just right. That's OK—you can always insert or delete a cell, a row, or a column.

Whenever you insert or delete cells in a worksheet, Excel shuffles everything around to make room. If you delete Row D, for example, Row E moves up into Row D; the folks in F move to E, and so on. Most of the proper change-of-address forms get filed, so everyone knows where to find everyone else.

The best way to insert or delete anything is with the right-mouse-button shortcut menus. Make a selection, then pop up the shortcut menus and choose Insert or Delete. Excel will pop up a dialog box like the one in figure 15.7, asking you how you want the worksheet rearranged.

Fig. 15.7
When you select a cell and choose Delete, Excel asks how to rearrange the worksheet.

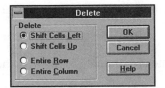

 Q&A

> ### I deleted a column, and now some of my formulas don't work any more. What went wrong?
>
> When you delete a cell, Excel removes every trace of it. If formulas elsewhere on the worksheet referred to that cell, Excel will get hopelessly confused and say something like #REF! No, it's not a computerized cuss word—it means Excel has lost track of a reference and can't evaluate the formula.

Working smarter with worksheets

Some people just stuff papers into file folders and leave it at that. If your approach to organizing information is that casual, skip this section. Otherwise, read on for instructions on keeping the worksheets in each workbook neatly arranged and clearly labeled.

Renaming a sheet

How would you like it if you went in search of important information in a file cabinet, and found that all the folders were labeled Folder1, Folder2, and so forth. How could you possibly know that your January expense report was in Folder143?

The default labels on Excel worksheet tabs are nearly that useless. Sheet1, Sheet2? How uninformative. You'll get more work done if your sheets have plain-English names like Sales Forecasts, Departmental Expenses, or Golf Scores, right?

To rename a worksheet, just double-click on the tab for that sheet, type in a new name, and click OK.

Of course, there are a few rules for naming your worksheets:

- You get **31 characters** for each tab.

- **Spaces** are allowed.

- **Square brackets** ([ ]) are not allowed (but parentheses are OK).

- You can't use any of the following characters: **/ \ ? * :** (slash, backslash, question mark, asterisk, or colon). Other punctuation, including commas and exclamation points, are allowed.

How do I switch to another sheet?

Workbooks let you keep all your similar worksheets in one place, where you can get to them in a hurry. To move from one worksheet to another, just click on the index tab of the sheet you want to work with. If you can't see all the tabs, click on the arrows to the left of the tabs to riffle through the sheet tabs you can't see.

(!) (Tip)

I usually don't need more than one or two worksheets in my workbook, so I lowered the number of blank sheets that Excel puts in a new workbook from 16 to 4 (you can set it to any number between 1 and 255). This also makes your files smaller and saves disk space. To change the setting, choose Tools, Options, click the General tab, and fill in a number in the box labeled Sheets in New Workbook.

Moving, copying, inserting, and deleting sheets

Go ahead and treat worksheets in your workbook as though they're sheets of paper in a three-ring binder. If you need a new one, add it. If you've made a mess of a worksheet and want to start over, tear it out and throw it away. You can also rearrange sheets in any order by dragging them around:

- To **insert a new worksheet**, select any sheet tab and right-click. From the shortcut menu, choose Insert, and pick Worksheet from the list of options. The new sheet will be added to the left of the selected sheet.

- To **delete a worksheet**, select its tab and right-click; then choose Delete from the shortcut menu.

- To **move a worksheet**, select its tab and hold down the left mouse button until the mouse pointer turns into an arrow with a sheet of paper (as shown in fig. 15.8). Slide the pointer along the sheet tabs until the small black arrow is pointing to the place you want to move your worksheet and release the mouse button.

- To **copy a worksheet in the same workbook**, hold down the Ctrl key and drag the sheet tab to the left or the right. If your old worksheet was named Sheet1, your new sheet will be called Sheet1 (2).

- To **copy a worksheet to another workbook**, use the right-mouse-button shortcut menus to copy the sheet and paste it in the new book.

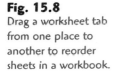

Fig. 15.8
Drag a worksheet tab from one place to another to reorder sheets in a workbook.

16

Making Great-Looking Worksheets

When each section is clearly marked off with lines, boxes, and bold type, it's easier to see the big picture.

How important is organization and clear labeling? For an instant object lesson, take a trip to your local supermarket.

If you're a really good shopper, you can get in and out of the grocery store in ten minutes. A quick raid on the produce section, a quart of milk from the dairy cabinet, and a fast pass down the frozen-food aisle on your way to the checkout stand. You find your way around fast because someone organized the store that way. Every section is clearly marked, all similar products are organized together, and when you can't find something, you just look at the signs over each aisle.

That's the way to organize an Excel worksheet, too. It doesn't matter whether you're preparing a financial analysis for yourself or crunching numbers for a big presentation to the boss. When each section is clearly marked off with lines, boxes, and bold type, it's easier to see the big picture. And when key information is enhanced with colors, shading, and distinctive typography, the most important information—like the bottom line—jumps off the page.

What's formatting, and why should I care?

When you enter a value in a cell, Excel doesn't always display exactly what you typed. Instead, the program looks in the workbook to see whether you've left instructions about how to display the contents of that cell. If Excel can't find any instructions from you, it looks at the data and tries to figure out how you probably want to see it. Whatever Excel does with the characters in the cell is called **formatting**.

You use formatting instructions to tell Excel precisely how to display the characters in a cell or a range. **Make this sentence bold**. Put these three words in a different font. Put the bottom line in color, please: **($38,592)**.

True, there are shortcut buttons on the Formatting toolbar. But the best assortment of Excel formatting options pops up when you make a selection, click the right mouse button, and choose Format Cells. Then click a tab in the dialog box shown in figure 16.1 to adjust one of these six choices.

Fig. 16.1

Use the Format Cells dialog box to adjust the look of any cell or range.

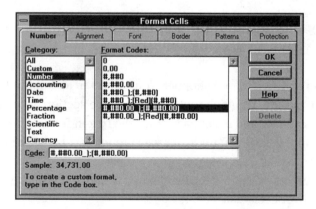

Look at the tabs across the top of the the Format Cells dialog box. Here's the scoop on each of these tabs:

- **Number** formatting tells Excel how many decimal points you want to see for each number in a given cell, whether there's a dollar sign or a percentage, whether the number is a date, and so on.

- **Alignment** tells Excel where you want your cells to line up. Usually, numbers press against the right edge of the cell, text leans to the left, and labels are centered.

- **Font** defines the size, shape, and thickness of each character in the cell. Fonts are measured in **points**—more points mean bigger letters. The default Excel font, 10-point Arial, is a good choice for most worksheets.

- **Lines and boxes** (controlled by the Border tab) allow you to draw a literal "bottom line" to set off your total beneath a column of numbers. You can also use borders to put parts of a worksheet into their own boxes.

- **Color and shading** (controlled by the Patterns tab) let you draw attention to a section of the worksheet, such as titles and totals. Remember, though, you can only see color on paper if you have a color printer!

- The final formatting option (Protection) lets you add a **lock** that makes it impossible for you or anyone else to change the contents of a cell.

①(Tip)

To select the entire worksheet, click in the tiny, unmarked gray button at the top left corner of the worksheet window. (It's just above the row heading for 1 and to the left of the heading for column A.) When you select the entire worksheet, any formatting options you choose will apply to the entire worksheet.

To deselect, click on any cell in the worksheet.

 **<Caution>** When does 2+2=5? When you've entered **2.3** or **2.4** into two cells, then reformatted both to show no decimal places. When Excel uses those values in a calculation, it uses the actual amount stored in the cell, not the clipped-off version you see. And if the total comes out to 4.7, the no-decimal format will display that number as 5. The moral? It's always best not to have Excel do the rounding off.

How do I make my worksheets more readable?

How do you turn the wallflower worksheet from figure 16.2 into the slick, easy-to-read sheet shown in figure 16.3? All it takes is a few clicks.

Fig. 16.2
Worksheets don't get much duller than this. If you just type, Excel puts every word and number into this normal font.

	A	B	C	D	E	F	G	H
1	Good Sports Travel							
2	Annual Expense Worksheet							
3	1/25/95							
4								
5								
6	Acct #	Account Description	Jan	Feb	Mar	Apr	May	Jun
7								
8	Employee Costs							
9	110	Payroll	33228	33228	34436.4	33228	34436.4	3588
10	120	Payroll Taxes	9102	9102	9428.4	9102	9428.4	9818.
11	130	Commissions	1660.8	11970	10830	11970	10830	1160
12	140	Insurance	4464	4144.8	4290	4144.8	4290	446
13								
14	Facilities Overhead							
15	410	Rent	6660	6660	6660	6660	6660	666
16	420	Parking and security	1620	1620	1620	1620	1620	162
17	430	Cleaning	540	540	540	540	540	54
18	440	Telephone	706	706	706	706	706	70

Microsoft Excel - GSTEXPNS.XLS

File   Edit   View   Insert   Format   Tools   Data   Window   Help

A1   Good Sports Travel

Arial   10

Expenses / Sheet1 / Sheet2 / Sheet3 / Sheet4 / Shee

Ready   NUM

Fig. 16.3
A worksheet make-over. Select the right cells and click a few buttons to make this easy-to-read worksheet.

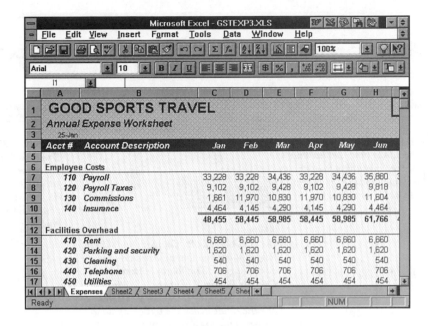

Here's how to give the worksheet example a make-over:

- Reformat every number, and make sure all the columns align properly.

- Make worksheet and column titles bigger and bolder, so they clearly define each column. Use a dark background and bold, italic, white type to make the titles impossible to ignore.

- To really make the bottom line pop off the page, use the Borders button to add an emphatic double underline beneath the month columns. Add a thinner border under the subtitles.

- Use soft yellow shading throughout the data section. This shading is easier on the eyes than the standard harsh white.

- Turn off the normal Excel gridlines. You'll be amazed at how unclut-tered the worksheet suddenly looks.

- You can format a cell (or a group of cells) even if it's empty.

You can apply formatting to a cell or a range using buttons on the Formatting toolbar. Think of it as the 7-11 approach to formatting. For simply changing font size or centering a label, you can't beat using the toolbar. But when you want to fine-tune a worksheet's formatting, you'll need to visit the formatting superstore: Excel's Format Cells dialog box.

What can I do with the Formatting toolbar?

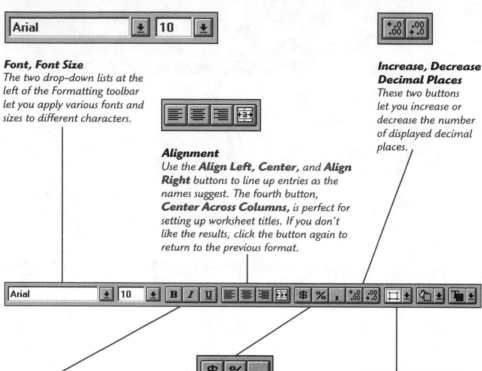

Font, Font Size
The two drop-down lists at the left of the Formatting toolbar let you apply various fonts and sizes to different characters.

Alignment
Use the **Align Left**, **Center**, and **Align Right** buttons to line up entries as the names suggest. The fourth button, **Center Across Columns,** is perfect for setting up worksheet titles. If you don't like the results, click the button again to return to the previous format.

Increase, Decrease Decimal Places
These two buttons let you increase or decrease the number of displayed decimal places.

Bold, Italic, Underline
Use these buttons to make text or numbers **bold,** *italic,* or <u>underlined</u>. You can also use the keyboard shortcuts Ctrl+B, Ctrl+I, and Ctrl+U.

Dollar, Percent, Comma
These three buttons let you apply preset dollar, percent, and comma styles with one click.

Borders, Background Colors, Text Colors
Click any of these three down-arrows to take your pick of borders, background colors, and text colors. Or click the buttons themselves to apply the most recent selections.

How do I make sure my numbers look right?

When you get right down to it, spreadsheets are all about numbers, so it stands to reason that there are lots and lots of ways to display those numbers. When you type a number and press Enter, for example, how should Excel display it? You have dozens of choices; fortunately, Excel keeps them neatly organized into categories. In the Number tab of the Format Cells dialog box, pick a category from the list on the left, select a format from the list on the right, and look at the sample at the bottom of the dialog box to see what will appear in the cell if you click OK.

Table 16.1 gives you a summary of the most popular choices for displaying numbers.

Table 16.1   Popular display options

Describe the kind of numbers you plan to enter	Choose a format from this group	The numbers in your worksheet may look like this
I don't know yet. Could be anything.	General format	-34.7 34 34731
I'm adding numbers to a profit-and-loss report.	Number or Accounting	34,731 (34,731) $34,731.92 [in red]
I'm working with dollars and cents.	Currency	$34,731 $34,731.00 $34,731 [in red]
I'm playing with percentages.	Percentage	34% 34.7% 34.731%
I'm dealing with dates and times.	Date or Time	2/1/95 01-Feb-1995 10:05:43 pm

*{Note} These are just a few of the many, many format options available. Chances are, if you need it, you can find it. If not, you can create your own!

?Q&A

My cell says `1.03E+08`***—but that's not what I typed. What's going on?***

You must have slept through that part of your high school algebra class (just like me). That's scientific notation, and Excel uses it when you type a number with more digits than it can display in the General number format. Take the number before the E and move the decimal eight places to the right (if that were a minus sign, you'd move the decimal to the left). So your number is actually 103,000,000.

⊗<Caution> Be careful how you enter percentages into your worksheet. If you use one of the Percentage formats, and then enter a number like **7**, it will appear as 700% (and your calculations will be off by miles). To enter percentages into a worksheet, remember to use the percent sign (**7%**) or the proper decimal point (**.07**).

How can I emphasize certain words and numbers?

The manager at my local supermarket is no dummy. He puts the Snickers bars and the National Enquirer at eye level, right next to the checkout stand. By the time I get to the front of the line, half the candy bar is gone, there are chocolate fingerprints all over the newspaper, and I'm probably going to pay for both.

You can make parts of your worksheet nearly as irresistible. How? By using bigger, bolder fonts, of course. The default font is fine for endless rows and columns of numbers, but titles and totals can always stand a little punching up. Here's how to do it:

- To **select a new font for a cell or range**, just select the cell(s), and choose a font from the drop-down Font list on the Formatting toolbar. Use the Font Size drop-down list to make it bigger, and click the Bold button to add some oomph to those labels.

- If you want, you can **apply different fonts and sizes to different characters in the same cell**. Maybe your lawyers want you to add a copyright symbol,©, but you'd prefer that it not be *too* obvious. Click in the formula bar, select the character you want to reformat, then use the Formatting toolbar to adjust fonts and sizes.

When should you use the Font section of the Format Cells dialog box? Whenever you're not sure what a given font looks like, you'll welcome the preview window shown in figure 16.4. This dialog box also offers some formats not found on the the toolbar, like strikethrough and double-underline.

It's 34731.9583—do you know where your kids are?

When you type a simple date or time into a cell, you set off a complicated chain of events. Consider dates. In Excel's world, you see, every date is actually just a number, and the world began in 1900. Confused? Here's what's really going on.

When you enter **2/1/95** into a cell, Excel examines it carefully: "Hmmm, looks like a date." Instead of plunking that date into the cell, though, Excel grabs its built-in Franklin Planner, and counts the number of days that have passed since January 1, 1900. (The answer, in this example: 34,731.)

Of course, this all happens in a few millionths of a second, and Excel continues to display the date you entered, so you're not even aware anything happened. If you added the time to your date, **2/1/95 11:00:00 PM**, Excel would simply figure what percent of the day had passed and tack that fraction onto the end of the number. So figure it's 34731.9583 with a few more decimal points thrown in for good measure.

Want to know more? Sorry, it's .7083333, and I'm knocking off for the day.

Fig. 16.4
Use the Font tab when
you want to see what
your change will look
like before you click
OK and make it so.

Pick a font, a font style, a size, and a color.

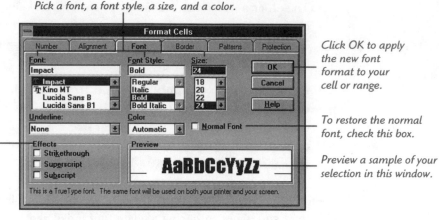

*Click OK to apply
the new font
format to your
cell or range.*

*For special effects,
including a choice
of underlines,
click here.*

*To restore the normal
font, check this box.*

*Preview a sample of your
selection in this window.*

 **{Note}**

If you have a long line of text that doesn't fit in a cell, have Excel wrap it to a
second or third line. Pop up the Format Cells dialog box, click the Alignment
tab, and check the Wrap Text box. Now, instead of running out of sight when
they hit the edge of the cell, your words will begin filling up a second line in
the same cell.

Format Cells also includes a few other options that come in handy:

- **Center across selection** lets you enter text into one cell and center it
  across a range of cells in one row. This is great for worksheet titles, grouped
  columns, and so on.

- Try changing the **vertical alignment** of a headline to Center;
  that way, it will seem to float in space instead of sitting on the bottom of
  the cell.

- Excel also lets you **change the orientation** and stack a cell on its side so
  it can act as an ultra-slim column title.

How can I make certain sections stand out?

There's no mistaking the produce section down at the local supermarket.
It's got wider aisles, different lighting, and those little spritzers that keep
the lettuce from wilting until it gets to your refrigerator.

You can create the same sort of distinctive identity for sections of a worksheet by using boxes and colors. Excel lets you use thin lines, thick lines, and double lines to add borders to cells and ranges.

You can also add colorful backgrounds (and change the type to complementary colors): dark backgrounds and white type to create powerful worksheet titles; soft, light backgrounds to make columns of numbers more readable; alternating colors or shading to make it easy to tell one row from another in a wide worksheet.

Pop up the Format Cells dialog box and choose the Border tab (see fig. 16.5) to draw a box around a selection. With the dialog box displayed, follow these steps:

1 Where do you want the lines? Outline draws a box around the selection, while Bottom underlines it.

2 Choose a line style—thick, thin, doubled, dotted, or dashed.

3 Click OK to add the borders to your worksheet.

 (Tip)

Turning gridlines off on-screen doesn't mean they won't print. If you add your own boxes and borders, turn off Gridlines (Sheet tab) under File, Page Setup.

Fig. 16.5

Use borders, boxes, and colors to distinguish sections of your worksheet.

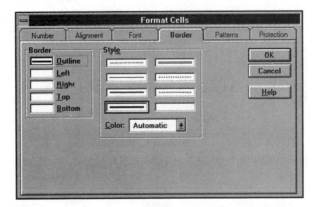

Recycling the best formats

You may tinker for an hour trying to find the just-exactly-perfect formatting for one section (or even one cell) on your worksheet. That's OK this time, but if you do that every time, your computer isn't exactly a labor-saving device, is it? Fortunately, Excel has a solution when you find a format that works.

Just like Word, Excel lets you collect favorite combinations of cell formats and store them in reusable **styles.** Instead of clicking in six different dialog boxes, you choose Format, Style to display the dialog box shown in figure 16.6. Then you choose a name from the drop-down list, and click OK. Here's how to work with styles:

- To **create a style**, select a cell with the formatting you want to save (such as Arial 24, bold, and underlined), then choose Format, Style. Type a name in the Style Name box and click OK.

- Styles only apply to the workbook you designed them in. But don't worry—you can cheat! To **copy styles from another workbook,** first open the workbook containing the styles you want to copy. Click the Merge button, and pick the workbook name from the list that pops up. After you click OK, your styles will be available in the current workbook, too.

Fig. 16.6
Create a masterpiece of a cell format? Save it using Excel's styles, then reuse it in another worksheet or even another workbook.

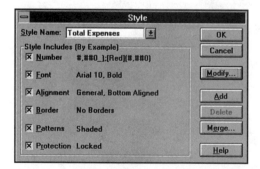

Can't I just copy formatting from one place to another?

When you don't particularly care about saving your format for posterity, there's a quicker way to copy formats from one cell to another. The Format

Painter works just like the paintbrush pictured on its button. You dip the brush in one cell, and it picks up all the formatting in that cell. Swipe the brush across another cell, or a whole range of cells, to "paint" the identical format into the new location. Here are the steps:

1 Select the cell whose format you want to copy.

2 Click the Format Painter button. (If you plan to copy the format to more than one place, double-click the button to lock the Format Painter in place.) When you move the pointer back over the worksheet, you'll see that there's now a paintbrush alongside the regular Excel pointer, as shown in figure 16.7.

3 Click on the cell where you want to copy the formatting. To "paint" the formats across a range of cells, hold down the mouse button and drag the paintbrush across the entire range.

4 If you locked the Format Painter on, press Escape or click the button again to return the pointer to normal.

Fig. 16.7
Click the Format Painter button and use this pointer to copy formats from one cell and "paint" them in another.

To automatically convert a fraction to its decimal equivalent, enter a **0** and a space first. If you don't, Excel will convert some fractions to dates (5/8, for example, would become May 8) and others to text labels. But when you enter **0 5/8** into a cell, Excel correctly stores the number as 0.625, and displays the fraction you entered.

I need to resize rows and columns

When you first begin working with a worksheet, every row is the same height, and every column is the same width. It soon becomes obvious that that state of affairs can't last. A column that contains only two-digit numbers doesn't need to be as wide as one that's filled with descriptive labels. And rows need to get bigger when the data inside them gets bigger.

Fortunately, Excel takes care of that last problem for you. Rows automatically adjust in height when you change the font size of the text within the cells. If you want to adjust a column width, or make a row just a little taller, you'll have to master a simple adjustment technique. (Don't worry, no tools are required!)

- To **drag a column or row to a new size**, point to the thin line between the row or column headings until the pointer turns to a black bar with two arrows pointing away from each other (see fig. 16.8). Hold down the mouse button and drag the edge of the column or row until it's the size you want, then release the button.

- To **automatically size a column or row**, make a selection, then choose Format, Row, AutoFit; or Format, Column, AutoFit Selection.

Fig. 16.8
When the pointer turns to this two-headed bar, you can drag a column or row and resize it.

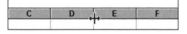

 (Tip) Double-click the right border of a column heading (or the bottom border of a row heading) to automatically adjust column width or row height to fit the widest or tallest entry.

AutoFormat: let Excel do it all for you

I don't know about you, but my favorite aisle in the grocery store is the microwave section. Popcorn in three minutes? Yes! Soup in 90 seconds? All right!

And a perfectly formatted Excel worksheet with one mouse click? Sounds too good to be true.

AutoFormat, Excel's instant do-it-all formatting feature, works pretty much as advertised on most simple worksheets. It's a simple process, really:

1 Select a range. If you skip this step, Excel will try to guess how much of your worksheet you want to be automatically formatted.

2 Choose Format, AutoFormat to display the AutoFormat dialog box shown in figure 16.9.

Fig. 16.9
Most of the time, AutoFormat will make your worksheet look better, although you'll still want to polish the final product.

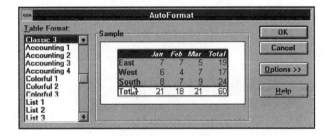

3 Pick one of the built-in formats. As you scroll through the list, you can see a sample in the preview window at the right.

4 Click the Options button to keep Excel from resizing columns, changing fonts, and so on.

5 Click OK to see the results.

If AutoFormat doesn't quite work out the way you expected, hit the Undo key right away to return to the previous worksheet formatting. Then try a smaller range or a different format.

Fancy Excel Stuff

17

In this chapter:

- How do I work with lists?

- I need to search for data with forms

- How do I link data between workbooks or worksheets?

- How can I get started working more quickly?

You can use Excel for many of your daily tasks, including those that have nothing to do with number-crunching.

We haven't even begun to scratch the surface of what Excel can do for you and your business. The more you work with it, the more exciting features you'll discover. And once you discover the power hidden within this program, you may find yourself using it for many of your daily tasks, including some that have nothing to do with number-crunching. In this chapter, we show you how to take your rows and columns of numbers beyond mere calculations.

Clearing up the clutter with lists

Are you a collector? A friend of mine collects sports caps of all sports in all leagues—professional, college, even Junior League. They're all hanging on his office wall. Hundreds of them. I asked him once how many baseball caps he had. It took him 20 minutes to go around the room and count them, because they were spread out randomly all over the place. Next I asked him how many caps came from California. I haven't heard from him since 1992.

Collecting data is important, but managing it is crucial. Just the fact that the data exists doesn't mean you can get to it quickly and make sense out of it. You need to be organized. You need a database-management system.

A **list** is Excel's term for a database. If you have the Professional Edition of Microsoft Office, you may be using Access 2.0, the database-management program. Even if you are, Excel databases are simpler to use because you run them from the familiar Excel interface.

Plain English, please!

A **database** is a collection of **records**. Your phone book has thousands and thousands of records. What's in a record? Here's one:

Smith, Mary, 234 Elm Street, Anytown, 555-2345

In this case, there's a last name, a first name, a street address, a city, and a phone number. Each of these categories is called a **field**. Fields make up the structure of the database. You can search on a field ("Is there anybody called Smith in Anytown?") or sort the database according to any field, name, city, and so on.

Creating lists by the rules

Excel databases are regular worksheets, but you must follow some rules:

- Field names must be in the top row (Excel calls it the **header row**).

- Each row must be a separate record.

- You should avoid having blank rows between records, or between the header and the first record.

Efficient databases break down the fields to the smallest element possible, so you can use the information more flexibly. For example, a Name field should be split into Last Name and First Name, so you can use the First Name only in the salutation.

Figure 17.1 shows an example of a list.

Fig. 17.1
It looks like a simple worksheet, but it's a powerful database-management tool, letting you get at your data more quickly than looking through folder after folder full of documents.

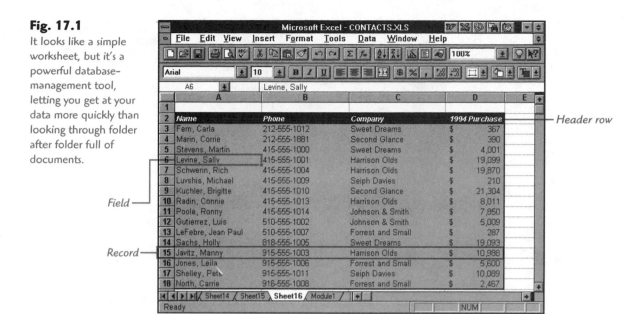

Filling in forms

Once you've created the list, Excel generates a **form**, which is a convenient data entry and search tool. If you've followed the simple list-creation rules given earlier in the chapter, just click anywhere within the list, and follow these steps:

1 Choose Data, Form to display a dialog box like the one in figure 17.2.

2 Click on New to enter a new record.

3 Enter the data in the blank text boxes. Press the Tab key after each entry to go on to the next field.

4 Click on Close when you're done entering data.

(X)<Caution> The title on the form is actually the worksheet's name, so be sure to name it, or else you'll end up with a very uninspired Sheet8 in your form.

Fig. 17.2
How smart is this form?
It knows which fields
are in it and how many
records you have; it
even displays the
database title.

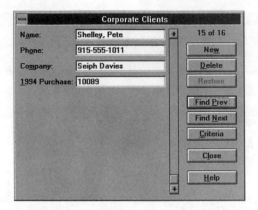

Sorting your data the easy way

Just like your file folders, which are placed in alphabetical order in your cabinet, a good database should be **sorted**. You can sort it by Name, City, State, or whatever. Unlike using your file cabinet, though, you don't need to shuffle dozens of file folders when you want to sort or re-sort. Let's say you need to sort data by State, and within these, by City (so that Alabama comes before Alaska, and Anchorage comes before Cicely). Here's how you do that:

1 Click on any cell within the database.

2 Choose Data, Sort. Excel identifies the list, selects it, and presents you with the Sort dialog box, shown in figure 17.3.

3 Click on the drop-down arrow next to Sort By, and select the key sort field (State, in this example).

4 Click on the drop-down arrow next to Then By, and select City.

5 Make sure that both are marked Ascending, which is the natural order (A-Z).

6 Click on OK.

Fig. 17.3

If you don't have a header row, click next to No Header Row, and your sort options will be the mysterious Column A, Column B, and so on.

Desperately searching for data

I have a terrific filing system. There's a folder labeled 1995, where all my letters, receipts, and invoices go. When I need to find one of them, I... well, give up and hope the IRS didn't really mean business when it asked for those receipts.

If you only have a few documents to file, that system may make sense to you. And if there are only 20 records in your database, you can just glance at the screen and find the one you're looking for. But if you have hundreds or thousands of records, you can't take the time to scroll down the list until you find the customer you're looking for (with your luck, he will be record number 2198). You can use a form to quickly find the information you're looking for.

To quickly find records that match your search criteria, click on the first record, and then:

1 Choose Data, Form.

2 Click Criteria. As you see in figure 17.4, the form's contents are cleared.

3 Type your search criteria in the appropriate boxes. For example, if you're looking for your Cicely, Alaska contacts, type **Cicely** in the City box and **Alaska** in the State box. Press Enter to start the search.

4 You may have more than one match, so click on Find Next to see the next record. Repeat the process until you hear a warning beep, telling you there are no more matches. You can also click on Find Prev to go back. Only records that match the search criteria will be displayed.

5 Click on Close to exit.

Fig. 17.4
You can search on any combination of the fields in the list.

(Tip)

Don't feel like typing out **Connecticut**? And is that client called Sanderson or Sandersen? Don't worry. You don't need to type it all in the Criteria form. Just type the first few characters, followed with an asterisk (*). For example, enter **Conn*** or **Sander***.

Filtering out what you don't need

Forms are an acceptable search tool if your needs are simple, but the true search tools in your Excel list are **filters,** which are search criteria that display the list in its original table-state, but you only see the data specified by the filter. The advantage of this method is that you can continue working with the worksheet as you're used to, but you don't clutter the screen with information you don't need to see. Let's say you only want to look at your Cicely, Alaska contacts. To activate a filter, follow these steps:

1 Click anywhere in the list.

2 Choose Data, Filter, AutoFilter.

3 Look at figure 17.5. Notice the drop-down arrows next to each field name? Click the one next to State, and select Alaska. Click the one next to City and select Cicely. Magically, the only records on display are those that match these search criteria.

Fig. 17.5
On your color monitor, the drop-down arrows next to State and City change color to signify that you've selected a filter.

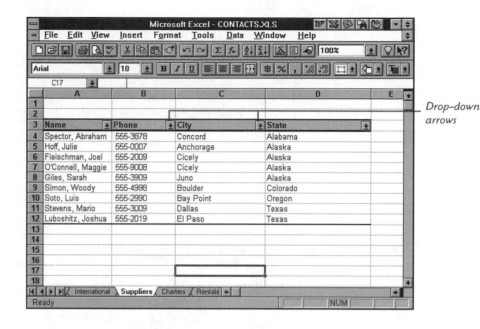

Drop-down arrows

Printing selected records is easy if you use filters. Just click the Print button in the toolbar; only the visible records get printed.

Creating subtotals

Your worksheet is complete. All the data is in. Your totals are all calculated, and you're ready to call it a day. But, wait! You forgot the subtotals. Now you need to insert blank rows and enter more formulas. It's time for Monday Night Football, but you won't get home until Tuesday morning. You know there's an easier way, don't you? Tell Excel to plug those subtotals in, and you'll be home in time for the pre-game show.

Before you apply subtotals, make sure your list is sorted on the field you want to perform the calculation. For example, if you want to total the sales-per-company data, sort by the Company field.

Here's how you insert subtotals in a list:

1 Click anywhere within the list.

2 Choose <u>D</u>ata, Su<u>b</u>totals to launch the dialog box you see in figure 17.6.

3 Click on the drop-down arrow next to <u>A</u>t Each Change In, and select the category on which you want to perform the subtotal calculation.

4 Make sure that Sum is selected under <u>U</u>se Function.

5 Under A<u>d</u>d Subtotal To, click next to the field you want to sum.

6 Click OK.

Fig. 17.6
Inserting subtotal rows into a long list is as effortless as making a selection in this dialog box.

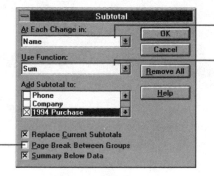

This menu includes all the fields in the list.

Your subtotals don't necessarily have to be sums. You can find the average, maximum, minimum, or number of entries within the group.

Need to print each group on a separate page? Select this checkbox.

 Q&A

> ## Can I just look at the subtotals without the rest of the data?
>
> The subtotal structure is a collapsible outline. Look at figure 17.7: on the left side of your screen, you see the **outline buttons**. Just click on the button labeled "2" to see the subtotals. To return to full view, click on the button labeled "3".

Fig. 17.7

Take a peek at the subtotals by using this handy outline feature.

Outline buttons

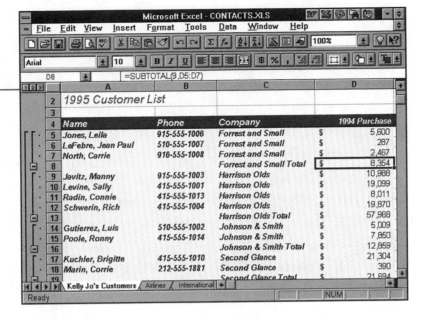

Search and replace

Suppose you get a postcard from the phone company, informing you that all the phone numbers that start with 555 are changing as of April 1. The new prefix is 111. This is a data entry nightmare. What do you do? Hire a temp? Spend a week re-entering numbers? Of course not. Just tell Excel to replace all instances of 555 with 111. Here's how:

1 Choose Edit, Replace (or press Ctrl+H) to launch the dialog box you see in figure 17.8.

2 Type **555** in the Find What box (don't press Enter), then press Tab to move to the Replace with box.

3 Type **111** in the Replace with box (still, no Enter).

4 Click Replace All.

5 Click Close to exit.

Sometimes your search doesn't go quite as expected. For example, if you have Zip codes in your database, and you replace all instances of 555, some of your Zip codes might be corrupted. No problem. Select the Edit menu, and choose Undo Replace.

Fig. 17.8

Wrist rest: to avoid unnecessary typing, rely on shortcuts like Search and Replace.

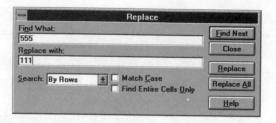

If you want the Search and Replace action to apply to only part of your worksheet, select that area before you start. Even when you choose Replace All, the changes apply only to the pre-selected range.

Linking data between workbooks or worksheets

You often need to consolidate data from different sources into one worksheet. You may have a separate sales-tracking worksheet for each month and one year-to-date worksheet. Or you might have one for each division in your company, and one for the entire company. One thing you want to avoid like the plague is repetition of data entry. And, Excel can help.

Establishing a link may seem a bit tedious, but you'll only do it once. After you establish the links, you'll never have to go through this again. Follow these steps:

1 Open all the related workbooks.

2 In the source worksheet, go to a cell you want to link to a master worksheet or workbook, and press Ctrl+C to copy it to the Clipboard. (See Chapter 20 for more about copying to the Clipboard.)

3 Go to the master worksheet or workbook, and click on the cell in which you want to insert that information.

4 Choose Edit, Paste Special.

5 From the Paste Special dialog box (see fig. 17.9), choose Paste Link.

Fig. 17.9
When you establish this link, you open a line of communication between the two worksheets: any change at the source work-sheet is automatically reflected in the target one.

Speeding up the file-open process

Don't you wish there were a few minutes every day when you could just kick back and check out the latest office gossip? Excel makes it easy because while you wait for your workbooks to open, you can take a walk, make a phone call, go grocery-shopping, and so on. The larger the files, the longer it takes to open them. But there are a few things you can do to automate the file-open process. Read on.

Quick start

You're a person of habit. Every morning you launch Excel, open the Budget file, then the Payroll file, then the Sales Tracking spreadsheet, and while you wait for your files to wake up, yawn and stretch, you go out for espresso and a bagel. Excel makes that process simpler for you. If you always open the same workbooks, tell Excel to open them at the same time it launches. Just save each of these files into the XLSTART subdirectory (located under the EXCEL directory), and each time you open Excel, these files will open by themselves.

If it's Tuesday, it must be payroll

You may have specific tasks you work on at different times. Sometimes you need to open all the payroll-related files, and other days you work with all the budget-type files. Luckily, you can save groups of files as one **workspace** file, which is an umbrella file containing several related workbooks. To create a workspace file, make sure all the files you want in it are open, then choose File, Save Workspace, and give it a name. Excel will add the extension XLW to that name. To open that workspace, just choose File, Open and choose the file from the list.

18

Creating and Enhancing Charts

Excel makes it easy (and fun) to create charts out of your data. It's as easy as pointing and clicking the ChartWizard.

There are two ways you can look at your Excel data: in worksheet form or as charts. While worksheets are necessary for plugging in the data and performing calculations, it's very difficult (practically impossible) to analyze the information just by staring at row after row after row of numbers. What was the best sales month in 1994? Did the '89 earthquake have an effect on sales? Who sold the most tickets in February? Let's take out the yellow highlighter.

Better yet, let's plot those numbers. Did sales drop after the earthquake? When you look at a line chart, if it's shaped like the Grand Canyon, and the lowest point is around October '89, the answer is immediately apparent.

Excel makes it easy (and fun) to create charts out of your data. A very handy wizard is always at your disposal. Just tell it which data to use, and it'll be plotted.

Navigating my way around charts

When you look for an address on a map, you usually consult the index. Suppose the street you're looking for is marked as M7. This reference means that the street is located within the M7 square: M is the horizontal axis, and 7 is the vertical axis. Axes make it easy to find information. Without them, you'd be going cross-eyed trying to find tiny Elm Court.

Charts are the same way. Unless you had axes as points of reference, you'd be looking at meaningless piles of numbers and words. Some people say that the Y axis is the vertical one and the X axis is the horizontal one. But they're wrong. The direction is not the point, only what's plotted on it. Here's how you can tell your axes apart:

- X axis: **categories**

- Y axis: **values**

For example, look at figure 18.1: the names are on the X axis, while the numbers are on the Y. Figure 18.2 shows the same information, but the axes are "flipped" for effect.

Fig. 18.1

This is the traditional way of looking at charts: The Y axis is on the left, and the X axis is on the bottom.

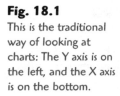

Y: *These are the numbers (or* **values***) we're plotting.*

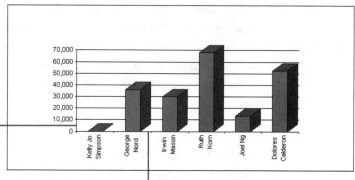

X: *This is the* **category** *axis. In this case, the category is people.*

Fig. 18.2
What's wrong with this picture? Nothing, really. This "sideways" chart is perfectly legitimate.

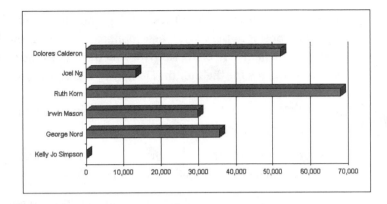

The ChartWizard—just add water

Creating a chart in Excel is as easy as pointing to the data and clicking on the ChartWizard. The wizard does most of the preliminary work for you, and all that's left for you is customizing and minor tweaking. Just like everywhere else in Office, this wizard takes you through a series of questions, then builds the chart according to your specifications.

Drag and plot

Look at the worksheet in figure 18.3. This is a sales-tracking worksheet, where each salesperson's figures are logged.

Fig. 18.3
Too many numbers? Wait till you see this as a chart.

	Jan	Feb	Mar	Apr	May	Jun
Good Sports Travel						
Sales Tracking						
Kelly Jo Simpson	0	32,099	0	61,300	0	9,870
George Nord	35,600	14,800	30,972	28,755	40,883	46,500
Irwin Mason	29,800	37,988	25,926	50,144	34,222	23,840
Ruth Korn	67,900	21,084	0	27,831	34,560	45,760
Joel Ng	13,290	46,980	11,562	62,014	15,262	0
Dolores Calderon	52,190	32,900	45,405	43,428	59,935	57,210
Total	$ 198,780	$ 185,851	$ 113,866	$ 273,472	$ 184,863	$ 183,180

Let's say we want to look at the overall picture for January. We will take this chart and post it in the employees' lounge. Using the mouse, select a range: in this example, we're using A5:B10, which includes the salespeople's names and their figures for the month. Then, follow these steps:

1 Click once on the ChartWizard button on the toolbar. Your cursor changes to resemble a tiny bar chart.

2 To insert this chart, click on another worksheet tab. This is optional: you can place the chart in the same worksheet.

3 Click in the cell that you want to become the top left corner cell of your data range.

As you see in figure 18.4, the wizard starts asking you questions. The first one is about the range you want to plot. Although you've preselected it, you can change it here, if you like. Simply highlight the range, type **$A$4:$B$11**, accept it, and go on to the next step.

Fig. 18.4
Even though you pre-
selected the range, you
can still override it; just
type a new name here
or select a new range
with your mouse.

In the Step 2 of 5 dialog box, you get to choose the chart type. Look at figure 18.5: there are several chart types. Three that might make sense for this data are Pie, 3-D Pie, and Doughnut. What's the difference? Just cosmetic. 3-D pies look more professional than the flat 2-D variety, and a doughnut is another appetizing prospect. Click on one of them, then on Next.

In the Step 3 of 5 dialog box, the ChartWizard gives you more options for customizing the chart. Select option 7, which will label each slice with the salesperson's name and the percentage that is his or her contribution to January's total sale amount. Then click Next.

Fig. 18.5
Don't worry if you make the wrong selection here. You can always go back and change it.

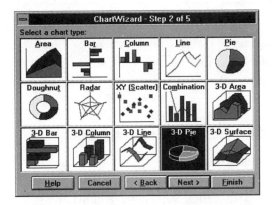

In the Step 4 of 5 dialog box, the ChartWizard (see fig. 18.6), gives you a preview of the actual chart you've created. The wizard was clever enough to discern that the values you wanted to plot (that is, the Y axis) are placed in a column, not a row. Let's see what happens if we select Rows under Data Series in. One pie, no slices. No good. Quickly, click next to Columns to restore the chart, and then click Next.

Fig. 18.6
Now is the time to evaluate. Is this the look you're after? If not, click on Back and try another one.

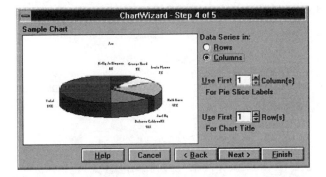

In the Step 5 of 5 dialog box, you enter a title for the chart: click the box under Chart Title, and type a title, such as **January Sales**. Click Finish; the chart is placed in the worksheet.

You can include more than one value series in a chart. For example, to chart the sales figures for January, February, and March, select columns A, B, C, and D before you start the ChartWizard.

 **<Caution>** Pie charts can depict only one value series at a time, regardless of the number of value series you select before you start the ChartWizard. The wizard will only act on the first value series from the left.

I want to resize the chart

To resize the chart, click once—anywhere on the chart—and notice the handles around the frame. Drag any of the handles in or out to reduce or enlarge the size, then click outside the frame to de-select it.

I want to move the chart

If you just want to move the chart within the current worksheet, click it once, then drag the entire frame to a new location. But if you want to move it to another worksheet, use the Clipboard to transport it, as follows:

1 Click once anywhere on the chart.

2 Press Ctrl+X to cut it and place it in the Clipboard.

3 Select the target worksheet's tab.

4 Move your cursor to where you want the chart pasted, click once, and press Ctrl+V to paste it. The cell you've selected is the upper left corner of the chart

I changed my mind. How do I change this chart to a bar chart?

Come to think of it, you may want that monthly sales chart to be a bar chart. Don't worry, you don't need to re-create the chart. Just click once anywhere within its frame, and notice the tiny chart toolbar that pops up. Click on the drop-down arrow next to the Chart Type button, and select any of the bar charts you see in figure 18.7.

Doughnut or pie... Which chart do I use?

Even if you slept through this class in high school, don't let charts intimidate you. All a chart does is give you a clearer idea of how your numbers look. Would you rather look at row after row of numbers, or a color picture that tells the same story? (You only get one guess.)

But which chart do you use? One size doesn't fit all. For some types of information you need pie charts, and for others, a line chart is more appropriate. Ever seen the Dow Jones chart on the evening news as a pie chart? Of course not.

When you want to portray a trend over a period of time, you use a line chart. If, on the other hand, you want to look at your portfolio and see what portion of your money is invested in junk bonds, use a pie chart.

Here's a breakdown of all the Excel charts and what they're good for:

Chart type	Button	What it does
Bar/Column		Comparison between values in one or more series. For example, you can show how much money each of your salespeople generated over a period of 3 months.
Pie/Doughnut/Radar		The relationship between the parts and the whole. For example, the ethnic background of your state. Only one series can be plotted.
Line		A trend, or the relationship between the values and a time period (so that the X axis is the time). Often used to depict stock activities.
Area/Surface		Illustrates cumulative values. You can use this chart for your sales figures, whereby each level adds to the total sale amount.
XY		Shows the correlation between several value series (for example, between weather data and sales figures).

Fig. 18.7
You don't get as many choices here as in the ChartWizard, but make a selection anyway, and you can later fine-tune it to have all the bells and whistles you need.

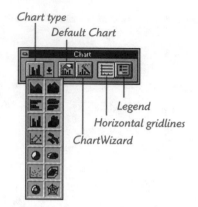

Chart type
Default Chart
Legend
Horizontal gridlines
ChartWizard

(Tip)

If the new chart looks strange, you can clean it up by clicking on the Default Chart button on the floating Chart toolbar. This may not be the chart you want, but in most cases, it's easier to customize from this point than if your chart has been previously bent out of shape.

{Note}

One final type of chart is a **combination chart,** which, like a combination pizza, gives you more than one thing layered on top of another. In this case, you can show a column chart with an area chart to show how trends in two areas are related (for example, how the trend toward two pizzas for the price of one affects the comsumption of pizza).

Fancy formatting

Your in-laws are dropping by for a short visit and the refrigerator is empty. You can buy a strawberry pie at your local grocery store, but you won't fool them: they'll recognize that ready-made look. Now is the time to prove to them that their daughter married the right guy: decorate that generic-looking pastry and dazzle them with your *famous, home-made* strawberry pie. They'll never know the difference. But be prepared: from now on you'll be expected to bring your *famous, home-made* pumpkin pie to every Thanksgiving dinner.

Your bosses are like your in-laws: They need to be impressed. So let's decorate that pie chart.

Here, have a slice

Look at figure 18.8. The slice labeled Joel Ng is too thin. It's practically hidden.

Fig. 18.8
You can see a dark line by Joel's name, but is that a slice or a hole? It's hard to tell.

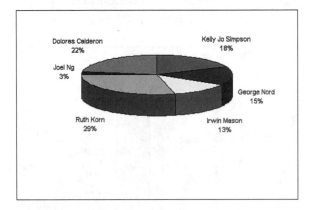

What you need is to take that slice and slide it out, so that it's easier to see. Follow these steps:

1 Double-click on the chart to switch to the chart editor. Notice that your menus are slightly different. Choose Format or Insert, and you'll see options you've never seen there before.

2 Click once on the slice you want to slide out. Notice the handles around it. This sometimes requires practice, so if it didn't work at first attempt, try again.

3 Gently drag the slice out as far as you want. Your pie should look like that shown in figure 18.9.

Fig. 18.9
I'll have that thin slice, please. I'm on a diet. A la mode? Sure.

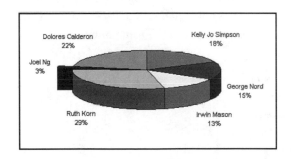

I can't tell which is which

If you use a multiple-value series, like the one in figure 18.10, where there is more than one value charted for each time period, it's hard to tell what each bar stands for. Each group of bars is identified on the X axis, but the individual bars are only identifiable by different colors.

Fig. 18.10
No, this is not the Manhattan skyline. It's an overcrowded bar chart. Too confusing for its own good.

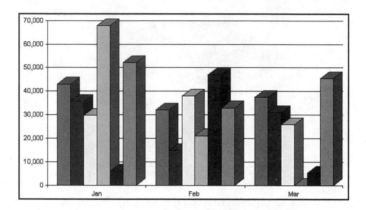

What you need are **legends**, which are labels you place outside the chart. To create legends, double-click anywhere on the chart, and click on the Legend button on the floating Chart toolbar. A **legend box** similar to the one in figure 18.11 gets inserted next to your chart. You can move it somewhere else within the frame, if you wish.

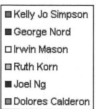

Plain English, please!

A legend on a chart is like the legend on your roadmap, which shows you that little lines stand for railroad tracks, and little bumpy shaded ridges represent mountain ranges. With an Excel chart, the **legend** helps the reader read the data that's been summarized visually—by relating the colors or shading pattern of the chart element to the name or type of data being displayed.

Fig. 18.11
Legends are labels. Clear and simple. What sets them apart from regular labels is that they're placed outside the chart, and not directly on the objects they're describing.

I can't tell what these bars represent

Legends are great for identifying what the different pieces of a chart represent. But they're not enough. Exactly how much money does that red bar represent? To label the different parts of your chart with their actual values, follow these steps:

1 Double-click the chart.

2 Right-click any of the value elements (bar, line, and so on). You'll get a shortcut menu with several options. One of them is Insert Data Labels, so click on it.

3 Select Show <u>V</u>alue and click on OK. As you can see in figure 18.12, the actual amounts are inserted as labels.

Fig. 18.12
Reading specific values for chart elements becomes a breeze when you place data labels on them.

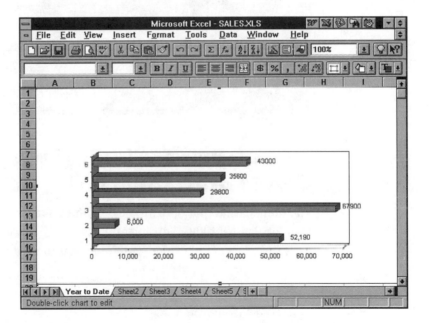

Q&A

> *My legend is confusing. Can't I label the slices, so that I don't need the legend?*
>
> No problem. Double-click the chart, then right-click anywhere. Select Insert Data Labels, and click on Show Label and Percent. You'll notice that the Legend box is still there, so click once on the Legend button in the floating Chart toolbar, and it disappears.

I want to place the labels somewhere else

Data labels can be placed above or below the bars in a chart (in all charts except pies), and you can even choose between vertical and horizontal alignment. To do so, double-click a chart, move your pointer to any of the labels, and right-click it. Select Format Data Labels. Then click the Alignment tab to display the Format Data Labels dialog box, shown in figure 18.13. Make your selection.

Fig. 18.13
For a nice effect, select Vertical orientation to place labels inside bars.

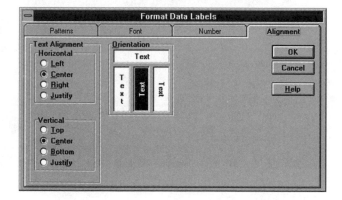

These labels are boring! Can't I dress them up?

You don't have to put up with the default font and color that Excel picks for your labels. Just right-click any of the labels, and select Format Data Labels. Let's say you want to use red Arial, 14-point fonts. Just follow these steps:

1 Click on the Font tab.

2 Select Arial from the Font list box.

3 Select the color.

4 Select the size, and choose OK to accept the changes.

The X axis is too crowded

Look at figure 18.14. Not all the X-axis labels are there because of the limited space.

Fig. 18.14
Looks like you've run out of real estate in this cityscape.

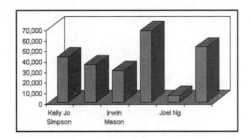

You can either try a smaller font or change the text alignment so that the words are written vertically. Double-click the chart, and right-click any of the X-axis labels. From the shortcut menu, select Format Axis, and click the Alignment tab. Now click in any of the vertical-alignment boxes, and, as you see in figure 18.15, your chart looks much better.

Fig. 18.15
Sure, you need to tilt your head to look at the labels, but at least they all fit.

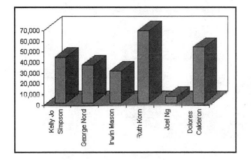

But what is this chart all about?

Your chart is meaningless unless you identify it with a title. As you saw earlier, you can specify a title in Step 5, the final step of the ChartWizard. But if you skipped that step or need to change the title, it's not too late:

- **Create a new title.** Right-click anywhere within the chart, and select Edit Object. Right click again anywhere within the chart box, but not on the chart itself, and select Insert Titles. From the Titles dialog box, select Chart Title, and click on OK. Type the title, and press Enter.

- **Modify an existing title.** Double-click the title, and make your changes.

- **Modify the title's format.** To select a different font or color, right-click anywhere within the title, and select Edit Object. Right-click within the title again, and select Format Chart Title. Click on the Font tab, and make your selections.

- **Move a title.** Double-click once on the title, then drag it to its new location.

Controlling the Y axis

One of the decisions the ChartWizard makes on your behalf is which values to place on the Y axis. The chart in figure 18.16 shows values from 0 to 70,000, with different value points at increments of 10,000.

There is a problem with this representation: a bar representing a value like 44,500 is hard to spot. As you saw earlier, you can add data labels to the bars, but they may clutter the display. A better way is to change the incremental value to something smaller than 10,000.

Fig. 18.16
There are three sets of labels on this chart, which make the chart too cluttered.

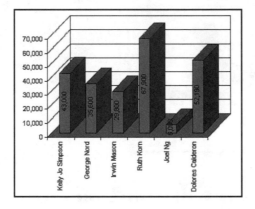

To control the minimum or maximum figures, or change the increment value, follow these steps:

1 Double-click the chart.

2 Right-click any of the Y-axis labels.

3 Select Format Axis.

4 Click on the Scale tab.

5 As you see in figure 18.17, all the values have been entered automatically for you. To change any of them, double-click the value box, and type a new value. For example, to change the increment value for Major Unit, double-click the value box, and type **5000**.

Fig. 18.17
Double-clicking the value box and entering a new value turns off the automatic mode (or you can turn it off by unchecking the box).

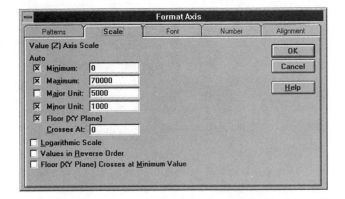

Something out of nothing: showing zeros in a chart

Where there's a zero in your data, your chart shows...well, nothing. But what if you want to highlight the zero so that it's obvious? This may be a sales-tracking spreadsheet. In figure 18.18, for example, it looks like something's missing where Kelly Jo's sales should be shown. Actually, though, Kelly Jo didn't have any sales at all. And Joel sold something, but he didn't do nearly enough because he had a sales quota of $20,000 (and he didn't meet it).

Fig. 18.18
Looks like a mouth with a missing tooth, right? Next, we'll fit it with a denture.

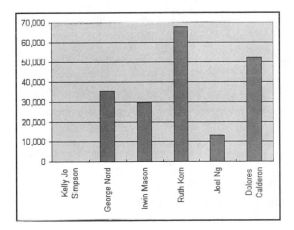

There's a way you can have the "underachievers" stand out. Just put their bars below the X axis:

1 Double-click the chart.

2 Right-click the Y axis.

3 Select Format Axis.

4 Click the Scale tab.

5 Notice the × next to Category (X) Axis Crosses At:? Turn off the automatic mode by clicking the check box, and replace the zero with **20000**. Click OK.

6 To make sure that everybody understands that $20,000 is the quota line, right-click that line; you get handles on each end.

7 Select Format Axis.

8 Click on the Patterns tab.

9 Select Custom. Play with different Style, Color, and Weight combinations, and watch the Sample box for the resulting effect.

10 When you're happy with the result, click OK. The chart in figure 18.19 makes it very clear that Kelly Jo and Joel are in trouble.

Fig. 18.19
The bars below the 20,000 line are pointing the other way because Kelly Jo made no sales, so her reverse bar is at the zero point. Joel sold a little over $13,000.

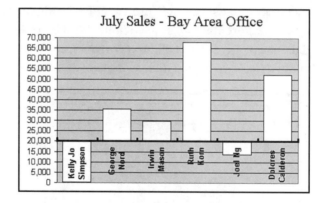

Yuck! These bright colors are nauseating!

Don't worry: just as you'd expect, you don't have to put up with the default color schemes. You can easily apply your own colors. This action is different from chart type to chart type, so read on.

Much as you'd like to, you can't change all the colors in a pie chart, line chart, or a multiple-series bar chart in one fell swoop. You need to deal with each element individually, as follows:

1 Double-click the chart.

2 Right-click the line, bar, or slice you want to modify.

3 Select Format Data Point.

4 From the middle of the dialog box shown in figure 18.20, select any color you want.

5 Click OK.

Fig. 18.20
Although these colors may look fine on your monitor, if your printer is of the black-ink variety, try playing with different patterns instead of colors.

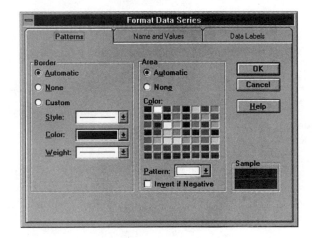

(Tip)

Single-series bar charts normally display all the bars in the same color, so right-clicking any of the bars will apply to all of them.

Q&A

I modified my worksheet, but I don't see any changes!

If you're configured for automatic recalculation, which you can do in the Tools menu through the Options command, the changes to your worksheet are automatically reflected in your chart. If not, you'll need to press F9 to refresh the chart.

Printing your chart

When it's time to print your chart, you have two options: you can print the chart as part of the worksheet or on a page by itself. Your CPA may need to do some serious analysis, which requires the combo printout, but your employees only get to see the motivational charts you want to show. Also, if you prepare overhead transparencies for a presentation, you'll need to print the chart as a full page.

 {Note}

See Chapter 23 for information on embedding Excel charts in a PowerPoint presentation.

 (Tip)

Although your screen may be able to display your chart in color, you may have a black-ink laser or inkjet printer. Always preview your selection before you print it—the preview screen shows the colors translated to shades of grey. You may want to replace some colors or play with patterns to make the chart more legible.

Printing the chart with the worksheet

To print the chart alongside the worksheet, select the print area, then click the Print Preview button on the toolbar to make sure that it all fits nicely. If you don't like the layout, and want to move the chart a bit or resize some of the text, click Close, make your changes, and then return to Print Preview.

Printing only the chart

When you need to print the chart on a page by itself, double-click the chart and select Print Preview. Happy? Click the Print button.

19

Printing Your Worksheets

In this chapter:

- What's the best way to print a worksheet?
- How do I select a printer?
- How do I rearrange the pieces on the page?
- How many pages will this worksheet need?
- Can I squeeze my entire worksheet onto one page?

Excel worksheets come in all different sizes and shapes. So how do you fit big worksheets onto small pieces of paper?

My hometown is a tiny place, a few miles from end to end. If you blink while you're driving through, you'll miss it completely. The people who live here love the place. So do the folks who publish maps, because they have no trouble fitting every street and avenue on the standard-sized fold-out maps you get at gas stations.

It's not so easy to put together a map of a really big city, though, like Los Angeles or Chicago. How do you squeeze 400 square miles onto one of those fold-out maps? Well, if you're a map publisher, you use every trick in the book. You shrink the streets and avenues into smaller sizes. You divide the big city into smaller neighborhoods and give each one its own map. You spend a lot of time making sure all that information fits on the paper.

Like cities, Excel worksheets come in all different sizes and shapes. The trouble is, you'll almost always want to print your worksheet on plain old letter paper—8 1/2 × 11 inches. How do you fit big worksheets onto small pieces of paper? You use the same tricks the mapmakers use: You shrink rows and columns to a size that will fit on the page. You divide the worksheet into smaller sections, then give each of these "neighborhoods" its own page.

Best of all, you don't have to worry for even an instant about folding up your printout and stuffing it the glove compartment.

Can't I just push a button and print?

 On Excel's Standard toolbar, there's a button you can click to print your worksheet automatically. If you want instant results, just click the Print button and wait for your pages to fly out of the printer. Be careful, though!

Here are just a few of the things that can go wrong when you click the Print button:

- Your worksheet doesn't quite fit on the page, so your column full of totals winds up lost and lonely on its own page.

- One or two columns aren't wide enough, so you see ###### instead of the numbers you expect.

- You've selected the wrong printer, so you have to wander through the halls like a bloodhound, trying to track down your hard copy.

OK, so what's the best way to print a worksheet?

There's one surefire way to get perfect printouts every single time. It's a simple three-step process:

   1 Click the Print Preview button. Excel changes the display so you see exactly what your printout will look like on paper. See figure 19.1 for a typical example.

2 Use the Setup button to make any necessary adjustments to the margins. Position the selection where you want it on the page, and add headers and footers if you want. You can even ask Excel to force your worksheet to print on a specific number of pages.

   3 Now that your worksheet looks just right, it's OK to click the Print button.

Fig. 19.1

When you click the Print Preview button, Excel shows you exactly what your worksheet will look like on paper.

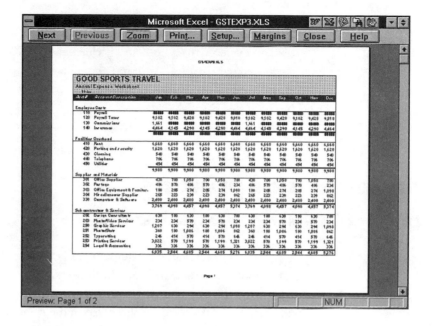

While you're previewing your worksheet, here are some tools that are available to help you make adjustments:

- If there's anything not quite right with your worksheet, click the **Setup** button. The Setup dialog box lets you fine-tune the look of your printout without wasting paper.

- Click on **Zoom** to switch between the big picture and a close-up view.

- Use the **Next** and **Previous** buttons to skip between pages. Look at the bottom left corner of the screen to see how many pages Excel has used for your selection.

- Use the **Margins** button, and Excel will show thin dotted lines along the margins for the page, headers, and footers. You can drag the lines up and down, left and right, to adjust margins instantly. You can also adjust column widths.

- **Print** lets you send the job to the printer. (Just make sure you've selected the right one!)

- **Close** sends you back to the worksheet editing view.

- Not sure what to do next? Click the **Help** button.

(Tip)

If most of your worksheets are simple one-page jobs, use Print Preview to confirm that everything fits. Quickly check that the Next and Previous buttons are grayed out. That way, you won't stand by helplessly (as I did once) while 60 pages of nearly blank printout pours out of the printer because you didn't set the print area correctly.

The secrets of printing great-looking worksheets

When you're building a worksheet, paper is the last thing on your mind. You're more concerned with making sure that the formulas are correct, that rows are the right height, that columns are wide enough to show the numbers inside, and that all your data shows up in the right bars on your charts.

That's OK, because once you switch into Print Preview mode, it's easy to rearrange nearly every aspect of the printout. Most often, you'll use the Page Setup dialog box, with its four tabs that let you control the way your printout looks.

Choose the pieces to print

You can have up to 1,069,547,520 cells in a single workbook. If you tried to print them all out, it would take more than 2 million sheets of paper, which means you'd probably have to buy your own acre of rain forest. Make it easy on Excel (and on the rain forest) by being specific about the section you want to print:

- **I've already selected the section I want to print.** You and Excel will get along just fine. When the Print dialog box pops up, choose Selection in the area labeled Print What.

- **I want to print the worksheet I'm working with now.** Then you don't need to do anything special. If you don't specifically set aside an area to be printed, Excel assumes that you want to print the current work-sheet. In this case, the print area starts with cell A1 and extends to the furthest cell that has a value or formula in it.

 Be careful when you ask Excel to print the entire worksheet, especially if you've added formulas or lookup tables below or to the right of the main worksheet. Excel considers everything you enter to be part of the worksheet. If you don't want your lookup table to print, you'll need to define the print area more precisely.

- **I want to print the same area every time.** If you have a complex worksheet, with lots of detailed sections that you don't want to see on your printout, you'll get tired of selecting the same area every time you print the worksheet. So don't. Instead, tell Excel which section you want to use as the standard print area. It's not difficult, but the technique is a little tricky.

To print the same area of your worksheet every time you print, use this procedure:

1 Choose File, Page Setup, and click the Sheet tab. You'll see the Page Setup dialog box, shown in figure 19.2.

2 Click in the Print Area box until the insertion point appears there.

3 Click in your worksheet on the cell that you want to use for the upper left corner of the print area. Hold down the mouse button and drag while you select the entire region you want to print. (You may have to move the Page Setup dialog box out of the way while you do this.) As you drag the selection, the cell addresses appear in the dialog box.

4 When you've made your selection, click OK to clear the dialog box, or click on another tab to continue formatting the rest of the worksheet.

Fig. 19.2
Use this Sheet tab of the Page Setup dialog box to define an area that will be printed by default for a given worksheet.

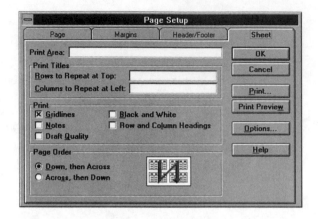

(Tip)

When you define the print area, Excel adds it to the list of named ranges. If you need to select it (maybe to zoom in and double-check some figures?), just click on the down arrow next to the name box (just to the left of the formula bar), and choose Print Area from the list. Voilá! The entire region is now highlighted.

<Caution>

Once you've defined a print area, Excel *always* prints that area—even if you've added other things to your worksheet (unless, of course, you redefine the print area to include your changes).

To temporarily override the defined print area, select the range you want to print, choose File, Print and click on Selection.

Pick the right paper (and turn it the right direction)

Most printers hold regular letter-size paper—8 1/2 × 11 inches. A few have trays that hold legal paper (14 inches long). Most printers can also handle special paper sizes, as long as you're willing to feed it in manually.

With Windows' help, Excel lets you choose the right size paper for your job. Then it asks you to make a more important decision. No, not paper or plastic—portrait or landscape?

- In **Portrait** mode, the page is oriented with the long side running from top to bottom. This is the way you typically see letters, and it's ideal when you're using Excel to print a list of three or four columns.

- In **Landscape** orientation, the page is turned on its side so that your rows read from left to right on the long edge of the paper. Choose this option when you have a lot of columns to show, as in a yearly budget.

To pick a paper size and orientation, choose File, Page Setup, and click the Page tab to display the dialog box shown in figure 19.3. Then set the options you want.

Fig. 19.3

If the naming clues aren't enough, Excel shows you a picture to remind you which is Portrait mode and which is Landscape mode.

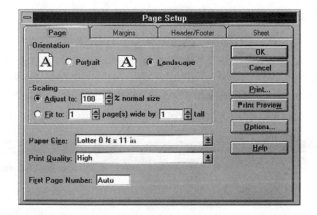

{Note}

There's one more good reason *not* to use the Print button on the Standard toolbar. If your printer is set for portrait orientation and your worksheet is designed for landscape mode, you'll get a printout with lots of white space along the bottom; meanwhile, your data will be distributed across two or three pages instead of being neatly arranged on one page.

Arrange your rows and columns

When you first create a workbook, Excel sets up common margins for every sheet in the book. These **margins**—which vary, depending on the kind of printer you're using—define how much white space will appear on each of the four edges around your worksheet. Think of the margins as being a fence around your worksheet. Inside that fence, you can move pieces of your worksheet around to your heart's content. But they can't leave the fenced-in area.

If you have a lot of data to show—as in a 15-month budget—you might want to push the fences out to give your data more room on the page. Or you can decrease the margins on the right if you want to leave yourself room to make comments.

I need help setting the margins

There's a tab on the Page Setup dialog box that lets you set margins by typing in numbers. But there's an easier way that also allows you to see exactly what your new margins will look like. From the Print Preview screen, click the Margins button. You'll see a string of small black boxes ringing the worksheet, plus thin dashed lines that represent each margin (see fig. 19.4 for an example).

Fig. 19.4
Click the Margins button, then drag the dotted lines to give your worksheet more (or less) white space.

Top and bottom margins are set off by four sets of dashed lines—one pair for the page and another pair that defines where the header and footer go.

Left and right margins are shown by single dotted lines on either side of the page.

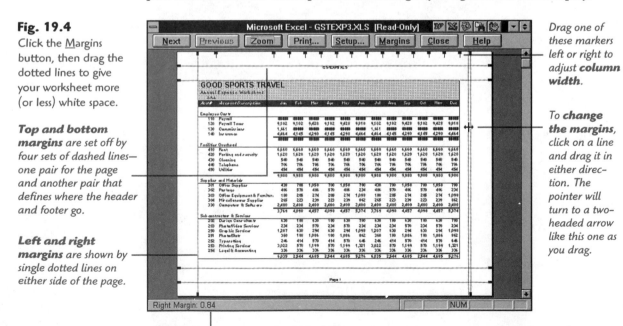

Drag one of these markers left or right to adjust **column width**.

To **change the margins**, *click on a line and drag it in either direction. The pointer will turn to a two-headed arrow like this one as you drag.*

To see the new **margin settings**, *look in the lower left corner. This number will change as you move the margin marker.*

I want my worksheet centered on the page

If you leave the printing up to Excel, your worksheet will be jammed into the upper left corner of your page, like a shy teenager at a high school dance. For a big worksheet, you might not notice the difference, but if your worksheet is small, the effect is ugly and a little strange. Fortunately, you can order Excel to automatically center your worksheet between the margins. Choose File, Page Setup, click the Margins tab, and then check the boxes to center either horizontally or vertically (as shown in fig. 19.5). Check both boxes if you want the worksheet perfectly centered.

Fig. 19.5

Doesn't the worksheet look strange jammed into the top left corner like that? Try using the Center on Page options.

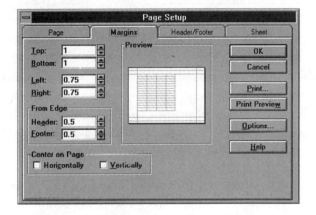

Use these guidelines for choosing your options:

- If the worksheet is relatively shallow—less than half a page deep—check only the box labeled Horizontally. This centers the sheet from side to side, but starts it near the top of the page.

- For larger worksheets that fill up all or most of the page, check both Center on Page options.

Add the finishing touches

How many vice-presidents and senior managers will be looking over your worksheet? If the answer is one or more, sweat the details. Here are three tips to help make your worksheet better looking and a lot more readable:

- **Get rid of those gridlines.** Look in the Sheet tab of the Page Setup dialog box, and make sure there's no × in the check box labeled Gridlines. If you want to help people follow rows and columns, there are much better ways than using Excel's gridlines. Either add borders to the cells you've selected, or use one of the AutoFormat options that includes shading for alternate rows.

- **Use titles if you need them.** If your worksheet extends over more than one page, your readers will need help figuring out what each column and row contains. On the Sheet tab, there's a space to define a row and/or column to use as titles. Click in the box, then choose the row or column that contains the titles for your worksheet. Now Excel will repeat the titles on each printed page, so you can see what's what.

If you've used background shading on your worksheet, you may have a great-looking screen, but the results can be horrendously ugly on the page because the tints are converted into gray smudges. The solution? Open the Page Setup dialog box, click the Sheet tab, and check the box labeled Black and White.

- **Use headers and footers to dress up your worksheet.** By default, Excel inserts the file name for your workbook in a header at the top of the page, and adds a page number along the bottom. Your boss probably doesn't care what the file name is, and that page number looks pretty silly on a one-page worksheet, doesn't it?

When you choose File, Page Setup and click the Header/Footer tab, you get access to all sorts of useful options for these labels (see fig. 19.6). Excel includes a set of preconfigured headers and footers that mix page numbers, worksheet names, dates, and your name.

If you can't find a header or footer on the list that matches what you want to say, go ahead and create your own, as I've done in figure 19.7. (Note that the header and footer options work exactly the same.)

Fig. 19.6
Does your boss really care about your workbook's file name? Of course not. Use these settings to make your own headers and footers.

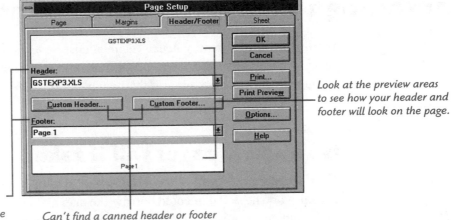

Look at the preview areas to see how your header and footer will look on the page.

Choose a prebuilt header or footer from the drop-down list. To remove it completely, choose (none) from the top of the list.

Can't find a canned header or footer that says what you want? Press one of these buttons to plug in your own.

Fig. 19.7
This custom footer puts a warning on the left, with today's date and time on the right. It's also formatted in bold so the footer will stand out more than usual.

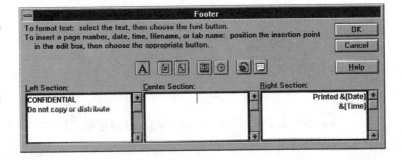

Type any text you want in the three text boxes. Everything in the middle box is centered on the page, while the left and right boxes are aligned against their own margins.

To insert a code for the date, page number, time, and so on, position the insertion point, and click one of the buttons in the center of the dialog box. Be sure the ampersand (&) is included—it tells Excel, "Okay, the next thing coming up is a code, not actual text."

To change the formatting of your header or footer, select the text, and click the button labeled with a large A. The dialog box that opens works just like the one you use to format a cell.

I'm through tinkering ... can I print now?

Thanks to Print Preview, you can get an almost perfect picture of what your pages will look like when they roll out of the printer. When you're ready to print, just click the Print button, set the number of copies (if you want more than one), and click OK.

How many pages will it take?

When you click the Print button, Excel automatically inserts **page breaks** in your worksheet. If you could borrow the map makers' printing press, you could put your worksheet on a single sheet of paper divided into 8 1/2 × 11-inch sections. On that printing press, each page break would create one of the lines where you'd fold the page.

How does Excel know where to put the page breaks? It doesn't, really. It just looks to see how many rows and columns will fit on each page, then plops in a page break at regular intervals. It's easy to spot these breaks, which take the form of dashed vertical and horizontal lines, right on your worksheet.

Can I add my own page breaks?

Absolutely. In fact, the best way to make sure that Excel prints your worksheet the way you want is to insert page breaks precisely where you need them. Select the cell that's one row below and one column to the right of the place where you want the page to break. Then choose Insert, Page Break. The page breaks (the dashed lines) appear above and to the left of the cell pointer, as shown in figure 19.8.

To select either a horizontal or vertical break only, select an entire row or column, and then choose Insert, Page Break.

To remove a page break, position the pointer in the cell just below or to the right of the page break, then choose Insert, Remove Page Break.

Fig. 19.8
These page breaks (the dashed lines) appear above and to the left of the cell pointer. You can also choose to insert page breaks between certain columns or rows.

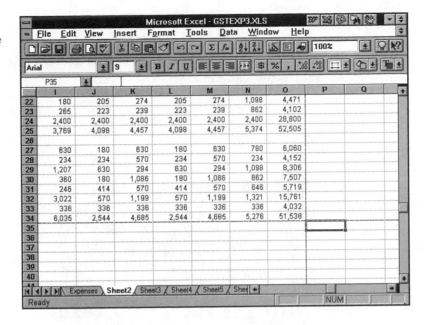

Q&A

I can't get my worksheet to print right. All the pages break at the wrong places. What should I do?

Remove all the manual page breaks and start over. First, select the entire worksheet (click on the gray area just above the heading for row 1), then choose Insert, Remove Page Break. Now click the Print Preview button, and try it again.

My worksheet's a little too big. Can I force it to fit?

I saved this piece for last, because it's probably the coolest thing Excel does. When you choose File, Page Setup, look on the Page tab for the section labeled Scaling. With a few clicks, you can reduce your printout to as little as 10% or as much as 400% of its normal size. By changing the scale, you can squeeze more rows and columns onto each page, just the way you can fit more streets and avenues on a map by using a smaller scale.

But how do you know what values to put in the scaling box? You don't need to know. Just tell Excel to fit your worksheet in a specific number of pages.

In our sample worksheet, for example, the final column doesn't fit on the first page. We could experiment with the scaling until we found the right setting, but it's easier to simply check the box labeled Fit to 1 page wide by 1 tall in the Page Setup dialog box.

With this box checked, as shown in figure 19.9, Excel automatically rescales the page to 87% of its normal size. The result is a perfect fit, as you can see in figure 19.10.

Fig. 19.9

Use Excel's shrink-to-fit box to squeeze your entire worksheet onto a single page.

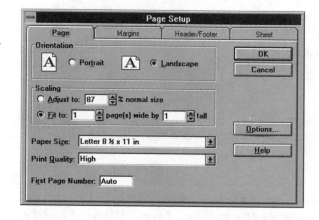

Fig. 19.10

The result is a perfect fit!

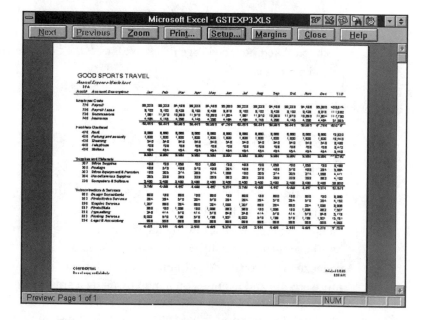

If your worksheet goes on for several pages, don't put anything in the box for the number of pages tall in the Page Setup dialog box.

20 Using Excel and Word Together

In this chapter:

- Where can I temporarily store stuff between applications?

- What if I need to do the same old report with different data next quarter?

- How do I move data back and forth between Word and Excel?

- When I change these numbers, can I make sure the numbers in my memo change automatically, too?

- I want to save a worksheet and a document as one file

Great teams do great work. OK, maybe Word and Excel don't belong on the same list as Lennon and McCartney, but they make a great team just the same.

reat teams do great work. If you don't believe me, just think of the most productive partnerships of our time. Laurel and Hardy. Ruth and Gehrig. Lennon and McCartney. Lemmon and Matthau.

OK, maybe Word and Excel don't belong on the same list as Lennon and McCartney, but they make a great team just the same. With all due respect to PowerPoint, these two are the superstars of the Microsoft Office. For day-to-day documents that mix words and numbers in convincing fashion, you can't beat this team. For more complicated jobs, the two occasionally bicker and step on each other's toes, and sometimes getting them to work with each other is like trying to get Simon and Garfunkel back together.

If you think Word is just for words and Excel is just for numbers, think again. All those words and numbers have a way of wandering from one document to another, depending on what you're trying to communicate. And when you have a complicated message to get across, Word and Excel are perfect partners. Most of the time, anyway.

How can Word and Excel team up to work for you? In this chapter, we'll look at the simple—and not-so-simple—ways you can move words into your worksheets and numbers into your memos and reports.

What is OLE? And why doesn't it work sometimes?

"oh-lay"

¡Olé! ¡Viva la revolución! ¡Hasta la vista! Oh, sorry, I got carried away. OLE is pronounced "oh-lay," just like the cheers you hear at a bullfight, but it's actually an abbreviation for the tongue-twisting phrase **object linking and embedding**. What a mouthful, huh? It might as well be in Spanish, or maybe even in Martian.

So let's break it down, piece by piece, and see what OLE really does when you use the Office programs together.

Objects are simply pieces of data, like letters, worksheets, charts, and tables. Technically, every file you create is an object, although most people would never think of it that way.

When you **embed** one object inside another, you create a **compound document**. For better or worse, you've played Dr. Frankenstein, taking part of another body and transplanting it into the body of your original document. With two or more objects in the same file, your document assumes a split personality. When you double-click on one of the **embedded objects**, for example, the menus and toolbars change, even though it looks like you're still in the same document.

Having a split personality isn't all bad. If you transplant an Excel range into a Word document,

for example, you can do much more sophisticated calculations than you can with a simple Word table.

If you want to get really fancy, you can create links between two documents. **Linking** is more like Mr. Spock than Dr. Frankenstein: when you link two objects, you create something like a Vulcan mind meld. There's no physical connection between the two objects, but if one changes, so does the other. Linking is the ideal way to make sure different people work with the same data, all the time.

And as long as we're talking about personality disorders, let's talk about an inescapable reality of all this OLE stuff. *Sometimes it just doesn't work.* It's not your fault; it's Windows' fault. On a scale of 1 to 10, this OLE stuff has a degree of difficulty of about 90. If you try to do complex object linking and embedding, you can expect your computer to do weird things, including unexpectedly refusing to work until you turn it off and then back on again.

If you want to experiment with OLE, go right ahead. But always make sure you save your documents first. And don't be surprised if it takes two or three tries before you get it to work.

I don't want to retype all this stuff

Your boss just sent you a piece of E-mail with a Word document attached. This memo (which looks a heckuva lot like the one in fig. 20.1) contains the names, birthdates, and departmental assignments of all the employees in your company. She wants you to transfer that information into an Excel worksheet, so you can add information about salaries, commissions, and accrued vacation time.

Fig. 20.1
How do you move this list of names from a Word document into an Excel worksheet? The first step is to copy it to the Windows Clipboard, so you can paste it into a fresh, new worksheet.

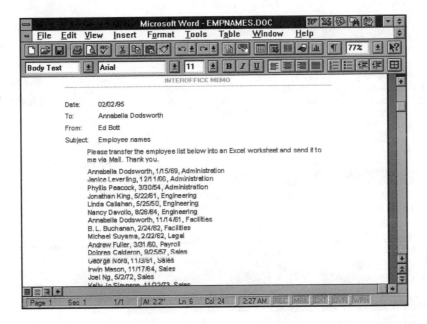

Count your blessings that the boss didn't print this memo on a piece of paper and leave it on your chair. If she had, you'd have to retype every word (and probably make a mistake or three along the way, if you're a two-fingered typist like me). Because it's in a Word file, though, you can automate the whole process. After you select the text from the Word document, copy it onto the Windows Clipboard, and then paste it into your Excel worksheet.

How Word and Excel share information

Kelly Jo Simpson	56,789	32,099	99,906
George Nord	21,122	14,800	18,376
Irwin Mason	45,210	37,988	39,333
Ruth Korn	67,900	21,084	0
Joel Ng	12,455	46,980	10,836
Dolores Calderon	29,088	32,900	25,307
Total	$ 232,564	$ 185,851	$ 193,757

Paste with formatting
The spreadsheet range becomes a Word table. Word tries to match fonts, colors, shading, and column widths, but some formatting glitches creep in.

	Jan	Feb	Mar
Kelly Jo Simpson	56,789	32,099	99,906
George Nord	21,122	14,800	18,376
Irwin Mason	45,210	37,988	39,333
Ruth Korn	67,900	21,084	0
Joel Ng	12,455	46,980	10,836
Dolores Calderon	29,088	32,900	25,307
Total	$ 232,564	$ 185,851	$ 193,757

You have a budget in an Excel worksheet. You have a Word document. What happens when you try to move the budget from Excel into Word? That depends on how you do it.

Paste as text
The numbers appear in the Word document just as if you'd typed them in directly. All of the Excel formatting is lost.

	Jan	Feb	Mar
Kelly Jo Simpson	56,789	32,099	99,906
George Nord	21,122	14,800	18,376
Irwin Mason	45,210	37,988	39,333
Ruth Korn	67,900	21,084	0
Joel Ng	12,455	46,980	10,836
Dolores Calderon	29,088	32,900	25,307
Total	$ 232,564	$ 185,851	$ 193,757

Paste as picture or bitmap
An image of the selection appears in the Word document. Double-click to edit it as a picture, although the numbers themselves are no longer there.

	Jan	Feb	Mar
Kelly Jo Simpson	56,789	32,099	99,906
George Nord	21,122	14,800	18,376
Irwin Mason	45,210	37,988	39,333
Ruth Korn	67,900	21,084	0
Joel Ng	12,455	46,980	10,836
Dolores Calderon	29,088	32,900	25,307
Total	$ 232,564	$ 185,851	$ 193,757

Paste with link
The spreadsheet range becomes a Word table. As long as the link is alive, any change in the worksheet causes a matching change in the Word table.

	Jan	Feb	Mar
Kelly Jo Simpson	56,789	32,099	99,906
George Nord	21,122	14,800	18,376
Irwin Mason	45,210	37,988	39,333
Ruth Korn	67,900	21,084	0
Joel Ng	12,455	46,980	10,836
Dolores Calderon	29,088	32,900	25,307
Total	$ 232,564	$ 185,851	$ 193,757

Embed as worksheet
The entire workbook file is stuffed inside the Word document. Double-click to start up Excel and change the numbers.

Yes, you can drag stuff from one program and drop it in another program window. But do you really want to do that? Drag-and-drop editing is fine for moving words and numbers around on the same screen, but it's just a gimmick (and it never seems to work right) when you're using two programs at once. Save yourself a headache. When you want to share data between programs, use Copy, Cut, and Paste instead.

The Clipboard? What's that?

This may be the first time you use the Windows Clipboard, but it sure won't be the last. Whenever two Windows programs get together, you can bet that the Clipboard is going to play a part. How does it work? If you've used a Polaroid camera, you've got a rough idea. Select something—a block of text in a Word document, or a range in an Excel worksheet—and then choose Copy from the shortcut menu to snap an instant photo of the selection.

In most Windows programs, you can press Ctrl+C to copy the selection to the Clipboard. If you never use any other keyboard shortcuts, you should memorize this one and its companions: Ctrl+X to cut and Ctrl+V to paste.

When you capture this chunk of text, Windows stores it in a special holding area while you move the insertion point to the place where you want to paste it. That's the Clipboard. When you reach your destination (in the same program or, as in this example, in a completely different program), choose Edit, Paste to plop whatever's on the Clipboard into the current document.

How do I copy stuff from one place to another?

Here's how to use the Clipboard to copy the list from Word into Excel:

1 In the Word document, use the mouse to highlight the text you want to copy.

2 Right-click the selection, then choose Copy from the shortcut menu.

3 Use the MOM toolbar to switch to Excel. Create a new workbook if necessary, then position the cursor in the cell where you want the pasted-in list to begin.

4 Click the right mouse button, and choose Paste from the shortcut menu. The text on the Clipboard appears in the first column, as shown in figure 20.2.

Fig. 20.2
When you paste a block of text into an Excel worksheet, each line lands in a single cell. It'll take one more step to split each line into three columns.

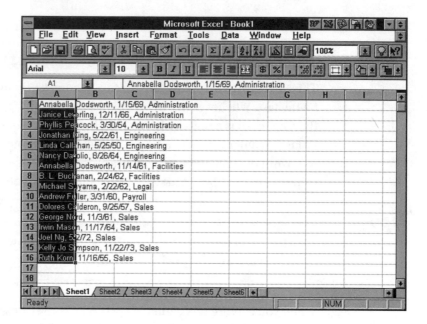

Well, that's not exactly what we had in mind, is it? Each line from the Word document landed in a single cell, even though there are three pieces of distinct information in each one. The trouble is, Windows took our request literally and pasted our snapshot of the Word text from the Clipboard into the worksheet.

How do I split text into columns?

Fortunately, there's an Excel wizard that specializes in splitting text into separate cells. To call the Text To Columns wizard, choose Data, Text To Columns. This wizard (shown in fig. 20.3) takes three steps to work its spell, and the only tricky part is helping Excel figure out where to split each line. The magic word is **delimiter**, and since the pieces in our list are separated by commas, we'll check that box. The preview window at the bottom shows us that the list will split quite nicely, thank you.

Plain English, please!

Although reminiscent of Cole Porter's song, "It's Delightful, It's Delovely, It's Delimiter," a **delimiter** has nothing to do with music. It's a code for your software, like a comma, that tells it that one command is over and the next is about to begin.

Fig. 20.3

How do you split a single line into separate cells? Tell the Wizard what separates each entry in the list (here, the **delimiters** are commas), and let it do the rest.

```
┌─────────────────────────────────────────────────────────────┐
│  —         Convert Text to Columns Wizard - Step 2 of 3       │
├─────────────────────────────────────────────────────────────┤
│  This screen lets you set the delimiters your data contains.  │
│  You can see how your text is affected in the preview below.  │
│                                                               │
│  ┌─Delimiters──────────────────┐   ☐ Treat consecutive delimiters as one │
│   ☒ Tab    ☐ Semicolon  ☒ Comma                              │
│   ☐ Space  ☐ Other: [   ]        Text Qualifier: ["    ▼]     │
│                                                               │
│  ┌─Data Preview────────────────────────────────────────────┐ │
│  │ Annabella Dodsworth │ 1/15/69  │ Administration       ▲ │ │
│  │ Janice Leverling    │ 12/11/66 │ Administration         │ │
│  │ Phyllis Peacock     │ 3/30/54  │ Administration         │ │
│  │ Jonathan King       │ 5/22/61  │ Engineering            │ │
│  │ Linda Callahan      │ 5/25/50  │ Engineering            │ │
│  │ Nancy Davolio       │ 8/26/64  │ Engineering          ▼ │ │
│  │ ◄                                              ►         │ │
│  └──────────────────────────────────────────────────────────┘ │
│                                                               │
│        [ Help ]  [ Cancel ]  [ < Back ]  [ Next > ]  [ Finish ]│
└─────────────────────────────────────────────────────────────┘
```

With a few touch-ups, the boss's memo makes a handsome worksheet. Add a row of bold column headings, resize the columns' fit, draw a box around the data, and give the worksheet a name. The finished worksheet looks like the one in figure 20.4.

Fig. 20.4

It only took a few mouse clicks to move the list of names from our Word document into a well-formatted worksheet.

```
┌─────────────────────────────────────────────────────────────┐
│          Microsoft Excel - EMPNAMES.XLS                       │
├─────────────────────────────────────────────────────────────┤
│  File  Edit  View  Insert  Format  Tools  Data  Window  Help  │
├─────────────────────────────────────────────────────────────┤
│ [toolbar]                                        100%         │
│ Arial        10      B I U                  $ % ,             │
│   A2           Annabella Dodsworth                            │
├──────┬──────────────────┬──────────┬─────────────┬──┬──┬──┬──┤
│      │        A         │    B     │     C       │D │E │F │G │H│
│  1   │ Employee Name    │ Birthdate│ Department  │  │  │  │  │ │
│  2   │ Annabella Dodsworth│ 1/15/69 │ Administration│ │  │  │  │ │
│  3   │ Janice Leverling │ 12/11/66 │ Administration│ │  │  │  │ │
│  4   │ Phyllis Peacock  │ 3/30/54  │ Administration│ │  │  │  │ │
│  5   │ Jonathan King    │ 5/22/61  │ Engineering │  │  │  │  │ │
│  6   │ Linda Callahan   │ 5/25/50  │ Engineering │  │  │  │  │ │
│  7   │ Nancy Davolio    │ 8/26/64  │ Engineering │  │  │  │  │ │
│  8   │ Annabella Dodsworth│ 11/14/61│ Facilities │  │  │  │  │ │
│  9   │ B. L. Buchanan   │ 2/24/62  │ Facilities │  │  │  │  │ │
│ 10   │ Michael Suyama   │ 2/22/62  │ Legal      │  │  │  │  │ │
│ 11   │ Andrew Fuller    │ 3/31/60  │ Payroll    │  │  │  │  │ │
│ 12   │ Dolores Calderon │ 9/25/57  │ Sales      │  │  │  │  │ │
│ 13   │ George Nord      │ 11/3/61  │ Sales      │  │  │  │  │ │
│ 14   │ Irwin Mason      │ 11/17/64 │ Sales      │  │  │  │  │ │
│ 15   │ Joel Ng          │ 5/2/72   │ Sales      │  │  │  │  │ │
│ 16   │ Kelly Jo Simpson │ 11/22/73 │ Sales      │  │  │  │  │ │
│ 17   │ Ruth Korn        │ 11/16/55 │ Sales      │  │  │  │  │ │
│ 18   │                  │          │            │  │  │  │  │ │
├──────┴──────────────────┴──────────┴─────────────┴──┴──┴──┴──┤
│ |◄ ◄ ► ►|  Sheet1 / Sheet2 / Sheet3 / Sheet4 / Sheet5 / Sheet6 │
│ Ready                                            NUM           │
└─────────────────────────────────────────────────────────────┘
```

Q&A

> ***I have several extra columns between my actual data. What happened?***
>
> If you have taken data separated by several spaces, rather than a comma or tab, and you are using a space as your delimiter, you will get blank columns. Be sure to delete any extra blank spaces between your data, or use a different delimiter.

I need to do the same old report next month

And the month after that, and the month after that...

You've added up this month's sales results in an Excel worksheet. The numbers look great (check out fig. 20.5, if you don't believe me), so you want to pass them around, along with an inspirational note and a few congratulations.

You could simply copy the data from your worksheet, paste it into a memo in Word, and print out a sharp-looking memo on your company's letterhead. But what will you do next month? If you simply cut and paste this month's numbers, you'll have to do it all over again when you get next month's sales results. And do it again the month after that, and so on and on and on.

What's your alternative? Instead of just snapping a picture of the data and pasting it into your document, create a link between the Excel spreadsheet and your Word document.

How do links work?

If doing a simple cut-and-paste is like placing a Polaroid snapshot on the page, then creating a **link** is like focusing a remote-controlled security camera on the data you want to copy. When you create a link in your Word document, you're telling Word, "Please keep an eye on this worksheet. If the numbers in the worksheet change, make sure the numbers in this memo change, too."

Fig. 20.5
When you want to create a permanent connection between numbers like these and a Word document, don't just cut and paste—use a **link**.

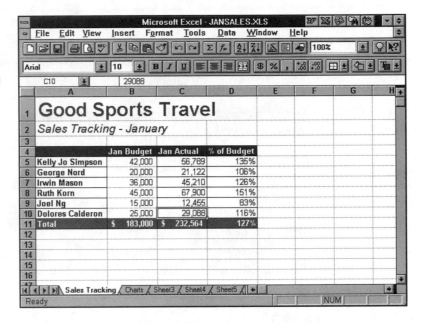

The result will look as if you'd simply pasted in your data, but there's a big difference: next month, when you update the sales worksheet with the new figures, your memo will automatically be updated as well. Add a new set of comments, and your sales report is ready to distribute.

How do I create a link?

To create a link between a document and a worksheet, you start by copying data to the Windows Clipboard. Instead of using the Paste command, though, use a fancier version of this command: Paste Special.

1 In your Excel worksheet, highlight the range you want to copy.

2 Right-click on the selection, and choose Copy from the shortcut menu.

3 Use the MOM toolbar to switch to Word. Create a new document if necessary.

4 Choose Edit, Paste Special. You'll see the Paste Special dialog box, seen in figure 20.6.

5 Choose Paste <u>L</u>ink, and make sure that Formatted Text (RTF) is highlighted. Click OK. It will take a few seconds, but eventually you'll see a new Word table in your document. It should look a lot like the range from your worksheet.

Fig. 20.6
To create a link, choose <u>E</u>dit, Paste <u>S</u>pecial and make sure Paste <u>L</u>ink is checked. The helpful text at the bottom of the box makes it easy to see what your choice will do.

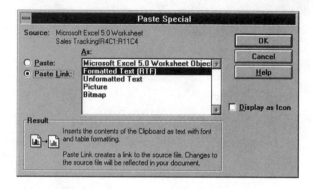

{Note}

RTF is short for **Rich Text Format**. It's a special set of instructions Windows uses to share formatted text between programs that otherwise don't have anything in common. Any time you're not sure how to move data from one place to another, look for an RTF option.

(Tip)

When you copy an Excel worksheet range and paste it into a Word document as a table, it doesn't always look as good as you'd like. That's easy to fix. Just position the insertion point in the table and choose Table, AutoFormat. Pick a format from the list and click OK. If you don't like the results, click the Undo button and try it again with a different format.

Links are especially useful when you're working on a set of documents with other people in your company. Let's say that your sales-tracking worksheet is on a shared directory where your coworkers can see it as well as you. If Bob in Accounting finds a mistake in your figures, he can update the Excel file stored on the network. The next time you open your monthly sales report memo, which is linked to that worksheet, Word will look at the data in the worksheet file and adjust the numbers in your memo. The two documents carry on their conversation without bothering you, and you're assured that the data in your memo is absolutely up-to-date.

With a little cleaning up and some AutoFormatting, the Word memo (with the linked table) looks like the one in figure 20.7.

Fig. 20.7
You can't tell by looking that the table in this Word memo is linked to an Excel worksheet. But if any of the numbers there change, the data in this memo will change, too.

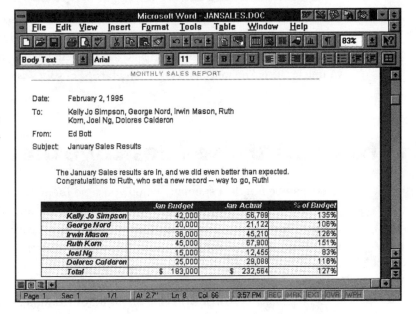

How do I change a link I've set up?

Word keeps track of links to other documents by hiding complicated formulas inside a document. If you need to change a link after you've set it up, choose Edit, Links. You'll see a dialog box like the one in figure 20.8.

Fig. 20.8
Choose Edit, Links to break a link or change the source document.

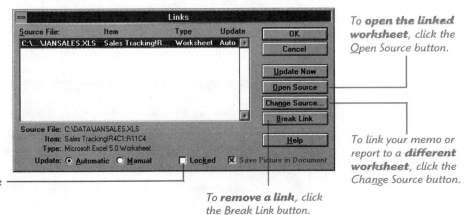

To temporarily **prevent updates** to your document, check the Locked box.

To **remove a link**, click the Break Link button.

To **open the linked worksheet**, click the Open Source button.

To link your memo or report to a **different worksheet**, click the Change Source button.

Q&A

I updated my Excel worksheet, but the numbers in my Word document didn't change. What happened?

Maybe the link broke. That can happen if you rename the source document or move it to a different directory. Try choosing Edit, Links and click the Change Source button to re-establish the link. If that doesn't work, you'll have to delete the linked range and insert a fresh copy of your worksheet range.

I want to keep these files together

Links can be fragile, especially when you send them somewhere away from your computer or your network. If someone accidentally wipes out or moves the source document—the Excel worksheet with all your numbers—Word will get hopelessly confused, and your carefully constructed link won't work any more.

This possibility is worth worrying about if, for example, you want to make sure all your regional sales managers have a copy of the sales-tracking worksheet, along with the accompanying memo.

You could copy both files to a bunch of floppy disks and mail them to all your managers, but you have no guarantee that the two files will end up in the right directories or even on the right computer. And if the two files get separated, the links don't work any more. How do you make sure the files stay as close as Siamese twins? **Embed** the Excel worksheet in your Word report.

How is embedding different from linking?

Instead of simply pasting a picture of the data in the second file, this option packs your entire Excel worksheet into the computer equivalent of a cardboard box, and stuffs it inside your Word document. Now you can distribute a single file that contains all of your data: words and numbers and formulas.

When you print out your Word memo, it still looks like you've pasted a picture of the worksheet data on the page. But instead of a simple snapshot, you have access to all the values, formulas, and formats of the original worksheet.

You don't have to worry about breaking links. You don't have to keep track of two different files. If you want to change the data in your sales-tracking worksheet, just double-click on the table in your Word document, edit the Excel worksheet, then resave it.

How do I stuff a worksheet inside a Word document?

Just like a copy or link, the secret of successfully embedding a worksheet into a document is to use the Windows Clipboard. Do this:

1 In the Excel worksheet, highlight the range you want to embed.

2 Right-click the selection, and choose Copy from the shortcut menu.

3 Use the MOM toolbar to switch to Word. Create a new document if necessary.

4 Choose Edit, Paste Special.

5 Choose Microsoft Excel 5.0 Worksheet Object from the list. Don't click the Paste Link button!

6 Click OK to embed the worksheet in your document.

At first glance, the names and numbers look like a Word table, but they actually behave very differently. In figure 20.9, for example, look at the status line along the bottom of the screen. To change the numbers, just double-click the object. Excel will start and load your embedded file.

Fig. 20.9

A Word document containing an embedded Excel worksheet. As the status bar along the bottom of the screen points out, you can double-click on the worksheet range to make changes to it.

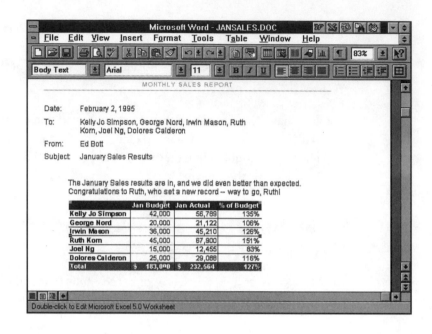

Part IV:

Using PowerPoint

21

Creating a New Presentation

To create a presentation with PowerPoint, you don't need a degree in multi-media productions from the Spielberg School of Whizz-Bang.

In this chapter:

- Where do I begin?
- What can I put on a slide?
- Adding stuff to a slide
- How does PowerPoint do the work for me?
- How do I do it from scratch?
- Viewing my presentation

"**A**nd here is Jackie, on our very first day there, in front of the hotel. And this is Jackie, talking to that nice couple from Iowa who rented the bungalow right next to ours. Oh, and in this one, Jackie is..."

How many times have you suffered through these uninspired slide shows put together by your best friends? And you didn't have the option to refuse the invitation to take a look at the world's dullest vacation.

Slide shows don't have to be sleep-inducing. When used right, they're powerful sales tools. Done professionally with special effects, they can turn the most reluctant audience member to an attentive participant. The good news is, you don't need a degree in multimedia productions from the Spielberg School of Whizz-Bang. In PowerPoint, you already have all the tools you need.

What's more, this program is very powerful, yet a breeze to use. Because so much of the work is done for you, you'll almost be embarrassed to accept your colleagues' compliments. But go ahead, take credit for these breath-taking sight-and-sound shows. After all, you were smart enough to let PowerPoint create them. Oh, and when you thank the Academy for giving you that award, don't forget to mention this book.

Where do I begin?

The road to a good slide show is paved with good intentions. And if you think this is a cop-out approach (which it is), plan ahead and make sure that you run the show, not the other way around. Jot down some ideas on how you want the presentation to look, but leave some room for spontaneous changes because PowerPoint is bound to give you a few brilliant ideas along the way.

When PowerPoint starts, it graciously presents you with some options for creating a new presentation or opening an existing one. Take a look at figure 21.1.

Fig. 21.1
The startup options: notice that there's something here for everyone, beginners as well as more seasoned users.

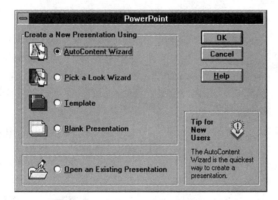

Two of the options feature the very resourceful **wizards.** The other options involve a bit more work on your part, and you'll turn to them as you become more comfortable with this program.

PowerPoint and its tools

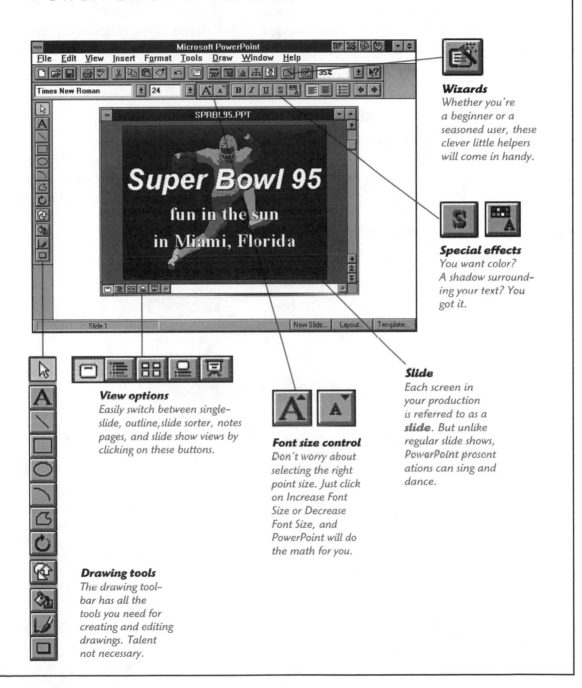

Wizards
Whether you're a beginner or a seasoned user, these clever little helpers will come in handy.

Special effects
You want color? A shadow surrounding your text? You got it.

Slide
Each screen in your production is referred to as a **slide**. But unlike regular slide shows, PowerPoint present ations can sing and dance.

View options
Easily switch between single-slide, outline, slide sorter, notes pages, and slide show views by clicking on these buttons.

Font size control
Don't worry about selecting the right point size. Just click on Increase Font Size or Decrease Font Size, and PowerPoint will do the math for you.

Drawing tools
The drawing tool-bar has all the tools you need for creating and editing drawings. Talent not necessary.

Sit back and let a wizard work for you

Lets talk about wizards: those wand-waving creatures whose sole purpose in life is to make *your* life easier by doing the grunt work for you. Wizards don't read your mind, though; they first interview you and then implement your wishes. And you? You just rest. Who says it's hard to find good help anymore?

AutoContent Wizard

In this 4-step interview process (see fig. 21.2), the Wizard finds out the purpose of the presentation (Are you selling a product or an idea? Is this part of a training program?), and creates a dummy presentation that you can customize by replacing text, changing colors, and applying special effects.

Fig. 21.2
The AutoContent Wizard creates a skeleton of a presentation, based on the information you provide. Change your mind? Just repeat the process, and the Wizard will apply your new input.

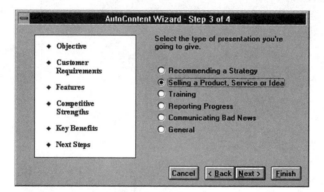

Pick a Look Wizard

While the AutoContent Wizard may appeal to your sense of order and structure, the Pick a Look Wizard, shown in figure 21.3, caters to your more aesthetic side by adding splashes of design to your slides. Tell it that you're creating overheads, 35mm slides, or on-screen presentations. You can choose from 60 different designs, each more exciting than the previous one. But more on that in Chapter 22.

Fig. 21.3
Step 3 of the Pick a Look Wizard may very well be the most fun you can have with a slide. Click on the button labeled More and a world of exciting backgrounds opens up.

Q&A

I don't like the way this presentation has turned out. Do I have to start over from scratch?

When you run the Pick a Look Wizard, it only applies a new look to your presentation; you don't lose any of the text or other elements you've added to your slides.

Starting without a wizard

Okay, so wizards may not be your thing. Maybe you're the hands-on type who likes to do everything on your own. Well, if you eschew the wizard route, PowerPoint offers a couple of other ways to get started.

Templates

Remember stencils? You used them in school, and, if you're creative, you probably still use them to decorate your home and make arts-and-crafts projects. Just follow the cut-out design with a pencil, and fill it in with paint, embroidery, or any other medium. PowerPoint **templates**, simply put, are electronic stencils. They are predesigned skeleton documents, which let you insert your own text and graphics in place of dummy place holders.

By the seat of your pants

So, you feel like taking the bull by the horns? Go ahead, give the Blank Presentation option a try. Nobody will be here to hold your hand, and no wizards will be conjured up. But you can't go wrong (well, not too terribly, anyway), and the experience may be good for you. Oh, and if your monitor starts smoking, don't call us, call Microsoft (see "Starting from Nothing," straight ahead).

Opening an existing presentation

Select this option to open a previously created masterpiece. Presentations are saved with the extension PPT, so if you're looking for your SPRBL95 (and now in English: Super Bowl 95) slide show, it'll appear as SPRBL95.PPT in the list that opens up.

Starting from nothing

It's that time of year again. You need to get your travel agents all pumped up for selling flight tickets and package deals for Super Bowl 95. There are two ways you can do this. The first one involves sending out brochures and following up with daily faxes that announce, "Only 5 months left to Super Bowl 95!" Very low on the excitability meter, you must agree.

Better yet, invite them to brunch, give them blue drinks with little umbrellas, and knock their socks off with a PowerPoint presentation, accompanied by Gloria Estefan sound tracks.

 Q&A

I've lost that start-up screen. Do I have to exit PowerPoint and rerun it to get to that screen again?

No. Just choose File, New, and a similar screen will open: the New Presentation dialog box appears.

How do I create a slide show on my own?

Though the wizards are wonderful design aids, you may find that it's just as thrilling to start with nothing but a blank canvas. Just select the Blank Presentation option from the start-up screen and let your imagination run wild.

Pick a layout, any layout

Take a look at figure 21.4. It seems that you're not on your own here, after all (whew...) because when you choose either to use a template or use a blank presentation, you can pick a layout from the New Slide dialog box. Title Slide is currently selected. How do you know? First of all, it has a thicker frame than the rest of the slides, and second, the words `Title Slide` are displayed in a box at the lower right side of this dialog box. Click OK to select this layout, or scroll down to view the other slides and select another one by clicking on it. Then click OK (or, if you're more mouse-savvy, double-click on the slide of your choice).

Fig. 21.4
Select one of the 21 templates and customize it. Resize any of the frames or duplicate or delete any of the objects. These are just suggestions, after all.

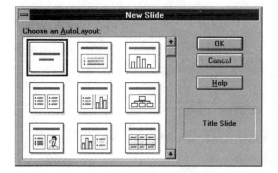

How do I start typing?

All the slide layouts represented in the New Slide dialog box—except for the last one at the bottom of the list titled `Blank`—feature clearly identified boxes, or frames. Their labels invite you to do things: like `Click to add title`. When you click anywhere inside a box—such as the one in figure 21.5—to take PowerPoint up on its offer, that message disappears, and a typing insertion point awaits your instructions.

Fig. 21.5
Color by numbers. OK, take a wild guess: what are you supposed to do here?

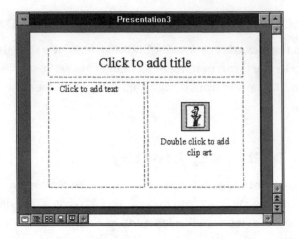

Once you've typed a title or any other text, you can select a different font or apply special text attributes such as bold, italics, or a different color. But before you do, you need to select the text with the mouse.

(Tip)

> To select all the text inside a frame, select the frame; any text-format changes will affect all text in the frame. You can also select all the text at once by selecting the frame and pressing Ctrl+A (Select All) instead of dragging the mouse over the words to select them.

Now I want to add special effects to the text

Paying special attention to the way your text is formatted— size, color, and special effects like shadows—is important if you want to make an impression. Here are several special effects to play around with:

- **To make your text larger**, you need to increase the font size. This can be tricky because if you're not sure what size you need, you may end up wasting time trying out different options in the Font Size pop-up list. The easier route is clicking the Increase Font Size button, which is located immediately to the right of the Font Size menu. Keep clicking until you're happy. If you want to keep the text on a single line, and the words wrap around to the next line, you've gone too far. Click the—what else?—Decrease Font Size button **to reduce the size of the text** until the text fits on the line.

- **To add more pizazz to a title**, click the Text Shadow button for a nice drop-shadow effect.

- **To add color to a title**, click the Text Color button, and select a color. For a further dash of excitement, pick a different font from the Font pop-up list. Make it bold, even italic. Since bold text is thicker than the plain variety, you may run out of space and the text will wrap around again, so click Decrease Font Size to adjust it. See if you can re-create the text in figure 21.6 (hint: you can do *much* better than that).

Fig. 21.6
Apply any fonts and special effects you like, but remember, the ransom-note look is no longer considered respectable.

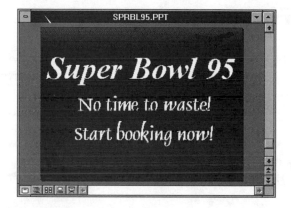

What can I put on a slide?

In an effective presentation, each slide should convey a complete thought or message. Other than text, there are a few elements you can—and should—add to your slides to make your point come across better or prove your claim (or both):

- **Graphics**. It's a cheap trick, but it works every time. Spice up your presentation with graphics, and you'll get their attention. Select from one of the dozens of clip-art images included with Office, or get your own.

 **<Caution>** Now that you've discovered graphics, you'll probably go haywire and want to use one (or more) in every slide. It's only natural. We've all been there... But don't give in to that temptation, because the result may look quite amateurish, even childish. Use graphics judiciously and sparingly.

- **Chart.** Nothing conveys numeric information like a chart. Place a pie chart in your slide to get their attention.

- **Table.** The best use of the screen real estate is placing your information in a table. It's neat and clean and easy to read and decipher.

Adding stuff to a slide

You probably have noticed by now that PowerPoint slides may feature several elements, one for every purpose under heaven. Well, almost... Here's how you add different elements to your slides.

Bite the bullet

Blame it on television, or blame it on junk food, but people have a short attention span. Rather than type a wordy paragraph into a slide, break up your thoughts into short ideas or topics, and point to them with tiny graphic markers called **bullets**. Here are some examples of bullets:

Standard bullet	•
Another common one	■
OK, so I'm a trekkie...	➤
Follow that finger!	☞

I sell travel services	✈
Have a nice day!	☺
We're a winning team!	✌
Miami, here we come!	✹

To replace the standard PowerPoint bullet with a more creative one, select the text frame, choose Format, Bullet, and click on the down arrow next to Bullets From. Select Wingdings, and a world of fun and wacky graphics is yours to explore. Select the character you want to use for your bullets by clicking on it, then click OK.

I want to add some text

If you've picked a prelaid-out slide (or template), such as the one shown in figure 21.7, you can click once anywhere in a text frame (any one labeled `Click to add...`), and start typing.

Fig. 21.7
How can you tell if the text is formatted as a bulleted list? Notice the tiny "•" character next to the words `Click to add text.`

(Tip)

If the text is formatted as a bulleted list, you'll get a new bullet each time you press Enter. Don't want a bulleted list? Select the entire text by pressing Ctrl+A, and click on the Bullets button on the toolbar. This is called a **toggle** feature: one click turns it on, another click turns it off.

{Note}

If you prefer to do your writing in Word, no problem. It's easy to turn a Word document into a PowerPoint presentation. See Chapter 23 for the step-by-step details.

I want to turn some numbers into a chart

There are two ways to insert charts into a PowerPoint slide (actually, there are more, but these two are the only ones that don't involve re-inventing the wheel):

- **Just add water.** If the chart exists in an Excel worksheet, copy it to the Clipboard (select Edit, Copy or press Ctrl+C), and then paste it into your slide (select Edit, Paste Special). See Chapter 14 for information on creating charts in Excel.

- **On the fly.** For simple charts, with just a little data, select Insert, Microsoft Graph. This opens a spreadsheet-like object called a **datasheet**. Click once on the upper left corner of the datasheet (a blank, grey rectangle) to select the whole datasheet. Press the Delete key on your keyboard to clear everything and type your data. Change the graph type, apply legends and titles, and you're done. Press Ctrl+F4 to insert the resulting chart in your slide.

I want to spice things up with a picture

Don't you wish you had a picture of a football player to place in a slide? Well, you do. Follow these steps:

1 From the menus, choose Insert, Clip Art..

2 There are many image categories to choose from. Scroll down the category list and click on Sports & Leisure (see fig. 21.8).

Fig. 21.8
Hey, it's Jerry Rice! Well, almost. This may not be the exact image you were looking for, but it's free.

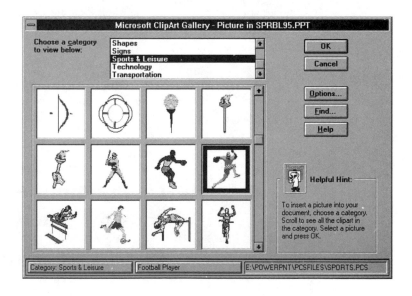

Using a chart to make your point

Although Microsoft Graph is not as easy to use as the ChartWizard in Excel, for simple charts it's more than adequate.

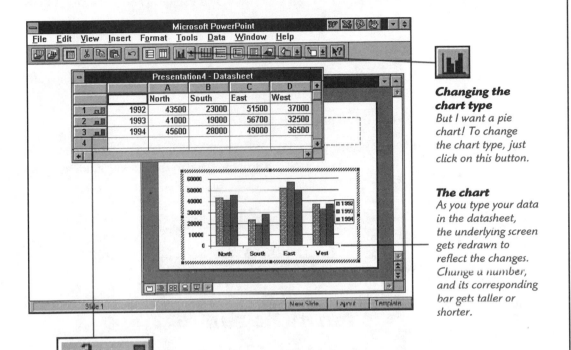

Changing the chart type
But I want a pie chart! To change the chart type, just click on this button.

The chart
As you type your data in the datasheet, the underlying screen gets redrawn to reflect the changes. Change a number, and its corresponding bar gets taller or shorter.

Knowing the chart type
The chart type you've selected is displayed on the datasheet, in case you can't see the underlying slide.

**{Note}**

There are hundreds of thousands of graphic images that you can purchase in any software store or from mail-order catalogs. They are often sold as libraries: packaged by topics such as sports, business, holidays, school, and so on. Since you're creating color slides, look for color graphics. For the more professional look, check out some of the many photo collections (usually sold on CD-ROM). Better yet, get your hands on a color scanner, and scan your own photos or graphics!

3 Scroll down the images, and click the football player graphic (notice the graphic's title on the status bar).

4 Click OK to place that image on your slide.

5 Oops, seems we've lost the text. No problem. From the menus, choose Draw, Send to Back; the graphic goes to the background, as shown in figure 21.9.

Fig. 21.9
The text layer should be on top of the graphic, not the other way around.

**{Note}**

In addition to pictures, PowerPoint also allows you to add sound and video clips to your presentation, which is very cool and makes you a multimedia producer! If you want to explore these options, you'll need certain hardware, sound and video files, and monitor-display capabilities. You insert the sound and video as objects through the Insert menu, just as you would a piece of clip media.

Different ways to view your presentation

Well, you've worked so hard that you deserve to take a look at your master-piece! Doing this is easy with the different viewing options in PowerPoint, as you can see in figure 21.10.

Outline View
No graphics, just text.

Notes Pages View
Be prepared for any disaster. See Chapter 23 for more information.

Fig. 21.10
The View toolbar.

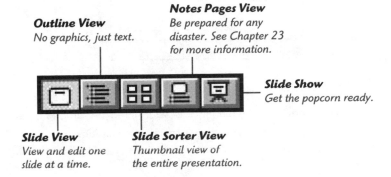

Slide Show
Get the popcorn ready.

Slide View
View and edit one slide at a time.

Slide Sorter View
Thumbnail view of the entire presentation.

I want to work on just this slide

There are two ways to view and work on just one slide. The easiest one is to click on the Slide View button at the bottom left corner of the screen. Alternately, choose View, Slides from the menu bar.

How about a panoramic view?

In Hollywood, before anybody ever aims a movie camera at that exploding car, the director must agree on the blueprints. These blueprints, in showbiz lingo, are called storyboards, and they depict tiny frames, with the general layout and action of each scene. Since you're the director (and camera person, and producer, and caterer) of this slide show, you must refer to a storyboard. PowerPoint calls it the Slide Sorter view. As you can see in figure 21.11, this is a visual overview of your entire presentation, though you can barely read the text (which is fine because you're looking at global issues, such as layout consistency, not details).

Fig. 21.11
Don't worry. You don't need new glasses. Look at the whole, not the details.

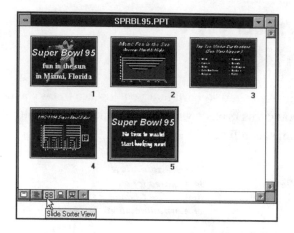

(!)(Tip)

Not happy with the sequence of your slides? No problem. Click on any slide you want to move, and drag it to its new location.

I want to see my whole presentation

It's the moment we've all been waiting for. It's show time! Click on the Slide Show button, and the slide show starts. Any mouse click takes you forward to the next slide. When you're done, you're back in Slide View. Don't worry if the show is on the dull side. It'll come to life in Chapter 22.

Fifty ways to leave your lover

If you haven't noticed this yet, there are several ways you can achieve any given task in Office. Here are different ways to move around your PowerPoint presentation:

- Press Page Up to go to the previous slide.

- Press Page Down to go to the next.

- Press Ctrl+Home to go to the first slide.

- Press Ctrl+End to go to the last one.

- Slowly slide the vertical scroll bar elevator, and watch the appropriate slide label pop up. Stop scrolling when you get to the desired slide.

To stop the presentation while in Slide Show mode, press Esc. This takes you back to Slide View mode.

Saving your work

If you're happy with the results of your first effort (and even if you're not), select File, Save As, and type a name. Remember, you're limited to 8 characters, no spaces. PowerPoint will add the PPT extension to that name.

Before you save, make sure you select a directory for your data. See Chapter 4 for more information.

22
Making Great-Looking Presentations

With a few mouse-clicks, a boring presentation turns into a crowd pleaser. So...lights, camera, action!

In this chapter:

- How do I choose a new background?
- I want to include smooth transitions
- I want to gradually build the elements on the slides

Sure, you're creative, and your slides are witty-yet-informative. But words alone are not enough to stop anybody from falling asleep. Your audience will settle for nothing short of an Oscar-winning show, and that includes color, special effects, graphics, and music. And when all else fails, door prizes.

PowerPoint has all the tools you need for bringing your presentation to life. different backgrounds, dramatic transitions, text flying in from all directions, you name it. With a few mouse-clicks, you can take the most boring presentation and turn it into a crowd pleaser. So...lights, camera, action!

How do I choose a new background?

To choose a new background, you can either let the Pick a Look Wizard guide you through the process, or just do it yourself. The advantage of using the wizard is clear—even veteran PowerPoint users shouldn't hesitate to rely on this tool because it saves energy and time.

I want to spruce up the whole presentation

If your presentation is dull and colorless, it's time for a makeover. With the presentation you want to modify on-screen, click the Pick a Look Wizard button, and click Next to go to step 2. This is where you tell the Wizard what kind of presentation you're working on. For this example, select On-Screen Presentation, and click Next.

Step 3 is where the fun begins. Now you'll tell PowerPoint which background you want for your slides. Look at figure 22.1. There are four templates to choose from. Click next to any of them and you'll get a preview. Pretty snazzy-looking, aren't they? But you didn't really think there were only four choices now, did you? See the button labeled More? Click it, and...open sesame! It's a treasure box full of colors, designs, and endless ideas.

Fig. 22.1
These four background templates are only the tip of the iceberg. The fun begins when you click on More.

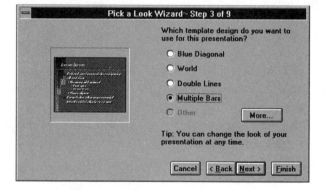

I don't know what these names mean

Each background template is a file, and the files are listed alphabetically. But what do they look like? And what does BLSTRIPS.PPT mean? Don't worry. You're not going to make a blind selection. As you can see in figure 22.2, it's easy to windowshop: just click once on any file name, and a small representation, called a **thumbnail**, appears in a frame at the lower right corner. So click on the top file name—it should be AZURES.PPT—and go down the list by pressing the down arrow key, one file name at a time.

Fig. 22.2
The **thumbnail** is a tiny representation of the actual template. You can easily browse and pick just the look you want.

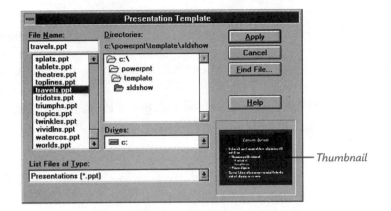

— Thumbnail

Don't worry if the thumbnail looks a bit grainy and out-of-focus; the actual slide will look much better. When you find the design you like, click Apply, and it'll be applied to all your slides.

The next step that appears, step 4, gives you a choice of what to print: full-page slides, speaker's notes, audience handouts, or outline pages. Deselect all but full-page slides, and click Next. This screen allows you to enter a name, date, or page number—but for now, just click Finish to leave the wizard and view your presentation.

 **{Note}**

If, after you click on More, your screen doesn't look like figure 22.2, you may not be in the right directory. Just double-click on the POWERPNT folder, then on TEMPLATE, then on SLDSHOW, and you'll see the choices shown in the figure.

I like this background, but I hate that color!

Every background template combines three separate user-customizable elements:

- **Layout.** Includes graphic elements, frames, lines, and so on.

- **Color.** The entire spectrum is available to you to choose from (providing your monitor can display all these choices).

- **Shade styles.** Colors don't just fill the slide. They're placed as **gradients**, with varying dark and light shades of the selected color.

For example, if you select TRAVELS.PPT as your background because you want to have an airplane in the background, you can set the sky's color to purple, and have the gradient fill flow from dark at the upper right corner to light at the bottom left.

Now that you've selected a background template, here are the different things you can do to customize it. By the time you're done with it, even its own mother won't recognize it.

I want to change the background color

True, the sky is blue. But you want it purple. Choose Format, Slide Background, and click on Change Color. There are 88 colors (plus black and white) to choose from on this screen, but if you can't find the exact shade of purple you're looking for, you can always click More Colors and, as you can see in figure 22.3, the entire rainbow is at your fingertips. Just click anywhere within the color palette, and watch the square labeled Color: That's the color you've selected.

Fig. 22.3

Slide the selection cursor over the palette to see all available colors. If you're "color-impaired" and can't tell all these colors apart, get a friend to help you.

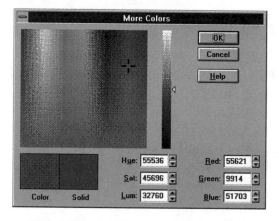

You can fine-tune that color by increasing or decreasing the levels of three of its elements:

- **Hue.** This is just a fancy way of saying "color." Click on the up or down arrows next to Hue, and you can fine-tune your selection. That's the same as sliding the selection cursor (the one that looks like a broken plus sign) across the palette.

- **Saturation.** Notice the bottom of the palette: the level of your selected color in the Color square is very low. Click the up or down arrows next to S̲at. The higher you go up the palette, the more intense the color.

- **Luminance.** Click the up or down arrows next to L̲um to select just the right level of darkness or lightness in your selected color.

To apply that new color scheme, click on OK twice, then on Apply̲ to All; the entire presentation changes before your very eyes.

I want to change the gradient fill

This is one of the most impressive and professional-looking effects in your slide. Notice the TRAVELS.PPT background in figure 22.4. It's darker at the top, slowly becoming lighter toward the bottom of the slide.

Fig. 22.4

Gradient fills add a flare to the overall look of your presentation.

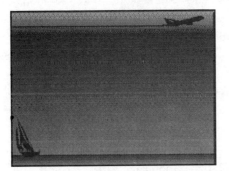

You can alter the direction of the gradient to go horizontally, vertically or any which way (choose Fo̲rmat, Slide Background). To reach the effect you desire, pick any combination of shade styles and variants, as shown in figure 22.5. Select N̲one, and a very boring square with no gradient appears. Trust me, you don't want that.

Click next to V̲ertical, and look at the four variant options. Continue clicking next to each shade style, and watch the variants. You can also change the color's luminance by scrolling the Dark/Light slider. Made your choice? Just click on the two selections that make that desirable combination and choose A̲pply to modify just the current slide (or Apply̲ To All for the entire presentation).

Fig. 22.5
To fine-tune your gradient fill, play with its three elements: color, shade, and variant.

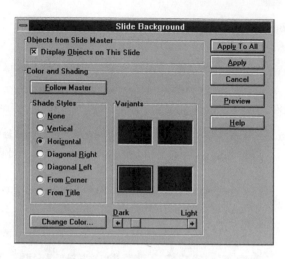

?Q&A

How do I change the background in just one slide, or a few selected ones, but not the entire presentation?

In Slide Sorter View, click on the slide you want to modify. If you want several slides, press Shift+click on each of them, and notice the thicker frame around each slide, indicating that it's been selected. Now, let's try changing the color. From the Format menu, choose Slide Color Scheme. Click on Color Scheme, then select two colors in the Background and Text & Line Color boxes. PowerPoint fills in the color scheme. Click OK, and choose Apply to change just one slide.

⊗<Caution>

Now that you can mix and match patterns, colors, and gradient fills, you need to develop a good eye for what works. Not every combination is aesthetically acceptable, and one thing you want to avoid at all costs is making your audience nauseous. If you're not sure of your judgment in this matter, designate a friend or colleague as a dry-run audience. Even Hollywood producers arrange these previews before the release of a new movie, which gives them a last chance to redo problem areas.

I want to remove all layout objects

You may want to remove all layout elements from a slide that's already too "busy" with graphics and text. To do so, choose Format, Slide Background, and click next to "Display objects on this slide" to check it off. If you see an × in that check box, click again to remove it. Click Apply to modify just the current slide (or click Apply To All for the entire presentation).

How do I modify a graphic's color?

Suppose your favorite football team wears red and gold, and the football player you inserted in Chapter 21 seems to play for some competing team. We can't have that! Just right-click on the graphic, and a shortcut menu displays. Select recolor. In the Recolor Picture dialog box, you get two palettes—the one on the left (Original) shows the existing colors in the picture, and the one labeled New lets you replace each color with any color you want (see fig. 22.6).

Fig. 22.6
The colors in the Original column are all the colors in the current picture. So if you select a black and white image, you can replace the black and white with another color.

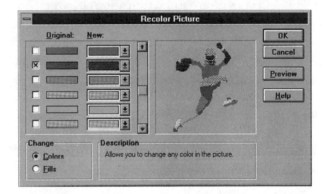

For example, to replace the orange with gold, follow these steps.

1 Slide down the scroll bar until you find the orange color in the Original column.

2 Click on the down arrow next to the orange color in the New column, click Other Color, and then click More Colors.

3 Find the exact shade of gold you're looking for by sliding the selection cursor across the palette. Watch the Color square for the current color.

4 Click OK twice to return to the main screen and look at your slide with the new graphic colors.

5 Click on Preview to see what the new color looks like. You may need to fine-tune the color a bit, so repeat steps 1 through 4. Also, there may be

more than one shade of orange, so you'll need to slide the scroll bar a bit lower to continue replacing all the instances of that color with the appropriate shades of gold.

Break a leg: dress rehearsal

No slide is an island. Your presentation should be one entity, melded into a captivating whole. One way to ensure that is to establish continuity between the slides. Here are a few things you can do to smooth out the rough edges.

I want smooth transitions

In movies and television shows, transitions between scenes have become an art form. You can't show dueling knights in one scene and then show a wedding scene a fraction of a second later, without any warning. The technique used to make these transitions smooth and natural are numerous, and some are more creative than others.

Sometimes a scene briefly "fades to black" (especially in those juicy love scenes) before the next one appears. Occasionally, you see an overlap between the two scenes, which makes the exiting scene look a bit transparent while the new scene comes into focus.

These effects are added in at the editing phase. And now you can be a movie editor too, because PowerPoint has 46 different transitions you can use in your presentation. Well, not exactly. There are 10 types of transitions, each with several variations. What they all have in common is the gradual transformation from one slide to the next:

- **Blinds.** Just like your window treatments, these come in the horizontal or vertical variety, gradually opening until you see the entire new slide. *Very impressive.*

- **Box.** A square shrinks into the center of the slide or grows to show the entire slide. *Slick.*

- **Checkerboard.** Small squares cover the new slide, then disappear either sideways or downward. *Three wows.*

- **Cover.** The new slide "flies" in from the top, bottom, sides, or corners, and covers the previous slide. *Ooooo and Aaaaaah.*

- **Cut.** This is a more abrupt transition, lacking the animation of the other transitions. *Yawn.*

- **Dissolve.** Tiny dots that make up the new slide gradually take over the previous one. *Magical.*

- **Fade through black.** A familiar Hollywood "fade-in" effect. The new slide materializes from black. *Classy.*

- **Random bars.** Thick and thin lines (vertical or horizontal) gradually display the new slide. *Dizzying.*

- **Split.** Think of it as pulling curtains over your slide, vertically or horizontally. *Knock their socks off.*

- **Strips.** The new slide reveals itself by covering the previous one in a diagonal direction with a jagged edge. *Interesting.*

- **Uncover.** Unlike Cover, where the new screen flies in all at once, Uncover does a little striptease, peeling off the on-screen elements gradually, in any of eight directions, as the new slide reveals itself. *Teasing.*

- **Wipe.** Gradually reveals the new slide, as if sliding a piece of paper off the transparency on an overhead projector (see fig. 22.7). *Smooth.*

Fig. 22.7

A wipe in mid-transition is half one image, half another for an instant.

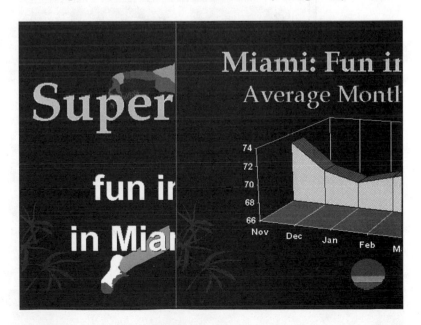

- **Random Transition.** Feel like gambling? Select this one—every time you run the show, you'll get different transitions for different slides. *Great if you're going for the annoyance factor.*

- **No Transition.** *No fun.*

I want to apply the same transition to the entire presentation

Select the Slide Sorter View, and click Select All to select all the slides. The thicker frames are your indication that the slides are selected. Now open the Transition Effects pop-up list, and select the transition you want to apply. Look at figure 22.8. Notice the tiny Transition icon under each slide? That's your indication that a transition has been applied to that slide.

Fig. 22.8
You can preview the transition by clicking on the Transition icon under the slide's thumbnail.

Transition icons—

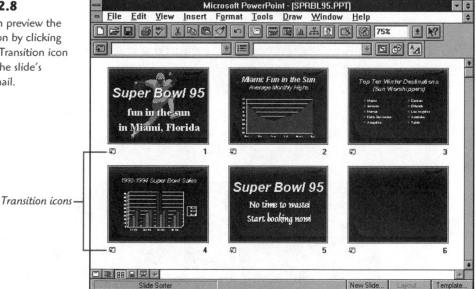

I want to apply a different transition to just one slide

I'll show you how to do this, as long as you promise not to mix-and-match too many different transitions. First, make sure that you've applied one global transition to the entire presentation, and only then override individual slides' settings. While in Slide Sorter View, click on the slide you want to affect. It should have a thicker frame, as shown in figure 22.9. Now click in the Transition Effects pop-up list, and select a transition.

Fig. 22.9
The thicker frame is an indication that you've selected this slide.

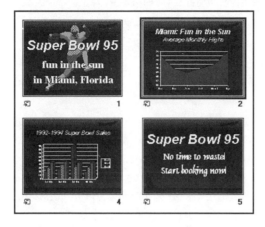

<table>
<tr><td>Super Bowl 95
fun in the sun
in Miami, Florida</td><td>Miami: Fun in the Sun
Average Monthly Highs</td></tr>
<tr><td>1</td><td>2</td></tr>
<tr><td>1992-1994 Super Bowl Sales</td><td>Super Bowl 95
No time to waste!
Start booking now!</td></tr>
<tr><td>4</td><td>5</td></tr>
</table>

(Tip)

> If you want to apply a different transition to more than one slide, select them by clicking the first one, then Shift+clicking on any additional ones.

The transition goes by too fast

So you've put all that effort into selecting just the right transition, but your computer is fast, and those checkerboard squares fly by too fast to impress anybody. No problem. First switch to Slide Sorter View, then select all the slides you want to affect. Click on the Transition button to the left of the Transition Effects pop-up list, and you'll get the dialog box you see in figure 22.10.

Fig. 22.10
This is the best place to get a preview of the different transitions. Play with each configuration, and watch the transitions between the dog and the key.

Transition

Effect:
Cover Down

OK
Cancel
Help

Speed
◉ Slow
○ Medium
○ Fast

Advance
◉ Only on Mouse Click
○ Automatically After
☐ Seconds

Click on each of the speed options, and look at the preview screen (the one showing alternating pictures of a dog and a key) to get an idea of how fast they go. This is different from computer to computer, so if you create the presentation on your desktop computer but use a notebook computer to display it, there will be a slight difference.

Keep them in suspense

Seasoned presenters know that no matter how good they are, or how interested the viewers are in the subject matter, minds will wander. To minimize distractions, you need to tease them with the promise of things to come. Imagine telling your best joke of the week, while everybody's busy reading what's on the slide. You won't even get a polite chuckle.

People who use overhead projectors have known the answer to this for years: reveal only one bit of information at a time. What they do is put a piece of paper over the transparency, and slide it down when they need to reveal a new item. And, not surprisingly, PowerPoint can do this for you, in a variety of fun and entertaining ways.

 Plain English, please!

PowerPoint calls the gradual introduction of text to the active slide a build. When you show a slide, each mouse click brings another line or item to full view, building the slide one item at a time. 🙴

How do I select a build?

There are nine general build categories, but really only two methods: your words can either fly in, already formed from all directions, or materialize out of thin air and form their shape on-screen.

To select a build, click in the Build Effects box, and make your selection. Unlike transitions, there's no way to preview this selection while in Slide Sorter View, so click on the Slide Show button to see it live. Every left mouse-click invokes a new line (see Chapter 21 for more information on moving within the presentation). When you've had enough, press Esc to stop the slide show.

When you first try out the different builds, you'll think they're all impressive and exciting. However, the honeymoon will soon be over, because once the novelty wears off, some of these effects can be pretty irritating. And if you're weary of them, just imagine how your audience will react (they'll hate your guts and never buy your product). So view them one by one, decide on the ones you like the most, and stick with them.

As in the case of transitions, you want to use the same builds throughout the presentation to assure cohesiveness and continuity.

I want to cover my tracks

It's true what they say: presenters are control freaks. Or at least they should be. If your slide features a bulleted list, you want to display each item only when you're good and ready. But as you progress, you also want to make sure that everybody's attention is focused on the newly displayed items. People may go back and read previous points if you just let them. So here's what you do to divert their eyes just to the line you want to read:

1 Switch to Slide Sorter View, and make sure that all the slides you want to modify are selected.

2 Click on the Build button next to the Build Effects box. The Build dialog box, shown in figure 22.11, displays.

3 Click in the check box next to Dim Previous Points.

4 Now you need to select the dimming color. For best results, try to find a shade that's similar to, but slightly lighter than, the background color. If the background is dark navy blue, go for a lighter shade of blue.

5 Click OK.

Fig. 22.11
Dimming previous points is the equivalent of sliding a piece of paper over an overhead transparency to cover text you don't want the audience to read.

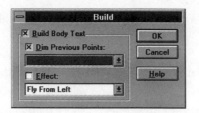

I want to dress up the text

Text formatting is one of the most powerful tools at your disposal. You can dress up your words with fonts, colors, and drop shadows, as long as you remember two cardinal rules:

- There must be a consistency to the presentation. If you apply a different font to each slide, you'll lose the continuity.

- Too many fonts conjure up images of ransom notes. See Chapter 8 for more information on fonts.

23
Using Word and Excel with PowerPoint

In this chapter:

- What if I like creating my outlines in Word?
- How do I include a Word table in my slide?
- I need to add Excel data and a chart to my presentation
- Can I place a PowerPoint slide in Word?

Granted, Word by itself is wonderful and PowerPoint is a great little program, but what they need is some chemistry, some romance.

—*I'll take Software for $300, Alex.*

—It's the number one reason for investing in Microsoft Office.

(buzz)

—*What is entertainment value?*

—Wrong!

(buzz)

—*It's so easy to learn, you don't need to buy a book.*

—You didn't phrase that as a question.

(buzz)

—*What is integration?*

—Right!

You know there was a reason for investing in Office instead of in a bunch of stand-alone programs. But what was it? OK, the price tag was very attractive, but there are lots of inexpensive alternatives out there. And, no, it wasn't the cute salesperson in the software store (let's pretend you didn't say that).

I've said it several times already, but it bears repeating: Office's unique power is its capability to integrate its different components. Granted, Word by itself is wonderful and PowerPoint is a great little program, but what they need is some chemistry, some romance in their lives. Go ahead, see for yourself— marry these two, and soon your computer will be filled with the pitter-patter of little OLE objects.

 Plain English, please!

> **OLE** means **object linking and embedding.** It all has to do with taking a little file in one parent application, and placing the file (embedding) or the information (linking) neatly inside another application. To **embed**, you have to open the file in the original application to edit it. To **link**, you edit it in the original application and it updates through a link with the receiving application. Think of it as electronic daycare for your files.

In this chapter, we'll explore the different ways you can integrate Word, Excel, and PowerPoint to enhance your productivity.

I'd rather work in Word

If you're like most people, you get to feeling at home in certain programs— maybe you use Word more often than PowerPoint. You're probably most comfortable working in Word, because some Word operations have become second nature, and you don't have to pause and think about them. And some features don't exist in PowerPoint. True, there's a spelling checker, but there's no thesaurus. Not to mention styles or macros—those personalized tools, the ones you reach for automatically. However, some people are right at home entering their outlines in PowerPoint, which has just enough word processing features to suit them. Realizing your predicament, PowerPoint is gracious enough to let you use its own tools or do quite a bit of your work in your favorite word processor, and then integrate it into your presentation without an effort. Here are a few examples.

I want to create my outlines in Word

Creating a few individual slides is easy. The difficulty is in putting together an effective presentation that delivers the right message and has the right impact on the audience. This takes planning and precision. Even Steven Spielberg couldn't have produced Jurassic Park without a good screenplay. And neither can you.

Each PowerPoint presentation has an underlying structure called an **outline**. An outline is, in essence, a screenplay (a non-graphical blueprint) for the presentation. You can create and modify the outline from within PowerPoint, in Outline View. But if you're more comfortable with Word's Outline mode, go ahead. PowerPoint can use a Word outline.

Here's what you do to turn a Word outline into a presentation:

1 Start PowerPoint without using a template, wizard, or opening another file, then choose File, Open.

2 Click on the down arrow next to the List Files of Type box, and choose Outlines, as shown in figure 23.1.

The Open dialog box displays.

3 In the Directories list box, go to the directory where you keep your Word files.

4 Select the file name, and click OK.

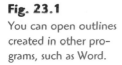

Fig. 23.1
You can open outlines created in other programs, such as Word.

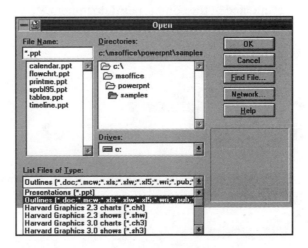

That's it! Your outline appears with each outline element on-screen as a bulleted item, and each bullet represents a slide in your presentation to be formatted and finalized. You're in Outline View, so switch to Slide Sorter View and apply any background, color, and other visual effects you want.

 **{Note}**

> Are you intimidated by outlines? You're not alone. To many users, this is not the most natural way to work. The good news is, an outline is just a hierarchical list. You don't need to create it in Word's Outline mode if you don't want to. Type your list regularly, and just remember that any items separated by hard returns (that's the Enter key) will be interpreted by PowerPoint as separate slides. To create bulleted lists within a slide, just indent each line with the Tab key.

I want to use a Word table

You can create tables in PowerPoint. But if you've already created a table in Word, you can—and should—use it in your presentation. Link your Word table to a slide and take advantage of the two-way street called **OLE.**

There are three advantages to using linked Word tables in PowerPoint:

- No need to reinvent the wheel. The table already exists in a Word document.

- You can edit the table from within PowerPoint, and all changes will be updated in the source Word document.

- Any change you make to the original Word document will be reflected in your slide. Automatically.

How do I place a linked table in my slide?

Before you place the table in your slide, you must copy it to the Windows Clipboard, which serves as a temporary storage area for all your programs. Just follow these steps:

1 In Word, select the table by placing the cursor anywhere within the table, then choose Table, Select Table.

2 Press Ctrl+C. This copies the selection to the Clipboard.

3 Switch to PowerPoint by clicking on the PowerPoint button on the MOM toolbar.

4 Go to the slide in which you want to insert the table, or create a new slide by pressing Ctrl+M. In the New Slide dialog box, select an autolayout, then click OK.

5 Switch to Slide View.

6 Choose Edit, Paste Special. This brings up the Paste Special dialog box shown in figure 23.2.

7 Click on Microsoft Word 6.0 Document Object, then select Paste Link. If you select plain Paste, you'll cut all ties to the source document.

8 Click on OK.

Fig. 23.2
The table you've copied to the Clipboard carries with it some identification: notice the source file name at the upper left corner.

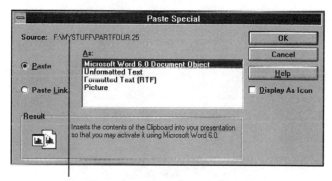

Source file name

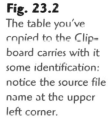

If you close the source document in Word before you paste the table into a slide, you'll lose the identifying information (file name), and you won't be able to establish a link. So make sure you leave the document open until you've gone through the Paste Special menu.

Adjusting the size of the pasted table

PowerPoint can't read your mind. So you probably won't like the size and placement of the pasted table. No problem. You can easily resize and move the table as follows:

- To **resize the table**, grab any handle (those tiny squares surrounding the table when you select it by clicking on it) and drag it anywhere you can—vertically, horizontally, or diagonally.

- To **move the table**, click anywhere inside the table, and drag the entire selected object to a new location.

Cropping odd-sized tables

Ever taken a shot of your cat and ended up with a print showing mostly your peeling stucco in the background? To correct that unsightly frame, you take your scissors and cut around the cat, so that the print is smaller, but the cat is better positioned in it. Look at figure 23.3. The handles extend beyond the table's frame, which makes it difficult to resize and move the table.

Fig. 23.3
You need to crop the extraneous space around the table before you can resize or move it.

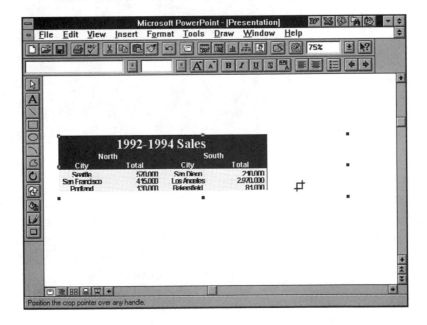

You need to adjust the handles so that they're attached to the table. So get out your electronic scissors, because we're about to **crop** (remove) the extra space around the table:

1 Right-click anywhere within the table.

2 Choose Tools, Crop Picture from the shortcut menu. Notice the cropping tool? Place it over a corner handle you wish to adjust, and drag it diagonally until it's close to the table.

3 If you've gone too far and are now missing part of the image, reverse the cropping direction.

4 Click anywhere outside the table to remove the cropping cursor.

5 Now you can resize and move the table.

How do I make changes to that table?

Since that table was originated in Word, you need to launch Word when you want to modify it or edit information in it. But before you go any further, remember: this is OLE; it'll do it for you. Just make sure that you're in Slide View and double-click on the table. Presto! Word is launched with the source document.

The Clipboard: tools of the trade

Just like everything else in Windows, you can access Clipboard operations by making menu selections or by using the keyboard. The more you use the Clipboard, the more you'll appreciate the speed and efficiency of the keyboard shortcuts, so here's a cheat-sheet. If you never memorize anything else, at least remember these:

Shortcut	Action
Ctrl+C	Copy to Clipboard
Ctrl+X	Cut to Clipboard
Ctrl+V	Paste from Clipboard
Alt+E, S	Paste Special (there's no shortcut for that, but here's a quick way to access the menu)

Make your changes and close the document by pressing Ctrl+F4. To return to PowerPoint, select its button from the MOM toolbar. If the recent changes aren't reflected in the slide, don't worry. Right-click on the table, and the menu you see in figure 23.4 displays. Select Update Link, and OLE will refresh the table in PowerPoint.

Fig. 23.4

You may need to give OLE a little nudge, to remind it to update the changes in the table.

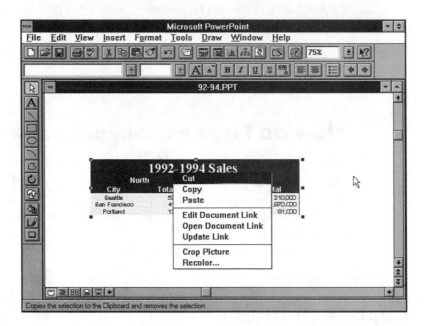

②Q&A

> ### What if I modify the source document and PowerPoint is not running? Will I lose the link?
>
> Think of an OLE link as a commitment, a wedding vow. You know, "Till death us do part." Once you've established a link, it's there to stay unless you delete the source document. That'll leave your embedded table widowed. Meaning, when you next open the PowerPoint presentation, you'll get an error that a link couldn't be established, but the table itself will still be there. More accurately, all you're left with is a "snapshot" of the table, and you won't be able to edit it any more.

I want to use an existing Word table, but I don't need a live link

Linking is good whenever you need to go back and edit data in the embedded table. But if you just want to use a table from a Word document, and you know that you'll never use this document again (or plan to delete it altogether), you don't need the extra baggage that comes with OLE (it does tend to be a bit "heavy" on your program, adding to its size, and slowing you down somewhat).

Follow these steps to copy a Word table into your presentation:

1 In Word, select the table by placing the cursor anywhere within the table, then choose Table, Select Table.

2 Press Ctrl+C. This copies the selection to the Clipboard.

3 Switch to PowerPoint by clicking the PowerPoint button on the MOM toolbar.

4 Go to the slide you want to insert the table in, or create a new slide by pressing Ctrl+M. In the New Slide dialog box, select an autolayout, then click OK.

5 Switch to Slide View.

6 Press Ctrl+V to paste the selection from the Clipboard.

(Note) Though you can't edit this table in its originating document, you can still edit it using Word. Just double-click on the table, and... look at your toolbars: are you in PowerPoint or in Word? This is the twilight zone called OLE: these are Word's toolbars, but you're still in PowerPoint. Make your changes, and click anywhere outside the table to save the changes and return to a regular PowerPoint screen.

What about data from Excel?

Worksheets are like new walking shoes. First they hurt a bit, and you curse the salesperson who talked you into getting them. Then you walk for miles and miles until they're comfortable, and once all the blisters have healed, you're afraid to try on a new pair. Similarly, you've created a worksheet in Excel and spent a long time formatting it so that it's just right, and working in it becomes second nature.

You don't want to bother with another spreadsheet, no matter how easy it is to use. And Microsoft Graph is like a new pair of cheap, no-name walking shoes. If you're an Excel user, you just don't need this substitution. Luckily, you don't have to.

The two Excel elements you'd normally want to add to your presentation are:

- **Worksheet.** Due to obvious reasons (limited screen real estate), you can use only small chunks at a time. If you have more data to share with your audience, you'll need to resort to—shudder—hard copy.

- **Chart.** True, Microsoft Graph has many of the tools you need to create charts from within PowerPoint, but they're not nearly as easy as using the Excel ChartWizard.

To link or not to link?

As with a Word document, you can create a live link to the source worksheet so that all changes in the source document are automatically reflected in your slide. Alternately, you can just paste your worksheet into a slide and cut all links to the originating document. Why would you use either method? If you're planning to reuse the presentation over a period of time, the data in the original worksheet may be constantly evolving, so you need to establish a link so that your presentation will reflect the changes. If the presentation is a one-time deal, don't bother creating a link.

How do I link an Excel worksheet to a slide?

Once again, we're going to rely on the Clipboard to transfer data between the programs. Open your Excel worksheet, and follow these steps:

1 Mark your selection with the mouse, and press Ctrl+C to copy its contents to the Clipboard. You should get an animated dashed border around your selection, similar to the one in figure 23.5.

Fig. 23.5
When you copy this selection to the Clipboard, you not only copy the data (words and numbers) but also formatting information, such as color, fonts, and lines.

Dashed border —

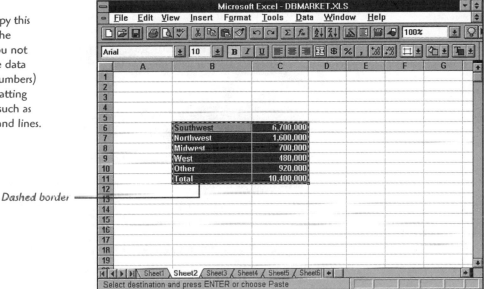

2 Switch to PowerPoint by clicking on its button in the MOM toolbar.

3 In Slide Sorter View, go to the slide in which you want to place the worksheet, or create a new one by pressing Ctrl+M. In the New Slide dialog box, select an autolayout, then click OK.

4 Choose Edit, Paste Special.

5 Click Microsoft Excel Worksheet Object, and select Paste Link.

6 Click OK.

I don't need to link that worksheet to the source document

No problem. Follow the same steps for linking a worksheet, but select <u>P</u>aste instead of Paste <u>L</u>ink in step 5. Better yet, bypass steps 4, 5, and 6 by pressing Ctrl+V for a quick paste from the Clipboard.

How do I place an Excel chart in a slide?

Placing an existing Excel chart in a slide is just as easy. All it takes is Clipboard savvy. Here's what you do:

1 In Excel, click once (don't double-click!) on the chart you want to use. You should get handles around its frame, signifying that it's been selected.

2 To copy the chart to the Clipboard, press... *right!...* Ctrl+C (aren't you glad you've been paying attention?)

3 Click on the PowerPoint button in MOM's toolbar.

4 In Slide Sorter View, go to the slide in which you want to place the chart, or create a new one by pressing Ctrl+M. In the New Slide dialog box, select an autolayout, then click OK.

5 Choose <u>E</u>dit, Paste <u>S</u>pecial, and click on <u>P</u>aste or Paste <u>L</u>ink. Your choice.

24

It's Showtime! Giving a
Great Presentation

*Simply put, a PowerPoint
presentation is a sales
pitch. And nobody ever
wants to lose a sale.*

There's an old adage that says that whatever you do, you're always
selling something. Sometimes you sell a product or a service, other
times you sell an idea, and often you're just selling yourself or the image
that you want to project. So, a PowerPoint presentation is simply a sales
pitch. And nobody ever wants to lose a sale.

PowerPoint presentations are used by college students, sales people, executives, and spin doctors of all kinds. They're all trying to get a point across,
and sometimes the difference between success and failure is the wrong
shade of green in a slide show.

Getting ready

One of the greatest presenters of all time was Demosthenes, who lived in Greece in the 4th century B.C. Of course, he was called an *orator* then, not a *presenter*, (because PowerPoint hadn't been written yet), but we can still learn some important lessons from him. Most importantly, he used to practice the clarity of his speech by talking with a mouthful of rocks. And while your dentist may not approve of this, you can still prepare yourself for a successful presentation by rehearsing over and over. And over.

My name is... my name is...

Forgetting lines is the most common ailment plaguing people who practice any form of public speech. Even seasoned actors and masters of ceremonies freeze in front of the camera every once in awhile—not able to remember their own names. Teleprompters can help, but if one technical problem occurs, you're on your own—on a stage, with the spotlight on you, and millions of people looking at you, whispering and giggling. OK, wake up! It was just a bad dream. You have PowerPoint—you'll be prepared.

PowerPoint has a couple of tools to help you prepare yourself for the presentation:

- **Rehearse Timing**. Script in hand, you go through a dry run of the presentation, and PowerPoint times each slide. When you're done, you get a report.

- **Notes Pages View**. You can type notes next to each slide and not leave any stone unturned.

Pace yourself

To rehearse your timing, switch to Slide Sorter View and click on the Rehearse Timings button on the toolbar. The first slide comes up, showing a running digital stopwatch at the bottom left corner (see fig. 24.1).

Start talking through the presentation as if you have a live audience, and PowerPoint will keep track of your progress. Click the left mouse button, and then press Enter or PgDn when you're ready to move to the next slide.

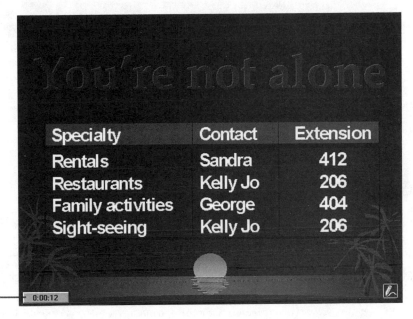

Fig. 24.1
—"How do you get to Broadway?"
—"With lots of practice."

Stopwatch

When you're done, you'll see a dialog box that reports the total length of the presentation and asks whether you want to record the slide timings so that you can see them in Slide Sorter View. Since it's a good idea, click OK.

As you can see in figure 24.2, each slide has a time stamp under it. Now is a good time to tweak your presentation. Did it take too long? Where can you reduce some time? Adjust your script accordingly, and try again until you reach the desired length. What's worse, running out of time and leaving out important information, or finishing too fast and having to improvise? (Hint: both scenarios are to be avoided at all costs).

Fig. 24.2
If your boss has given you only 15 minutes to make your point, you have to look at each slide and see where you can make changes.

Time stamp

---

① (Tip)

If you're having trouble cutting appropriately to get through the presentation in the time allowed, consider using Timing to automatically forward your slides at regular intervals. Of course, the key here is to cut your patter appropriately and keep up with the slides, so you don't end up five slides behind at the end!

The presenter's motto: be prepared

In a perfect world, you're in full control of the audience during your presentation. In reality, though, there's always a heckler at the back of the room who'll ask you about stuff you're not ready to discuss. To prepare yourself for such surprises, you'll want to bring as many notes with you as your briefcase can carry. Use the Notes Pages View (see fig. 24.3) to write down anything you can think of, including your script and rebuttals for any off-the-wall questions.

Fig. 24.3
Use the Notes Pages View as your script, and read from it during the presentation.

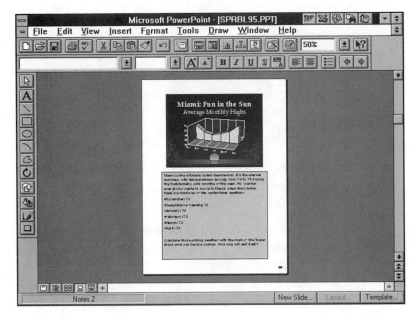

Choosing the medium

That's it. You're done. The presentation is perfect. All that's left is, well, the difficult part. Now you need to face your audience and dazzle them. But how? Will you use a computer-based slide show? Do you need 35mm slides? Are you going to hand out hard copies of the presentation? Or perhaps your equipment is limited to an overhead projector. Once you establish which medium you're going to use, PowerPoint can generate output to match your specifications.

Installing a slide show on another computer

If your presentation is a computer-based slide show, you need to set it up on a computer. In all likelihood, it won't be the same computer you've used to create the presentation. Many people run their slide shows off a notebook computer because it's easy to move from place to place.

There's only one problem: you don't *want* to install PowerPoint on your notebook, because your hard disk space is limited.

No problem. You can install just a portion of PowerPoint—the mini-program that lets you display your slide show (the PowerPoint Viewer). Before you install it onto another system, however, you need to create a Setup disk, as follows:

- If you have the disk version of Microsoft Office, locate the disk labeled PowerPoint Viewer, and copy it to another high-density disk. To be on the safe side, make sure the original disk is write-protected first.

- If you have the CD-ROM version, copy the contents of the \SETUP.ADM\DISK31 directory to a formatted, high-density disk.

Now that you have a Setup disk, insert it into the floppy drive on the notebook system, and run the VSETUP program by selecting File, Run from Program Manager.

Copy the presentation itself onto a disk, and copy it over to the PowerPoint directory on the notebook (unless you're on a network, in which case you don't need to use a disk to transfer files). That file should have the extension PPT. In our example, the file name is SPRBL95.PPT.

Running a slide show

To run a slide show from the PowerPoint Viewer, double-click the PowerPoint Viewer icon in Program Manager. Figure 24.4 shows the resulting dialog box. This is where you can choose to run the presentation continuously—if you're showing it at a trade show booth, for example—or to use automatic timings. If you want to select either, click the appropriate box in the bottom left corner. Select the presentation you want to run from the file list on the left, and click Show.

Fig. 24.4

The PowerPoint Viewer: Think of this as "PowerPoint Lite." It's not the whole program, but just what you need to show your presentation on a computer where PowerPoint isn't installed.

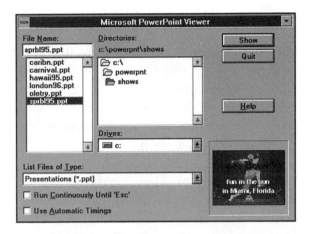

The PowerPoint clicker

Here are the keys you press during your presentation to navigate through the slide show:

If you want to...	Press
Use the Mouse	
Go to the next slide	Left button
Go to the previous slide	Right button
Use the Keyboard	
Go to the next slide	Page Down
Go to the previous slide	Page Up
Go to a specific slide	The slide number, followed by Enter
Stop the show	Esc

Your secret weapons: hidden slides

There may be some sensitive information you'd rather not talk about, unless forced to. For example, if your CEO has disappeared to South America with 5 million dollars in cash, you wouldn't want to lie about it, but you don't want to advertise it freely, either. Just in case anybody has heard the news and wants to ask you about the impact on your cash flow, have a slide ready, but don't show it until you're cornered.

PowerPoint lets you create hidden slides that are part of the presentation, but can be displayed at your discretion. To hide a slide, switch to Slide Sorter View, click the slide you want to hide, and click the Hide Slide button on the toolbar. As you can see in figure 24.5, the slide doesn't vanish into thin air, but its number is enclosed in a box with a line across it.

Fig. 24.5
Don't let them catch you unprepared. Hidden slides are your ammunition against the unexpected.

 ———— *Slide number*

Q&A — **How do I reveal a hidden slide during my presentation?**

There are two ways to "unhide" hidden slides:

- **Mouse.** If you move the mouse during the presentation, you'll notice the icon at the bottom right corner of the slide preceding the hidden one. That's the Hidden Slide icon. Just click on it, and the next slide will appear normally.

- **Keyboard.** If you use the keyboard to advance to the next slide, just type **H** (or **h**, it doesn't matter) while you're on the slide preceding the hidden one.

 **{Note}** The Hide Slide button appears only while you're in Slide Sorter View. If you want to hide a slide while in Slide View, select <u>T</u>ools, <u>H</u>ide Slide from the menus.

"X" marks the spot

During football games, things can get confusing. Luckily for television audiences, there's John Madden in the background, explaining every move and drawing circles and arrows all over the screen. And no matter how clear your presentation, there may be times when you need to point out an important fact on a slide.

There are several approaches. You can talk about it and hope your audience looks at the right spot, or—and this is where it gets exciting—you point to it with your index finger. Both are effective methods, but if you need more flash, pretend you're John Madden and use the on-line annotation pencil. Here's how:

1 During the slide show, when you move your mouse in any direction, your cursor appears as an arrow and a pencil icon appears at the bottom right corner.

2 Click once on that icon. Your arrow pointer becomes a pencil pointer. (Click the icon again, and the pencil icon changes to back to an arrow icon.)

3 Proceed to draw circles, arrows, or whatever you like (see fig. 24.6) by holding down either mouse button as you draw.

4 If you want to erase your doodles, press **E**. Otherwise, when you move on to the next slide, these annotations disappear by themselves and don't get saved with the presentation.

5 To get the arrow cursor back, click on the arrow icon at the bottom of the slide.

Fig. 24.6
It's a proven scientific fact: nothing draws attention to important details like circles and arrows (this is widely known as the Madden Axiom).

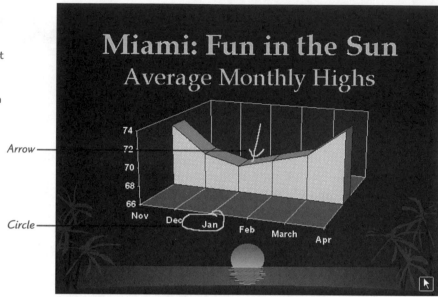

> ⊛ **{Note}** Your presentation can be as informal as gathering two of your colleagues around your desk and having them look at your screen. Or it can get as nerve-wracking as facing three hundred of your closest enemies and trying to convince them that you deserve that promotion. If that's the case, you can't have all these people huddle over your computer. For best results, make sure there's a screen projector in place.

Printing your presentation

Not all PowerPoint presentations are of the high-tech variety. Sometimes you find yourself in a place where setting up a computer is out of the question. But you can still make an effective presentation by handing out hard copies of your slides.

How do I make handouts?

Before you print out your presentation, you need to set it up. Choose File, Slide Setup. In the Slide Setup dialog box that displays, (see fig. 24.7), select the paper size and orientation.

Fig. 24.7

You can select any paper size for your printouts. Just select the Custom option in the drop-down list, and specify width and height.

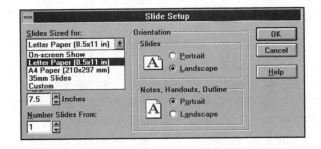

Now choose File, Print. From the dialog box shown in figure 24.8, make all the necessary selections:

- **Print What.** Do you want to print each slide on a separate piece of paper? Do you want to fit 2, 3, or 6 slides on one sheet? Or do you need the Notes Pages?

- **Copies.** Make as many copies as you want, but remember that you can make one copy and then photocopy it as many times as you need.

- **Slide Range.** Print the entire presentation or just selected slides.

- **Black & White.** Your colors will get translated into shades of gray.

- **Pure Black & White.** Colors in background graphics print out as white (not gray), but embedded graphics are still gray.

Once you've printed one type of item, like handouts, you have to return to this dialog box and print whatever else you need: speakers' notes, outlines, or the slides themselves (see fig. 24.8).

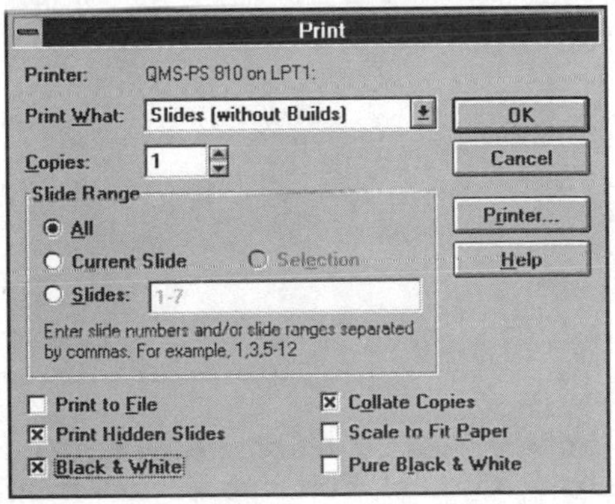

Fig. 24.8

Once you've printed all the handouts, you'll need to return to this dialog box to print your notes and/or outline.

What if I forget my lines?

Earlier in this chapter, we talked about teleprompters, those wonderful safety nets that any public speaker should have to fall back on. PowerPoint calls them Notes Pages. We also know them as **cheat sheets**. So now that you have a complete packet of handouts for your audience, make a separate one for yourself, complete with slides and notes. To do so, select Notes Pages under Print <u>W</u>hat in the Print dialog box, and you'll see pages similar to the ones in figure 24.9.

Fig. 24.9
If you tend to forget your lines, print out these pages and read them when you make the presentation.

Miami is the ultimate winter destination. It's the eternal summer, with temperatures varying from 70 to 75 during the traditionally cold months of the year. No wonder everybody wants to move to Miami when they retire. Here's a rundown of the winter-time weather:

•November: 73

•December: a freezing 72

•January: 70

•February: 72

•March: 73

•April: 74

Combine this exciting weather with the rush of the Super Bowl, and you have a winner. This one will sell itself!

> If you want to skip over the next couple of slides, you'll need to know which slide you want to skip to. To prepare this cheat sheet, print out the presentation in Outline View.

Can I use an overhead projector?

Before notebook computers, the most popular way to make a business presentation was by using overhead projectors with transparencies. You manually replaced each transparency when you needed to move on, and if you wanted to hide a piece of information or a portion of the text, you covered it with a piece of paper. (Makes one reminisce about the old days, when you had to actually turn a lever around in order to roll down your car window.)

But there are still plenty of overhead projectors and projection panels out there, and PowerPoint doesn't snub them. As long as your printer supports overhead transparencies, you don't have a problem. Buy a ream of transparencies and print regularly. If it's a color printer, make sure you *check off* the two Black & White options in the Print dialog box.

If your printer doesn't support transparencies, you can send your file to Genigraphics, and you'll get them in return mail within a couple of working days.

How about a slide projector?

To turn your slide show into a *real* slide show using 35mm color slides, you'll need to send your presentation file to Genigraphics.

> It's a good idea to give your audience a hard copy of the presentation. If there's important information in it, nobody's going to retain it, no matter how good a presenter you are. So whether you make an on-screen slide show or use an overhead projector, make printouts of all the slides.

What's the Genigraphics print driver?

No color printer? No problem. Whether you need to generate high-resolution overhead transparencies, 35mm color slides, or even posters, you can use Genigraphics, which is an outside service specializing in producing them out of your PowerPoint presentation files.

If you have a modem, you can upload (send) your files directly to Genigraphics. You need a 1200-baud or faster modem and the Graphics-Link program, included with Microsoft Office. Otherwise, you can mail or deliver a disk to the Genigraphics center nearest you. Call 800-638-7348 to find out more.

To generate the file used by Genigraphics, select the Genigraphics printer driver from your Print Setup dialog box, and print your slides.

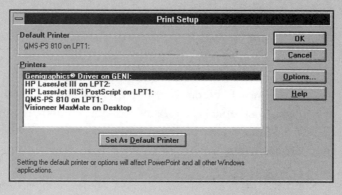

Part V:

Beyond the Basics

25
Making Office Work the Way You Do

After you work with Microsoft Office for awhile, you may want to redecorate! Rearrange Office programs until it feels like a comfortable place to work.

If you've ever moved from a cramped cubicle into a real office—the kind with walls and windows—you know the feeling. For the first few days (or weeks or months, if it's a *really* nice office), it's a small slice of heaven on earth. Look at all this extra room! Look at all this great new furniture! Look at this view!

And then one day the honeymoon ends. You've run out of space in the filing cabinets. The desk doesn't face the right way, and the chairs make your guests feel like they're in a waiting room at the DMV. And that view isn't so great when the blinding afternoon sun hits you right between the eyes.

After you've worked with Microsoft Office for awhile, you might notice the same phenomenon. The toolbars are arranged all wrong, you can't find what you want on the menus, and there's just not enough room for the stuff you're working on.

In this Office, there's a simple solution: redecorate. With a few clicks here and there, you can rearrange just about every aspect of the Office programs until it feels like a comfortable place to work.

Toolbars: have 'em your way

When you have a new chair delivered to your office, do you let a couple of musclehead delivery guys decide where it goes? Of course not. So when you first install Office, why should you leave all the toolbars arranged the way someone at Microsoft says they should be arranged?

The toolbars work the same in all three Office programs, and it's easy to move buttons around, delete the ones you never use, and add new ones. After you've worked with each program for a while, you'll develop a good sense of where the buttons would be best located for the way you work.

 **{Note}**———— You can rearrange the buttons on the MOM toolbar, too. See Chapter 2 for details.

I never use that button!

I'm not sure why some of the buttons on the default toolbars are there. But after I had gone an entire month without clicking certain buttons, I decided to put them out of sight and out of mind.

From the Standard toolbar, I removed AutoText (it's easier to press F3), and Drawing (I have no artistic talent). From the Formatting toolbar, I got rid of the Justify button (because on those rare occasions when I use justified text, I apply it using a style) plus the two indent buttons (because it's easier to just use the ruler).

Why get rid of these unused buttons? For one thing, they're distracting. When the screen is cleaner, I can find the buttons I do use a lot faster. For another, as we'll see in a minute, there are other buttons that deserve a place of honor on the standard toolbars.

Deleting a button, or moving it to a new location on the toolbar, is a simple three-step process:

   1 Right-click on any toolbar, and choose Customize from the shortcut menu.

2 Point to the button you want to move or delete. Click and hold the left mouse button—the thick dashed border means you've selected it.

3 To **delete the button**, drag it off the toolbar and release the mouse button (see fig. 25.1). Poof! It's gone.

Or

To **move the button**, drag it to the new place you want it to occupy on the toolbar, then drop it. (This takes practice. If it lands in the wrong place, pick it up and try again.)

Fig. 25.1
If you rarely use a button on one of the standard toolbars, get rid of it. Display the Customize dialog box, then drag the unwanted button off the toolbar.

I want to add buttons for things I do a lot

Easily done. Open the Customize dialog box again. All the Office programs have similar dialog boxes that let you scroll through a list of available buttons and drag the ones you want onto any open toolbar (see fig. 25.2). The toolbar buttons are good citizens. When a neighbor moves in or out, they automatically tidy up and adjust their spacing.

Fig. 25.2
All the Office programs let you add your own buttons to toolbars. Drag the button you want to add from this dialog box onto the toolbar.

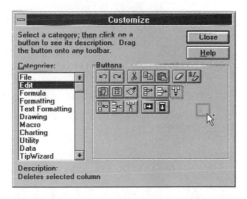

If you're not sure what a button does, just click on it, then read about it in the Description section of the Customize dialog box.

Q&A

> **My finger slipped and I accidentally created a new toolbar, which I don't really want. How do I get rid of it?**
>
> It's an easy cleanup. Choose View, Toolbars. From the list, choose the name of the "I didn't mean that" toolbar, and press the Delete button.

I want to see a toolbar (or put one away)

Toolbars come and go in Office programs more often than extras in a Spielberg film. Sometimes it's automatic: if you start drawing a picture, for example, a Drawing toolbar will appear automatically. But you can choose when and where toolbars appear and disappear. To display a list of available toolbars, right-click one that's already visible to display the shortcut menu shown in figure 25.3.

Fig. 25.3
You can have as many or as few toolbars visible on the screen as you want.

(Tip)

> I find the yellow ToolTips extremely useful, but some people absolutely detest them. If their constant appearing and disappearing drives you nuts, turn them off. Choose View, Toolbars, then uncheck the Show ToolTips box. After you click OK, the labels will no longer appear.

Q&A

> **Help! I cleared away all the toolbars, and now I don't know where to click to bring them back. What do I do?**
>
> Fortunately, all the Office programs work alike, and this is an easy problem to fix. Just choose View, Toolbars to display the list of available toolbars, check the ones you want, then click OK to make them reappear.

Should I redo the menus?

Some people never touch toolbars—they rely on menus for everything. If it works for you, that's fine. If you're tempted to boost your productivity by rearranging menus, I have some disappointing news: you can redo the menus in Word only, not in Excel or PowerPoint.

Frankly, I think it's too much bother to mess around with the pull-down menus. It's also a little dangerous: if you remove a command and then discover later that you need to use that command, even once, you'll have to prowl through the Customize dialog box and add it back to the menu before you can do it.

But the other menus in Word—the shortcut menus that pop up when you click the right mouse button—are worth changing if you use them regularly (and you should). For example, I've added Paste Special and Check Spelling to the Text (Shortcut) menu. If you want to do the same, follow these steps:

1 Choose Tools, Customize, and click the Menus tab to display the Customize dialog box shown in figure 25.4.

Fig. 25.4
Use this dialog box to change commands on Word's shortcut menus.

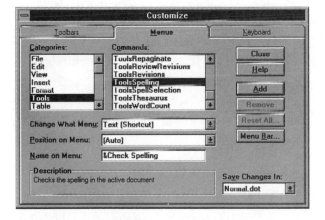

2 In the Change What Menu box, pick a menu. Word has 24 shortcut menus, one for every conceivable situation, so be sure you've picked the right one.

3 Pick a category from the left list box and a command from the right.

4 In the Position on Menu box, tell Word where to add the new command: The top of the menu? The bottom? Doesn't matter?

5 In the <u>N</u>ame on Menu box, give the new shortcut command a different
name, if you'd like. The ampersand (&) means the next letter will be
underlined so you can use it as a menu shortcut.

6 Be sure to click the <u>A</u>dd button before clicking Close.

Figure 25.5 shows a shortcut menu we've modified.

Fig. 25.5

Don't mess with Word's
pull-down menus, but
feel free to rework the
pop-up shortcut
menus. In this example,
we've added a quick
Check Spelling option.

Give Word a new set of shortcut keys

When you press a letter or number key, you know what Word will do with it.
If you press **C-A-T**, you'll see the word cat on the screen. But what happens
when you press some finger-twisting combination like Ctrl+Alt+L? Word
doesn't know, so it looks on its list of **keyboard shortcuts**.

You can assign a command, a style, a macro, or even an AutoText entry to a
key combination. If you want, you can turn your company logo into an
AutoText entry, and then set up Word so the logo will plop into your document every time you press Ctrl+Alt+L. There are hundreds of built-in shortcuts, and you can change them or create new ones with a few clicks and
keystrokes:

1 Choose <u>T</u>ools, <u>C</u>ustomize, then click the <u>K</u>eyboard tab to display the
dialog box shown in figure 25.6.

2 Choose a category from the list on the left and an item from the one on
the right. You can choose a command, a style, a font, or a special
symbol.

3 Click in the Press <u>N</u>ew Shortcut Key box, then press the key combination you want to use. Word will add the description of whatever
you press. The most useful combinations are Ctrl+Shift+*key* and
Ctrl+Alt+*key*.

Fig. 25.6
Word lets you take any key (or combination of keys) and do something special with it. Sorry—you can't do this with PowerPoint or Excel.

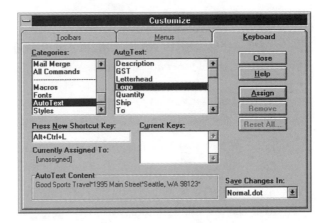

4 Look at the Current keys box to see which key combination(s) are currently assigned to the command you've chosen. There might already be a combination assigned that you don't know about. You can have more than one shortcut for the same command.

5 Look at the Currently Assigned To information to see what the key combination you've chosen does when you press it now. If you don't want to reassign it, try another selection.

6 Click Assign first, then Close to save your new key assignment.

ⓧ**<Caution>** You can actually reassign simple letters and numbers—A,B,C ... 1,2,3—so that they cause Word to do special functions. But if you do that, you'll have a *lot* of trouble composing a simple memo in English!

What else can I do with the Office programs?

When you choose Tools, Options from each of the Office programs, you get wildly different choices. That makes sense, since each program is intended to do wildly different things.

There's a lot of technotrivia buried in these dialog boxes, but there are also a few cool options that help you work faster, smarter, and more comfortably. Here's where to look.

Reworking Word

If you choose the Save tab of the Options dialog box (see fig. 25.7), you see a smattering of ways you can customize Word:

- **Allow Fast Saves** lets you get back to work a little more quickly, but it also makes Word files bigger than they would otherwise be. I turn it off.

- **Prompt to Save Normal.dot** lets you decide whether you want to make changes to the standard document style permanent. Good idea.

- **Automatic Save** will annoy you occasionally, but someday, when the lights go out unexpectedly, you'll be glad you put a check mark here.

Fig. 25.7
Some customization options can make your life with Office much more pleasant.

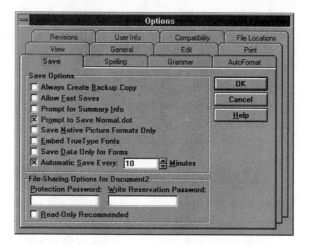

What else can you do with Word? Here are some highlights. Each boldfaced word refers to one of the tabs in that crowded Options dialog box:

- **User Info.** Add your name and address here to have it automatically inserted in letters and printed on envelopes.

- **View.** Decide whether to show tab characters, spaces, paragraph marks, and other oddball characters.

- **General.** Set the number of files (up to 9) to appear on the "recently used file" list.

- **Edit.** Here's where you turn off features like automatic word selection, drag-and-drop text editing, and smart cut and paste.

- **Print.** My laser printer stacks paper face up, which means that page 1 is always on the bottom of the stack. Ugh. So I've checked the Reverse Print Order box here. There's also a box that lets me specify which paper tray to use.

Making an easier Excel

If you choose the General tab of the Options dialog box (see fig. 25.8), you can customize Excel in the following ways:

- **Prompt for Summary Info** displays a box so you can add more information every time you save a file. Some people find it annoying; I like it.

- **Sheets in New Workbook** starts out at 16, which is too many for me. I've lowered the default number to 4.

- Add a **Default File Location** here so you don't have to wander through directories every time you want to open or save a file.

- The **User Name** you enter here is the one Excel will use when you save or mail a worksheet.

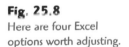

Fig. 25.8
Here are four Excel options worth adjusting.

What else can you do to make Excel easier to use? Choose one of these tabs from the dialog box in figure 25.8 to find these useful options:

- **Color.** Choose standard colors to use in worksheets and charts.

- **Transition.** If you know Lotus 1-2-3 inside and out, you can readjust Excel so that the familiar 1-2-3 keystrokes work.

- **Edit.** Lets you turn off in-cell editing and drag-and-drop copies. Set the default number of decimal places Excel uses here, too.

- **Calculation.** If you have a huge worksheet filled with formulas that seem to take forever to recalculate every time you change a value, change automatic calculation to manual here (but don't forget to turn it back on later).

- **View.** Lets you hide the formula bar, gridlines, row and column headers, and just about everything else on the screen.

Personalizing PowerPoint

Now let's look at PowerPoint's Options dialog box (fig. 25.9). Gee, compared with Word and Excel, PowerPoint isn't exactly overwhelming with options, is it? If you use the program a lot, try setting the number of recently used files to its maximum of 9. And if the startup dialog boxes bug you, turn them off.

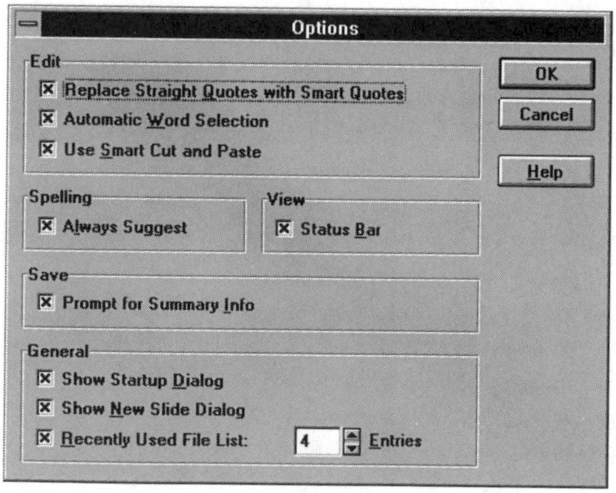

Fig. 25.9
PowerPoint has a limited number of options.

How do I save my setup?

The only thing you have to do to save your new setup is say Yes when the program asks if you want to save changes to the template or the default files or whatever it asks for. The next time you open the program, things should be just as you left them.

Of course, there's always a catch.

Someday, if you're a little unlucky, you might see an error message like the one in figure 25.10. Don't despair—it's not the end of the world, but it is a hassle.

When you customize the Office programs, your changes are stored in a handful of files that are scattered all over your hard disk. If anything ever happens to your PC and you have to reinstall one or all of the programs, you'll have to start over. And if you've made a lot of changes to your working environment, you'll find it a frustrating few days (or weeks).

Fig. 25.10
This error message means Windows has lost track of an important configuration file. If you've made a backup copy of it, though, you don't need to rerun the Office Setup program.

That's why I recommend you grab an empty floppy disk and copy these crucial files to it every so often. In every case, I've specified the name of the file and the default directory you'll find it in. If you specified different directories when you installed Office, you'll need to adjust these names accordingly:

- **Word.** NORMAL.DOT (in C:\MSOFFICE\WINWORD\TEMPLATE), and WINWORD6.INI (in C:\WINDOWS).

- **Excel.** EXCEL5.XLB and EXCEL5.INI (both found in C:\WINDOWS).

- **PowerPoint.** POWERPNT.INI (from C:\WINDOWS).

26

What Are All Those Little Programs?

In this chapter:

- I need to create quick charts

- I want to design my own logo

- How do I add cool images to my documents?

- How can I show my company's reorganization in a chart?

Most of the Office programs are small, and like Hollywood bit players, they have specialized roles to play.

The superstars in the Microsoft Office are easy to spot: Word, Excel, and PowerPoint get all the headlines. But the Office supporting cast is worth a look, too. Most of these programs are small, and like Hollywood bit players, they have specialized roles to play. Because these mini-applications are so small and specialized, they even have a nickname: **applets**.

Meet the Office applets

If you chose the Complete option when you first installed Office, you automatically added six smaller programs to your computer. In every case, these programs allow you to insert **objects** inside your Word documents, Excel worksheets, and PowerPoint presentations. The big program doesn't worry about what's inside the object; it just makes room on the screen for it. So you can have picture objects, graph objects, even sound objects that talk or play music when you double-click on them.

Plain English, please!

An **object** is something (a piece of text, graphic object, or sound object) that's created in one program, but can be available and manipulated in another program by a process called embedding. **Embedding** has nothing to do with mattresses: it simply means that the file containing the object lives with the receiving program, and can be moved and resized there. It can also still be opened and modified in the program where it was created.

These mini-programs don't look very much like the big Office programs. The toolbars (for those applets that have them) are different, menus don't match up, and things generally behave just differently enough that it's easy to get confused.

These are the six Office applets:

- **Microsoft Graph** turns numbers into simple charts.

- **Microsoft WordArt** twists words and phrases into unusual shapes for use as logos and letterheads, for example.

- **Microsoft ClipArt Gallery** lets you add canned drawings and cartoons to your documents.

- **Microsoft Organization Chart** lets you sort out who's who (and who answers to who) in any company.

- **Media Player** works with multimedia files to show movie clips and play sounds.

- **Equation Editor** will be a big help if you're working out a new theory of relativity.

How do these applets work?

You choose <u>I</u>nsert, <u>O</u>bject, then pick a name from the list of programs that Windows displays. You'll see other programs on the list, in addition to these six, depending on what other kind of software you have on your system.

Three of the applets—Microsoft Graph, Microsoft WordArt, and Microsoft ClipArt Gallery—will only run from inside another program. The doorway to get to the applet is basically through a dialog box in one of the major applications — it's like the applet itself has no "engine" to start it up; it relies on the other application to be launched. The other three can be used by themselves, although you might have to create Program Manager icons for each one first.

When you work with one of these applets, it takes over the screen, including the window that your document was in. It's like turning on your VCR: it temporarily takes over the screen for the movie you're showing (and you have to use the VCR controls to make things happen), but the TV programs and controls are still there underneath. Sometimes your document stays there, and only the menus and toolbars change. It's a slightly disorienting experience at first, but you get used to it.

How do you get the regular menus and toolbars back? Click anywhere in your main document outside of the new object. To edit the object, double-click on it, and let the applet take over your screen again.

Painting pictures with numbers: Microsoft Graph

For complicated charts, Excel is the best tool for the job. To plop a quick-and-dirty chart into a Word document or a PowerPoint presentation, though, this applet might be a better choice. Think of Microsoft Graph as "Excel Extra Lite."

You enter numbers into a **datasheet** that works like an Excel worksheet. Your chart appears in its own window inside your document. Toolbars and menus let you choose a different chart type, or format labels and numbers on your chart.

Take your choice of two techniques to make a Graph object:

- To start from scratch and enter numbers directly, just choose Insert, Object, choose Microsoft Graph, and replace the numbers in the sample datasheet. This is the most common way to insert a chart into PowerPoint (see fig. 26.1).

- If your numbers are already in an Excel worksheet, highlight the relevant cells in the sample datasheet, then click the Import Data button. Your new chart will go in just below the table.

Fig. 26.1
It may look like Excel, but it's really Microsoft Graph.

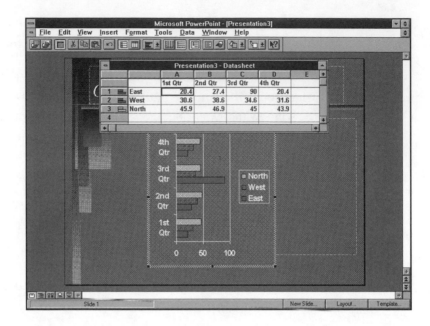

Making your text shine with WordArt

Look at the label on a Coca-Cola can (classic Coke, of course, not that New stuff). See the flowing script in the logo? It's a work of art that started out as eight letters and a hyphen. A graphic artist took the letters in the name and manipulated them into the most recognized logo on the planet.

Your market might not be as big as the billions and billons of Coke drinkers worldwide, but a good logo can still help your business grow. And the WordArt program, which helps you turn plain text into fancy artwork, is a good place to start.

What is WordArt, anyway?

WordArt is an extremely simple program that takes a few words and lets you stretch, bend, distort, and colorize them. Think of it as the computerized equivalent of what you used to do with Silly Putty and the Sunday comics.

There are a few things you should know before you use WordArt:

- The program won't run by itself. You have to start it from inside another program (like Word or Excel).

- It works only with TrueType fonts. If your printer uses a font that doesn't have a TrueType equivalent, you can't use it in WordArt.

- Any object you create with WordArt can be resized, moved, or copied into another document using the Windows Clipboard.

 (Tip)

> When you insert a WordArt object into a Word document, be sure to enclose it in a frame after you create it. (Select the WordArt object, click the right mouse button, and choose Frame Picture from the shortcut menu.) Once there's a frame around the picture, you can easily move it where you want it on the page.

How do I create a work of WordArt?

To get started, position the insertion point where you want your masterpiece to appear, and choose Insert, Object. Pick Microsoft WordArt 2.0 from the list. After the program finishes loading, your screen will be transformed. The title bar will still say Microsoft Word, but the menus will have changed, and there will be a small box waiting for you to enter some text in it, like the one shown in figure 26.2.

Fig. 26.2
To create this logo with WordArt, we used every trick in the book, including shadows and slanted type, to make a dramatic-looking image out of three simple letters.

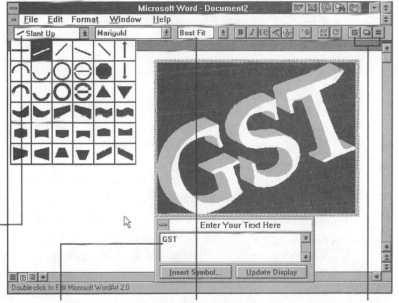

This drop-down palette lets you choose from three dozen special text-distorting effects.

Enter some text here.

Pick a typeface and a font size here. Sorry, you can't mix and match typefaces.

Use these buttons to apply special effects like color, shadows, and borders.

To return to your document, just click anywhere outside the WordArt object. You can also copy a WordArt object from one document to another. That means you can create your WordArt logo in a blank document; then, when you're satisfied with the way it looks, copy it to the Windows Clipboard and paste it into the document where you want to use it, as shown in figure 26.3. Don't forget to frame it now, so you can move it around the document easily.

Fig. 26.3

With a little fine-tuning and resizing, the logo we created fits perfectly in a variety of Office documents, like this invoice created in Word.

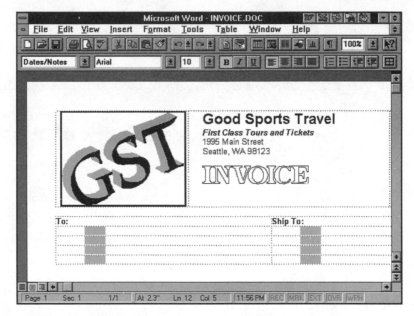

Browsing through the ClipArt Gallery

Most commercially available clip art comes in separate files, disorganized and impossible to find. ClipArt Gallery actually makes it easy to browse through hundreds or thousands of images to find the one you're looking for.

Like all the other applets, this one inserts an editable object in the file you're working on. It doesn't matter whether it's a Word document, an Excel worksheet, or a PowerPoint presentation—the picture sits comfortably in the midst of your work. There are some cool images in the collection (along with some clunkers), but all that clip art comes at a price. If you install it all, as figure 26.4 illustrates, you'll chew up nearly 14 megabytes of hard disk space.

Fig. 26.4

Go ahead and install all the images in the Microsoft ClipArt Gallery, but only if you have 14 megabytes of storage you don't mind giving up.

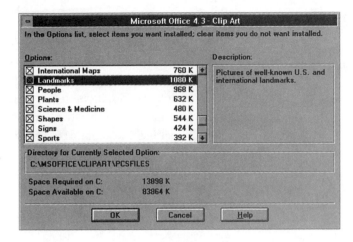

By this time, you should know how to start up this applet. Insert, Object. Microsoft ClipArt Gallery. Right.

Once you've started the program, you can do a surprising number of things with it. The simplest is to browse through thumbnail sketches of the images in your collection, organized by category (see fig. 26.5). If you find one you like, click OK to close the Gallery window and pop back into your program with the new image in place.

At that point, you can resize the image, put it in a frame, or copy it to the Windows Clipboard to paste into another program.

Fig. 26.5

Sort through collections of clip art until you find the right image, then click OK to insert the picture into your document as an object that can be resized, moved, and copied.

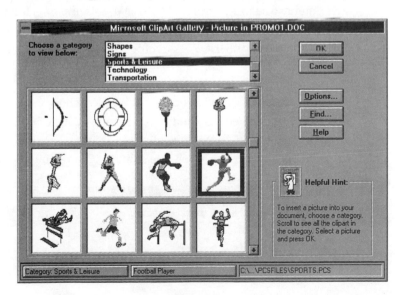

Microsoft Organization Chart

When you start Organization Chart, you get all the tools you need to rearrange your company's management structure from top to bottom (see fig. 26.6). It only takes a few clicks and drags to move an entire department from one division to another, halfway across the country. The program shows up on the Insert, Object list, but it can also be run on its own, and you can save files as separate files, not embedded in another application.

Fig. 26.6
Go ahead—give yourself a promotion with the help of Microsoft Organization Chart.

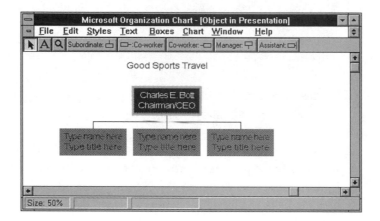

Jazzing up your world with Media Player

If you have a sound card and CD-ROM, this applet is for you. It's actually an upgrade to a mini-program that comes with Windows, which is why you'll find it in the C:\WINDOWS directory, instead of mixed in with the rest of the Office files.

Media Player lets you play back sound files, show video clips (in a little tiny window), and even play audio CDs through your CD-ROM player and sound board (see fig. 26.7). If you get hooked on multimedia, you'll outgrow Media Player in a hurry. But for simple sounds, it's just fine.

Fig. 26.7
This sound- and video-playing program from the Office package is an improved version of one that comes with Windows.

27

What Am I Supposed to Do with Mail?

Thanks to E-mail, you'll slap fewer yellow sticky notes on other people's monitors and you can get rid of those pink "While You Were Out" message slips.

In this chapter:

- Where is the mail program, anyway?
- How do I send a file through the mail?
- How do I read this file I received?
- How do I send a message?

You lick a stamp, slap it on an envelope, and drop it in the mailbox. You don't think twice about whether your letter will get to the person you've addressed it to. You just assume that someone responsible will pick it up and start the chain of events that will get it safely to its destination in Fort Lee, New Jersey (or wherever it's bound).

After you've used **electronic mail** for a month or two, you'll probably come to take it for granted, too. You'll think of it as your own private FedEx, delivering messages and packages that absolutely, positively have to be there right now. Thanks to E-mail, you'll slap fewer yellow sticky notes on other people's monitors, and you may even get rid of those pink "While You Were Out" message slips.

E-mail really pays off when you work with other people as part of a team. To share a file with your coworker, simply stuff it in an electronic interoffice envelope and press the Send button. When you need to gather reactions to this year's budget numbers or the first draft of the annual report, it's even easier. Office lets you staple an electronic routing slip to your worksheet or document, then start it on its rounds through the rest of your department.

If your PC isn't hooked up to a network, you can skip this chapter. But if your office uses Microsoft Mail, here's what you need to know to use it with Office.

Where *is* the mail program?

You can shake the Microsoft Office box until every last scrap of paper falls out, and you won't find Mail. If you have a high-powered microscope, you can use it to inspect every floppy disk in the package, in vain. No matter how hard you try, you won't find Mail anywhere.

Why not? Because along with your copy of Office, you received a **license** to run one copy of Microsoft Mail. You didn't get disks with software on them. In fact, you don't need them.

If all the computers in your office are connected to a network, you probably already have electronic mail. Whoever runs your network set up a **post office** on the main network PC, and you need to track down that person to find the software that lets you send and receive E-mail. Once this **client program** is loaded on your PC, you've just stepped onto the on-ramp of the Information Superhighway.

What is electronic mail, anyway?

Here are the basic facts you need to know about E-mail:

- You have to be able to access a **network** to use it. You need someone else's help to set it up. Trust me on this.

- Everything that zips around your E-mail system is a **message**. The actual contents of a message can be as simple as a few letters ("OK.") or go on for a couple paragraphs ("I've come up with 10 cost-cutting suggestions...").

- You can send packages, called **attachments**, through E-mail as well. These can be Word documents, Excel worksheets, PowerPoint presentations, or anything else you can stuff into a file.

- Every message has a pre-addressed **envelope** that tells the Mail system where to send your note and any accompanying packages.

- At your network's **post office**, there's a master address book that includes the name of everyone attached to your mail system. You can look in this book any time, and you can also create a personal address book that includes groups of people you communicate with regularly.

- New mail gets delivered to your **in box**, and when you compose a message to send to someone else, just like the mailbox in front of your house, you place it in the **out box** to be picked up.

- All your messages can be sorted into groups and stored in **folders** that you create yourself.

How do I send a file to someone else?

Let's say you're working on this month's budget forecasts. You've entered the numbers in your Excel worksheet and stared at them until you're cross-eyed. You think they're right, but you need a reality check. So you decide to send them off to the best number person you know. There's no need to leave Excel. You don't even have to save your file—Excel will handle that detail. Just be sure you've logged into Mail, and choose File, Send to display a blank message form. The effect is the same as if you'd summoned a messenger who brought along a fill-in-the-blanks form for you to use (see fig. 27.1). He takes the file that's displayed, and whisks it away.

Follow these instructions, and you don't have to lick a stamp:

1 Click in the To box, and click the Address button to pick names from a list.

2 Edit the subject line, if you want to.

3 Add a note to accompany the file, if you want to.

4 Click the Send button.

Fig. 27.1
When you want to send the file you've just finished to a co-worker, Mail handles the details. Add the name, add a brief note, then click Send.

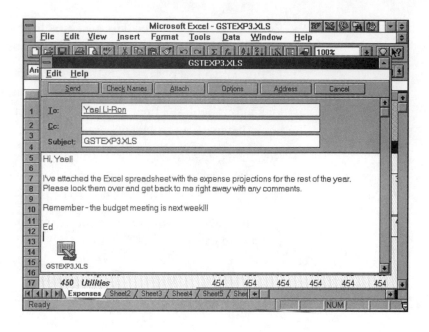

(Tip) ─── If a message is particularly urgent, you can prioritize it as high priority. When composing the message, click on Options, and you'll see three priorities: Low, Normal, or High. A high-priority message appears in your recipient's in-box with a unique icon so he'll know to open it right away.

{Note} ─── You can attach more than one file to a message if you want. See "How can I attach files to my message?"

What if I just want to send a message?

Sometimes, you simply want to use Mail to communicate with other people on your network. Then, Mail truly becomes like those little pink message slips. Anything from a quick comment to a 10-page diatribe can be sent through Mail, and the people who get the message can respond and carry on a dialog with you as if you were in a little electronic meeting room.

To send a message, click on the Compose button. In the Compose dialog box, you address the message, just as you did when you sent a file. Type a subject, and then click in the space below and start writing. When you're entering message text, Mail functions like a basic word processor: you can enter, delete, and cut-and-paste just like you normally do.

To get the message on its way, just click the Send button and off it goes.

How can I attach files to my message?

You can also use the Mail program itself to write a note, address it, and *then* attach the file you want to send. This is particularly handy when you have more than one file to attach. First you have to save the file, start Mail, and create a new message. Then click the Attach button. In the Attach dialog box shown in figure 27.2, find the file you want to attach, and finally click the Send button. Repeat the process to attach each additional file.

Fig. 27.2

Click the Attach button to browse for the file (or files) you want to add.

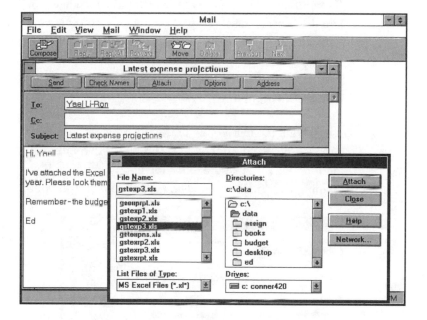

How do you know whether you've successfully attached a file? Look in the message itself. Your attached files show up as icons with labels underneath. The label shows the file name.

Someone sent me a file. How do I read it?

When FedEx shows up with a package, there's *always* an airbill on the outside. One-page letter or oversized box, it doesn't matter—at a minimum, you can tell who sent the package by checking that slip of paper.

E-mail works the same way. Whenever a file lands in your in box, it's attached to a message. You can see the outside of the package—there's an icon that may or may not give you a clue what's inside, plus a label that tells you its file name. When you look at the message, you can tell who sent it to you, and when it was sent. If the sender wasn't too rushed, there might be a message explaining what you're expected to do with the file.

All that information is in the envelope that's taped to the top of the box. If you actually want to see what's inside the package, you'll have to open it up. You don't need scissors—just double-click on the icon. Assuming that the program that created the file is also available to your computer, Mail will start up the program you need (or switch to it if it's already running), and load the attached file into it for you. Once that's done, you can begin working with the file right away.

If you want to save a copy of the file on your hard disk so you can use it later, choose File, Save Attachment from the Mail menu. You'll see a Save Attachment dialog box like the one shown in figure 27.3. If you don't care about keeping your mail, simply click the Delete button...poof! It's gone!

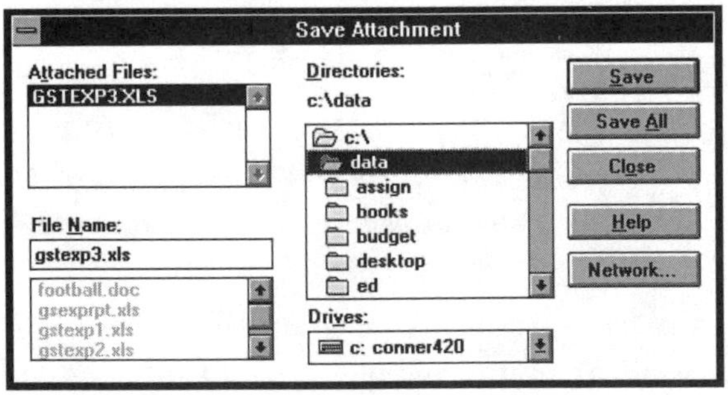

Fig. 27.3

If you want to save an attached file on your hard disk, give each file its own name, and click the Save button.

What happens to the attachment in your mail message? Nothing. It stays attached to the envelope until you click the Delete button and run both the message and its attachments through the electronic shredder.

⊛ **{Note}**

If you want to print your message (in direct opposition to paperless office advocates, I might add...), you can do so by clicking on the Print button, if it's displayed on your toolbar, or choose the File menu and select Print.

Does this have anything to do with the Information Super-you-know-what?

As long as it's just you and a few coworkers shooting messages back and forth, it's hard to argue that you've merged onto the Information Superhighway. When you're confined to your own local network, you haven't even shifted out of Park.

But you can get into gear quickly; all you have to do is set up connections between your mail system and other, similar mail systems in the outside world. If your company is big enough, or if enough of your customers and outside suppliers use E-mail, too, then it makes good business sense to do this.

By adding these **gateways**, you can use Mail to exchange messages with other people on other systems. It's not complicated: your Mail administrator tells the program to dial up another mail system at regular intervals—once an hour, once a day, whatever. When the two couriers connect, they exchange their sacks of mail. The outgoing messages get routed to their destination (maybe even in New Jersey), while incoming messages get sorted and delivered to local mail clients.

Today, you can use mail gateways to swap messages with CompuServe, America On-Line, even the legendary Internet, with its 20 million users. Eventually, Windows 95 will replace Microsoft Mail with something called the Message Center. When that happens, you'll be able to mix and match mail from just about anywhere with all the other kinds of messages you deal with every day.

There'll be a place for faxes in the Message Center; with the right modem, you'll even be able to dial up another company's fax machine and request specific faxes ("Have your fax machine call my machine..."). When someone figures out how to hook your telephone and your computer into the same wire, you'll even be able to store your voice mail in the same place.

When that day comes, you can consider yourself well-connected. You can also prepare for another unpleasant side effect of all that access: junk E-mail.

How do I make sure that everyone reads this file?

Simple attachments work well when you're working with a single partner. But what happens when you're part of a committee? Well, you could send the file as an attachment to the first person on the committee, along with a note saying please, *pretty please*, pass this along to the next person in the list when you're done. And like all important mail messages, odds are it will get lost in someone's in-basket, somewhere along the way.

Fortunately, there is a better way. With Word, Excel, and PowerPoint, you can clip an electronic routing slip to your document. Depending on how urgent your project is, you can fire copies of the document to everyone in your group, all at once. Or you can set up a list of people to receive the file, one after another. Each time a recipient looks at the attached file, Mail pops up a reminder that there's a routing slip attached to the document, and offers to send it to the next person on the list.

To add a routing slip to a document, follow these steps:

1 Choose File, Add Routing Slip. You'll see a dialog box like the one in figure 27.4.

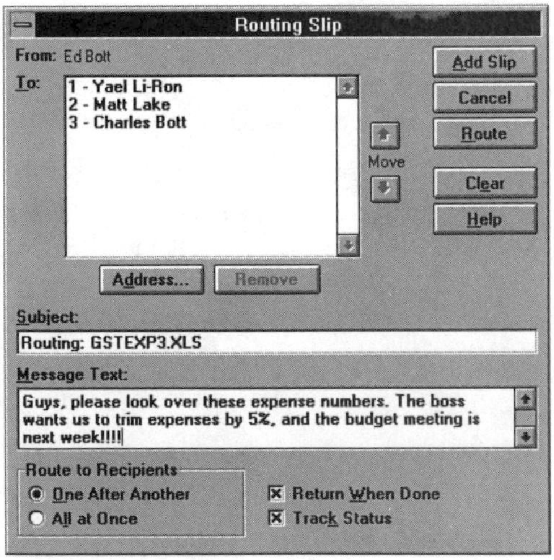

Fig. 27.4
Use electronic routing slips to pass a document from one coworker to the next, automatically.

2 Click the Address button and pick the names you want on your routing slip.

3 Edit the Subject line, if necessary.

4 Add a message to accompany the file as it works its way through your workgroup.

5 Tell Mail how to route the document, and specify whether you want to get status reports each time it moves to the next person on the list.

6 Use the Move arrows to reorder the names on the list. Press the Clear button to start the list over.

7 Press Add Slip to save the routing slip and continue working. Press Route to send the message right now.

What happens when the recipients open up a message with a routing slip attached? They'll see a message like the one in figure 27.5. Note that Mail has changed the title bar and added an explanatory note at the bottom of the message. With all those clues, it's hard to imagine that anyone could miss the routing slip!

Fig. 27.5

When you receive a message with a routing slip and attached file, it's filled with reminders. Double-click to launch the attached file.

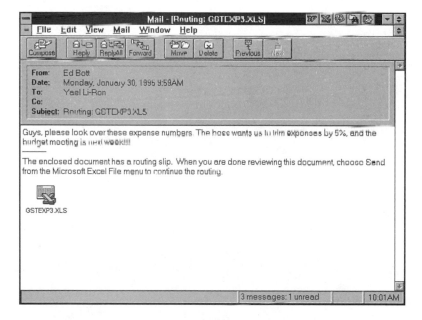

After the first person on the list has finished working with the file, he can choose File, Send to route it to the next person in line. When that happens, instead of getting a fill-in-the-blanks message form, he'll see a dialog box like the one in figure 27.6. If you leave the first selection, Route document to.... and click OK, it keeps moving down the line. The other option, Send copy of document...allows you to send a copy to someone who's not on the regular route.

Fig. 27.6

Mail remembers that there's a routing slip attached to a file, even if you forget.

{ Index }

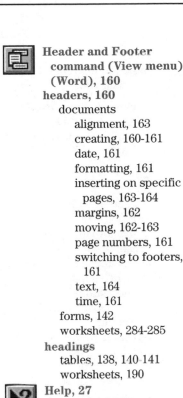